A World on Fire

A World on Fire

Sharing the Ignatian Spiritual Exercises
with Other Religions

Erin M. Cline

The Catholic University of America Press
Washington, D.C.

Library of Congress Cataloging-in-Publication Data
Names: Cline, Erin M., author.
Title: A world on fire : sharing the Ignatian spiritual exercises
with other religions / Erin M. Cline.
Description: Washington, D.C. : Catholic University Press, 2018. |
Includes bibliographical references and index.
Identifiers: LCCN 2017042379 | ISBN 9780813229775 (pbk. : alk. paper)
Subjects: LCSH: Ignatius, of Loyola, Saint, 1491–1556. Exercitia spiritualia.
Spiritual exercises. | Christianity and other religions.
Classification: LCC BX2179.L8 C55 2018 | DDC 248.3—dc23
LC record available at https://lccn.loc.gov/2017042379

For Siobhan Mary

And for Kevin, who inspired me
with the idea in the first place

Ad Majorem Dei Gloriam
For the Greater Glory of God

Contents

Acknowledgments

I owe a debt of gratitude to many people who helped me write this book, especially since it involved moving beyond my training as a philosopher and scholar of Chinese and comparative philosophy and religion to more theological work. First and foremost, I want to express my deepest gratitude to Kevin O'Brien, SJ, who initially invited me to make the Exercises and who served as my spiritual director. One day in his office, shortly before I began my retreat, Kevin told me about Father Nicolás's remarks about sharing the Exercises with members of other religions, and noted the need for someone to take on the project of working out what that might mean. I responded that this was a fascinating idea, and told him that I thought he should do it. He responded that he lacked the expertise in other traditions that would be needed. Then he suggested that at some point in the future, perhaps I would be interested in such a project. Well . . . I laughed like Sarah! It was inconceivable to me how I could ever possibly do such a thing. But one year later, as I considered the many ways in which my life had been changed by the profound experience I had with the Exercises, I found myself sitting in Kevin's office again, discussing the call I sensed to write this book. From the day I began to work on it until now, Kevin has been my constant guide, offering suggestions on every draft, sending me articles to read, putting me in touch with Jesuits and with others in Jesuit circles who might have insights to offer, and having numerous conversations with me about the history and practice of giving the Exercises. I would never have undertaken this project if he had not suggested it, and without his generous guidance and encouragement it would not have been possible.

For reading the entire manuscript and offering immeasurably helpful suggestions and feedback I am particularly grateful to Brian McDermott, SJ, and Anthony Moore, as well as three anonymous referees for the Catholic University of America Press. I have also benefited greatly from conversations with Francis X. Clooney, SJ, Howard Gray, SJ, John O'Malley, SJ, Benedict Jung, SJ, Jerry Blaszczak, SJ, Daniel Madigan, SJ, Christopher Steck, SJ, Karen Stohr, Jonathan Rice, Vicki Pedrick, Jim Keane, and Kate Cullen. All of these individuals offered suggestions that contributed to this book, and I am immensely grateful.

I presented material from this book or discussed the project in a variety of forums over the past few years, and I wish to thank the audience at the International Conference on Confucianism and Catholicism: Reinvigorating the Dialogue, held in March 2016 at Georgetown University, for helpful comments and questions on an earlier version of the chapter on Confucianism. I am especially grateful to Kevin Doak and Bill Farge, SJ, for their questions and our subsequent conversations about different kinds of religious practices in East Asia. I also thank the audience in the workshop on "Offering the 19th Annotation Retreat to University Faculty and Staff" at the Ignatian Spirituality Conference, held in July 2015 at St. Louis University, for their helpful questions and comments on my project. I would also like to thank my fellow participants in the Seminar on the Jesuit Constitutions at Georgetown as well as the Chaplaincy Directors at Georgetown for conversations about my project in relation to campus life at a religiously diverse Jesuit university today.

I received the generous support of a Jesuit Mission Grant from Georgetown University's Office of Mission and Ministry and the Office of the Provost, which allowed me to complete this book. I would also like to thank Georgetown's Office of the Vice-President for Global Engagement for an International Collaborate Grant that furthered my work on this project through the International Conference on Confucianism and Catholicism.

I want to express my appreciation to the entire editorial team at the Catholic University of America Press, who made this book possible through their hours of hard work. I am particularly grateful to John Martino for his interest and support for this project from the beginning, and for his very helpful feedback along the way. My special thanks to Theresa Walker for all of her editorial work, to Anne Needham for outstanding copyediting, to Brian Roach for his support on the marketing end, and to Kachergis Book Design for the beautiful cover.

I would like to thank Philip J. Ivanhoe and Michael Puett, two senior scholars in the field of Chinese philosophy and religion, who offered great encouragement to me as I pursued this project. From the day I told them about it, they saw it as an exciting and appropriate (as opposed to bizarre) departure from writing books about Chinese philosophy, and I am forever grateful for their vision and appreciation for what I am doing in this book.

Finally, thanks are due to my family. My parents, Michael and Dorothy Cline, and my brother, Kelly, and sister-in-law, Jamie, asked great questions about Jesuits and spiritual exercises while providing constant encouragement as I worked on this book. And as always, I owe the biggest debt of gratitude to my husband, Michael, who read each version of the manuscript, offering invaluable feedback and encouragement, and who had countless conversations about the adaptation of the Spiritual Exercises with me. Being married to a scholar of religion with special expertise in William James's *Varieties of Religious Experience* was a special asset as I took on this project, as was his generosity in lovingly caring for our children while I worked on it. I am grateful, too, to our two older children, Patrick and Bridget, who are always showing me how to find God in all things.

This work is dedicated to our youngest daughter, Siobhan Mary, and to her godfather, Kevin O'Brien. She is truly a child of the Exercises: during the year that I was making the nineteenth-annotation retreat, the question of whether to have another child was a matter of discernment for our family. Siobhan, you are nineteen months old as I write this, and the best part of my day is when you lay your head down on my shoulder each night before I put you to bed. May you one day discover for yourself the beautiful gift of the Exercises, which helped bring you to us.

Introduction

Teaching and studying theology means living on a frontier, one
in which the Gospel meets the needs of the people to whom it
should be proclaimed in an understandable and meaningful way.

—Pope Francis

O N SEPTEMBER 25, 2015, Pope Francis stood alongside Jewish,
Muslim, Hindu, Buddhist, Sikh, and Christian religious leaders in
an underground chamber at the 9/11 memorial, where the victims of the
World Trade Center attacks are memorialized. In one of the most memo-
rable scenes from his historic visit to the United States, each one offered
prayers or meditations first in their sacred languages, then in English,
and Pope Francis called on the religious leaders who surrounded him to
be a force for reconciliation: "In opposing every attempt to create a rigid
uniformity, we can and must build unity on the basis of our diversity of
languages, cultures and religions, and lift our voices against everything
which would stand in the way of such unity."[1] The scene was nothing
short of captivating, but Pope Francis's emphasis on personal encounter
with other religions, rather than on theological or doctrinal differences,
is not surprising coming from the first Jesuit pope. And the ideals that
Pope Francis articulates are not just hallmarks of the Jesuit order; recently Jesuits have begun to recognize the distinctive role that Ignatian spir-

Epigraph is from Pope Francis, *Letter of His Holiness Pope Francis to the Grand Chancellor of*
the 'Pontifica Universidad Catolica Argentina' for the 100th Anniversary of the Founding of the Facul-
ty of Theology, March 3, 2015, http://w2.vatican.va/content/francesco/en/letters/2015/documents/
papa-francesco_20150303_lettera-universita-cattolica-argentina.html.
   1. Pope Francis, *Interreligious Meeting, Address of the Holy Father, Ground Zero Memorial, New*
York, September 25, 2015, https://w2.vatican.va/content/francesco/en/speeches/2015/september/
documents/papa-francesco_20150925_usa-ground-zero.html.

ituality might be able to play in promoting interreligious understanding globally.

In recent years there has been a growing interest in interreligious dialogue, but an important question remains: How can members of different religions learn from each other not just at the level of theological reflection, political negotiation, or peace-building, but at the level of spirituality? Can we genuinely learn from one another in ways that will deepen and enrich our spiritual lives at the level of practice? And what is involved in adapting the spiritual practices of others to cross religious boundaries? While many Christians have benefited from engagement with meditative practices that have become popular in the West—particularly those derived from the Buddhist and Hindu traditions—does Christianity have similar spiritual riches to share with members of other faiths? This book focuses on how Ignatian spirituality can provide an answer to these questions, and how it provides an avenue to interreligious understanding that begins with understanding another religion from the inside out through spiritual practice.

The idea that Ignatian spirituality is eminently adaptable to different religious contexts is not new. In 2009 Fr. Adolfo Nicolás, then Superior General of the Jesuits, suggested in an address at Loyola Marymount University that important elements of Ignatian spirituality can be "fruitfully appropriated even by non-Christians." While acknowledging that the Ignatian Spiritual Exercises are "radically Christo-centric," Nicolás went on to say, "I would like to underline this idea that the Spiritual Exercises can be shared by non-Christians. Even though Christ is at the heart of the full experience of the Exercises, it is also true that their structure outlines a process of liberation—of opening to new horizons—that can benefit people who do not share our life of faith. This is something I would like to see explored more and more.... What are the dynamics in the Exercises that non-believers might make their own to find wider horizons in life, a greater sense of spiritual freedom?"[2] Called "spiritual exercises" because they reflect Ignatius of Loyola's belief that, like the body, the human spirit requires exercise in order to stay healthy (SE 1), these different ways

---

2. Adolfo Nicolás, SJ, "Companions in Mission: Pluralism in Action," Mission Day Keynote Address, Loyola Marymount University, Los Angeles, California, February 2, 2009, http://www.gonzaga.edu/About/Mission/docs/LoyolaMarymountUniversityAddressAdolfoNicolasSJ.pdf, 87–88.

of praying, meditating, and reading scripture give shape to the spiritual lives of Jesuits.[3] They also express, in an important way, the very heart of Christian spirituality—a spirituality that is grounded in following Christ. They offer a way of learning to recognize God's ongoing presence and discerning God's call in one's life and work, of deepening one's relationship with God and making decisions based on that relationship (SE 21). As such, the prospect of sharing the Exercises with members of other religions invites us to a deeper form of interreligious dialogue; indeed, it invites us to move beyond dialogue to genuine understanding through practice. Ignatian spirituality offers a practical way for Christians to share their spiritual riches with persons of other faiths—a way that is not bound up in technical terminology or confined to the armchair reflections of theologians and religious leaders, for it beckons us to interreligious understanding through religious experience.

The Exercises originated with the religious experiences of Inigo Lopez de Loyola, known to us today as Ignatius of Loyola (1491–1556). As a young Spanish courtier and soldier, he was injured in 1521 during a battle defending the honor of the Spanish crown and spent six months convalescing at his family castle. During this time, he began to notice movements of his soul: feelings, attractions, passions, ambitions, and dreams. While reading Ludolph of Saxony's *Life of Christ* and a version of the lives of the saints, Inigo began to imagine a life that differed from his life as a knight, which was filled with the pursuit of riches, fame, and worldly honors. He pictured a life similar to the saints he read about—a life dedicated to serving Christ—and when he imagined devoting his life to the service of God and others, he found himself uplifted by a deep sense of joy. In contrast, when he revisited his familiar daydreams of serving as a valiant knight, he was left with feelings of discontentment and unhappiness. Inigo came to believe that God was speaking to him through these interior attractions and reactions, and once he had recuperated he decided to test his desires on a pilgrimage. The result was a journey on which his soul was exercised through a profound set of experiences and

---

3. Throughout this work, all quotations from the text of the *Exercises* follow George E. Ganss, trans., *The Spiritual Exercises of Saint Ignatius* (St. Louis, Mo.: Institute of Jesuit Sources, 1992). They are cited parenthetically by section number (e.g., "SE 1" refers to *The Spiritual Exercises*, section 1). I will italicize "Spiritual Exercises" only when referring to the text; un-italicized references are to the practices that constitute the Exercises.

encounters with God. Throughout this time, Inigo kept a record of his insights and the movements of his soul, hoping that his experiences might be able to help others one day. He was right: his journal was the beginning of the manual of prayer that is now known as the *Spiritual Exercises*.

Ignatius, who went on to found the Jesuit order, used this manual to give the Exercises to others, but while the Exercises became a central feature of the Jesuit order, Ignatius always intended them for the benefit of the entire Church. Here we can see how close they are to the core of Christian spirituality more broadly. Indeed, in the text of the *Exercises*, he outlines three different ways of making the Exercises, which makes explicit his intention to give them to men and women from all walks of life, in a wide variety of forms based on the particular needs and backgrounds of different individuals (SE 18–20). In what is called an eighteenth-annotation retreat (because the adaptation is found in the eighteenth preliminary note that opens the *Exercises*), individuals experience some but not all of the Spiritual Exercises, often in a weekend or weeklong retreat. In the nineteenth-annotation retreat, a person is directed through the entirety of the Exercises over an extended period of time—perhaps nine months or a year—without being removed from her or his daily life and work. The twentieth-annotation retreat involves making the full and complete Exercises in a more traditional retreat house setting over thirty or more consecutive days, during which one is completely removed from daily life.

Ignatius divided the Exercises into four parts that he called "weeks," but these are not calendar weeks. Rather, they are phases or movements felt within a person who is praying through the Exercises, beginning with consideration and experience of God's boundless generosity and unconditional love, our own limited response and patterns of sinfulness, and continuing with the experience of praying through the life, death, and resurrection of Jesus Christ presented in the gospels. The journey through the four weeks of the Exercises is not always linear, though; Ignatius insisted on the importance of adapting the Exercises to meet each person's individual needs and background, which means that one should not mechanically run through all of the Exercises at the same pace or even in the same order as others. Rather, under the guidance of a spiritual director, each person should move through the Exercises following the lead of the Spirit. The discernment of spirits underlies all four weeks of the Exercises. Ignatius intended the Exercises to help people make decisions grounded in their faith, whether this means making what Ignatius calls an "election"—a momentous decision or life choice—or whether it simply means checking to be sure one is heading in the right direction or deepening a call one has already embraced. Many believe that the deepest election for all exercitants is their choosing, under grace, to allow Christ to take over more and more of themselves, with the result that the particular choices coming from the exercitant (during the Exercises and afterward), are shaped by that deeper electing.[4] The Exercises gives the exercitant tools for discernment through various forms of prayer, whether or not one is making a formal election.[5] Throughout the Exercises, one learns what Ignatius learned during his convalescence—that God speaks to us through our thoughts, feelings, desires, attractions, and resistances. The Exercises offer a school of prayer that helps individuals to discern God's call in their own lives in part through a careful and systematic examination of these interior movements.

Ignatius always had a global vision; he sent Jesuits all over the world for various missions, often concluding the letters of instruction and encouragement that he wrote to them with the words, "Go and set the world on fire!" However, it would have been difficult for him to envision the possibility that members of other religious traditions would one day express interest in making the Spiritual Exercises. Indeed, while the Exercises have long been given to Christians around the world, including not only Jesuits but lay Catholics and Protestants, Father Nicolás's remarks about the Exercises and non-Christians raise a number of new and interesting questions. Which elements of the Exercises can be fruitfully appropriated by non-Christians, and in what ways should they be appropriated? What would it mean for non-Christians to "share" the Exercises or to make particular dynamics of the Exercises their own? The

---

4. Thanks to Brian McDermott, SJ, for this point. See, for example, Herbert Alphonso, SJ, *Discovering Your Personal Vocation: The Search for Meaning through the Spiritual Exercises* (New York: Paulist Press, 2001). Cf. St. Paul: ". . . it is no longer I who live, but it is Christ who lives in me" (Gal 2:20). (All quotations of scripture are taken from the New Revised Standard Version Bible: Catholic Edition, copyright © 1989, 1993, National Council of the Churches of Christ in the United States of America.)

5. I follow the Ganss translation in referring to those who are making the Exercises as "exercitants."

group Nicolás speaks of—"non-Christians"—is extraordinarily large and diverse, including members of non-Christian faith traditions as well as atheists, agnostics, and those who are "spiritual but not religious" or un-affiliated. As a result, there are good reasons to expect that the answers to these questions will vary considerably depending upon *which* non-Christians one is addressing. Indeed, in his recent work *Christian Spirituality for Seekers: Reflections on the Spiritual Exercises of Ignatius Loyola*, Roger Haight, SJ, seeks to interpret the Exercises "for a broad audience, not excluding Catholics but more pointedly addressing Protestants and also people outside Christianity, perhaps members of other religions, perhaps with no religious affiliation, who are looking for spiritual depth."[6] Haight's work focuses primarily on "seekers," a term he uses to refer to those with no explicitly developed religious faith, who "may or may not have a comprehensive framework for understanding human existence but are looking for deeper meaning in their lives."[7] So while Haight's work aims to show how the Exercises could be accessible to anyone seeking greater spiritual depth, his book is geared toward those without close ties to a religious tradition. He does not discuss any of the specific theological challenges that would be posed by adapting the Exercises for members of other religious traditions, who are committed to religious views and practices that differ from and in many cases conflict with the Christian theological view that is central to the Exercises. This is important to note, not as a shortcoming of Haight's work—for any book must have a particular focus in order to realistically achieve its aims—but as a reminder that Father Nicolás's claim that important elements of the Exercises can be shared by non-Christians involves different challenges depending upon the theological commitments of the non-Christians one is addressing. While I think Haight offers a compelling case for giving the Exercises to non-Christian "seekers," a further set of challenges is involved in defending the claim that the Spiritual Exercises can and should be shared by members of other faith traditions, simply because—as I will argue—the practical and theological challenges involved in adapting the Exercises for those of other faith traditions differ substantially from the

---

6. Roger Haight, SJ, *Christian Spirituality for Seekers: Reflections on the Spiritual Exercises of Ignatius Loyola* (Maryknoll, N.Y.: Orbis Books, 2012), xii.
    7. Ibid., xii, 88.

challenges of adapting the Exercises for "seekers." Here we can see clearly the need to distinguish between different types of non-Christians in order to practically address the challenge Father Nicolás presents.

With the aim of outlining how a new form of interreligious understanding might occur, this book explores the prospect of giving the Exercises to a particular subset of "non-Christians": members of other religious traditions, including but not limited to Buddhism, Confucianism, Daoism, Hinduism, Islam, and Judaism. It begins by exploring in chapter 1 the normative question of whether the Exercises *ought* to be given to (and therefore adapted for) members of other faith traditions, examining different theological justifications for this practice, including how it relates to the aims and purposes of the Exercises and to the Jesuit mission and especially its potential for contributing to mutual understanding among members of different faiths. The book then turns to the question of *how* one might go about adapting the Exercises for members of particular faith traditions, and what some of the specific challenges in that process might be. In order to undertake the latter task in a detailed manner, after addressing some of the shared challenges and questions relating to such an adaptation in chapter 2, I have narrowed my focus in the remaining chapters to the largest and most influential religious traditions of Asia. I have done this for multiple reasons. First, in order to offer an in-depth exploration of the very different kinds of challenges that are involved in adapting the Exercises for members of different traditions, and also in order to allow for an examination of the diversity *within* each of those traditions, I have chosen to devote a full chapter to the possibility of adapting the Exercises for members of each of three traditions: Hinduism, Buddhism, and Confucianism (although the chapter on Confucianism deals with Chinese religion and culture more broadly). I have chosen to focus on these traditions both because of space constraints and because of where my own scholarly expertise lies. It would be impossible to cover even all of the "major" faith traditions of the world carefully in one book, and no scholar has adequate training for such a task—again, if these traditions are to be examined in a detailed, in-depth manner. Here I have intentionally chosen depth over breadth, because I think we can learn more about what would be necessary in adapting the Exercises for members of other faiths and in sharing with one another on the level of spirituality by offering detailed explorations of a few traditions rather than superficial explorations of many.

There are multiple reasons for focusing on Hinduism, Buddhism, and Confucianism in particular, beginning with my own expertise. This set of issues is of particular interest to me because I am a comparative philosopher and theologian specializing in Chinese philosophy and religion, with a primary focus on Confucianism and Daoism and secondary training in Buddhism and Hinduism. I am also a Christian whose life was transformed by the Exercises. While I specialize in the earliest texts of the Confucian and Daoist traditions, I have also spent considerable time conducting fieldwork in contemporary China, observing and documenting the work of Daoist priests and female spirit mediums, as well as daily activities in Buddhist, Confucian, and Daoist temples in China today. Unlike most specialists in classical Chinese thought, my research has dealt with contemporary religious life, including the religious practices of these traditions as well as their foundational sacred texts. Obviously, given the tremendous diversity and complexity of each of these traditions, no single chapter could adequately address the full range of theological issues and challenges that would be involved in adapting the Exercises for members of these traditions. My aim in these chapters is to highlight some of the key issues that would play a role in adapting the Exercises for members of each tradition. I do this by focusing on some of the core theological commitments that are shared by most members of these traditions (despite the differences among members' specific beliefs), while also highlighting the diversity that exists within each tradition. The task of adapting the Exercises for a Shin Buddhist, for example, would present very different challenges than adapting the Exercises for a Zen Buddhist, and for this reason the chapter on Buddhism presents different types of adaptations for different types of Buddhists. One of my overarching aims in these chapters is to make clear just how far beyond talk of "non-Christians" we will have to go in order to respond constructively to the kind of interreligious exchange suggested in Father Nicolás's challenge; it is not enough to discuss "Abrahamic traditions" and "Asian traditions," or even to discuss "Buddhists" in general if we wish to address how the Exercises might be adapted for members of various faith traditions. Much more will required of us because of the dramatic theological differences that are in play, both within and among these traditions. The other overarching aim of these chapters is to move beyond the more abstract theological questions that are raised by adapting the Exercises for members of other religious traditions, to the specifics of practice. Given the nature of the Exercises, I think the very best way of getting at the issues that are at the heart of this project is to talk about specific theological commitments in relation to specific religious practices, in order to demonstrate how the Exercises might actually be adapted and also in order to fully understand the challenges of doing so. This will allow us to see how and why Ignatian spirituality is eminently adaptable to different religious contexts.

While my reason for focusing my attention on Asian traditions lies first and foremost with my own training and expertise, there are additional reasons why I think these traditions are especially important for this study. To begin, a number of questions about these traditions—especially Buddhism—have been raised in recent discussions of the Exercises, and I would like to continue these discussions and explore these questions more systematically.[8] Another reason for focusing on Asian religious traditions, though, is that these traditions often do not receive the attention they deserve when it comes to interreligious dialogue. As I will discuss further below, when those in Jesuit circles are asked about giving the Exercises to members of other religious traditions, they typically think first of Jews and Muslims. This is perfectly natural; the Abrahamic faiths share much in common, and these are most commonly the faith traditions that are at the center of Catholic interreligious dialogue today, for very practical reasons. However, when it comes to the study of the Exercises, there are good reasons one might turn first to Asian traditions. Jesuits have lived and worked in Asia throughout their history, and these are traditions they have long encountered and engaged, but there are far more important reasons than this historical link. For one, these traditions have influenced extraordinarily large numbers of people throughout Asia and have exceptionally long histories and deep roots in the cultures of those places; thus, not only do they have wide-ranging

8. See for instance Ruben Habito, *Zen and the Spiritual Exercises* (Maryknoll, N.Y.: Orbis, 2013), and Javier Melloni, SJ, *The Exercises of St. Ignatius and the Traditions of the East* (Leominster, U.K.: Gracewing, 2013).

influence in numbers, but also considerable depth of cultural influence, even for those who do not regard themselves as "members" of those traditions. All of the cultures of East Asia and Southeast Asia, for instance, are saturated in Confucianism, even though few people in the world today would call themselves Confucians. While most members of these cultures are deeply influenced by Confucian values and beliefs, most of them are also members of other religious traditions, or are members of no tradition at all. As a result of the unique and widespread cultural influence these traditions have had and continue to have, those who are giving or who wish to give the Exercises in East Asia, Southeast Asia, and South Asia—or to those who identify with or have been shaped by Asian cultures elsewhere—can learn much by exploring how particular aspects of Ignatian spirituality might resonate or fail to resonate in particular ways with these traditions, even if they are not adapting the Exercises for *members* of those traditions.

Another reason why Hinduism, Buddhism, and Confucianism are good traditions to start with is that if one can successfully show how the Exercises might be adapted for members of these traditions, one will have gone a considerable way toward showing how the Exercises might be adapted for members of any tradition, and how Christian spirituality can be shared with members of any religion. This is not only a result of the exceptional diversity found within and among these traditions, but because, as I will argue, particular branches of these traditions pose the greatest challenges to the prospect of adapting the Exercises for members of other faith traditions: these traditions do not always entail a commitment to some form of monotheism, and some do not even entail a commitment to theism. In other words, among the diverse traditions of Asia, we find traditions that differ more dramatically from Christianity than many people expect *any* religious traditions to differ. In these very same traditions—Zen Buddhism being a prime example—we find some of the most popular and widely celebrated contemplative practices in the world.[9] This represents an additional reason why those in Jesuit

---

9. The term "contemplative practice" refers to a broad category of religious practices including different forms of meditation and prayer. The emerging field of Contemplative Studies focuses on the study and application of these practices, which aim to cultivate contemplative states of mind. Although they differ in many ways, these states are associated with religious experiences;

circles and Christians more broadly should be interested in how these traditions interface with Ignatian spirituality: I will argue that an understanding of the contemplative practices of other traditions can not only help to clarify the truly distinctive features and aims of the Exercises, but can also assist with the process of encouraging scholars who study contemplative practices to study also the Exercises. The emerging field of Contemplative Studies is currently dominated by the study of practices found in Asian traditions; practices from Islam and Judaism are often included as well, but Christianity has a more limited presence. This reflects a dominant trend in American culture more generally, including the popularity of Kabbala as well as Buddhist and Hindu forms of meditation. The Ignatian Spiritual Exercises are worthy of greater attention in contemplative studies and in the wider culture, but unless there is greater engagement with practices that in at least *some* ways serve analogous functions in other religious traditions, and an attempt to articulate the distinctive features and contributions of the Exercises within this larger family of practices, such attention is unlikely. Relating the Exercises to Asian traditions—and Christian spirituality to other forms of spirituality—is an important first step in this process.

A word of further explanation and clarification about my discussion of other religious traditions, and the Asian traditions on which I focus most extensively, is required here. When I first began to work on this project and began talking with those in Jesuit circles about members of other faith traditions making the Exercises, two interesting things happened. First, I found that many people assumed I was including Protestants among "members of other faith traditions," and they subsequently began to present arguments that Protestants could make the Exercises and gain much from them, despite the theological differences between Protestants and Catholics. I agree wholeheartedly, and my sense is that this is a relatively settled issue among most who give the Exercises today. This is why, I think, Father Nicolás encouraged the exploration of how the Exercises can be shared by "non-Christians" (as opposed to "non-Catholics"). But I want to linger over this issue momentarily, because in order to appreciate the challenges that are involved in giving the

---

they are typically the highest states of calm and are often accompanied by a deep sense of oneness, unity, or emptiness.

Exercises to members of other faith traditions, it is important to begin by appreciating all that is shared by Christians, despite their diversity. As a philosopher and theologian in a Catholic theology department, and as a Protestant who has been a part of faith communities from a number of different denominations and also has a deep affinity for Catholicism, I have an especially keen appreciation for the theological diversity within the Christian tradition. By no means do I want to minimize this diversity or oversimplify it. However, as a comparative philosopher and theologian who specializes in Asian traditions, I am also aware that the theological differences between Catholicism and Protestantism are not even close to being on the same scale as the differences between Christians and Buddhists. I think it a worthy and important task to address the particular challenges of giving the Spiritual Exercises to Protestants who, for instance, likely do not share Catholic beliefs about Mary and indeed may never have encountered Mary prayerfully before, or Pentecostal Christians who place a much greater emphasis on the role of the Holy Spirit than the Exercises do. But I do not think these challenges—or the adaptations of the Exercises that might be required in order to address them— are potentially fatal to the integrity of the Exercises in the way that some of the challenges involved in giving the Exercises to members of other faith traditions are.

A second interesting thing that happened when I began to work on this project is that I talked to a number of Jesuits who were aware of Jews and Muslims who were interested in making the Exercises, some of whom had made the Exercises in a modified form during a weekend or weeklong retreat. The modifications that I heard about drew upon scriptures from the Hebrew Bible that are shared by Jews, Muslims, and Christians. There are some important things to note here. First, these three faith traditions have some shared scriptures. This is not insignificant and at the very least gives us a natural place to begin when adapting the Exercises for Jews and Muslims. Those who give the Exercises to members of these traditions would be familiar with at least some of the sacred texts that are important to Jews and Muslims, because they, too, regard them as sacred texts. In the following chapters it will become clear that not only the shared scripture and history of these traditions but also their shared belief in a single God who shares many of the same characteristics—including the belief that God wishes to have a relationship with human beings—is incredibly important when it comes to adapting the Exercises. This is because one of the fundamental aims of the Exercises is to help individuals to develop that relationship, and a number of shared values follow from a belief that God desires a relationship with humans. While many Christians assume that all religious traditions have an analogue to God, often described as a conception of "the Divine" (and note here the tendency to use language that refers to a single entity), as we shall see, this assumption is not easy to defend. This work will deal substantially with the question of how we should understand the purposes of the Exercises and of Christian spirituality more broadly, and if one of those purposes is to help one to create or deepen a relationship with God, then one can at least begin the process of adaptation on firm ground with Judaism and Islam.

The shared Christian, Jewish, and Muslim belief in a God who wishes to have a relationship with humans helps to explain why some Jews and Muslims have indeed made modified, partial versions of the Exercises. The latter point is not one to pass over lightly, though. The eighteenth, nineteenth, and twentieth annotations to the Exercises outline three different ways of making the Exercises, but only the latter two entail making the full and complete Exercises. Despite the shared belief in God and the shared scriptures and history, the fact that the Exercises are, as Father Nicolás puts it, "radically Christo-centric" presents substantial challenges for Jews and Muslims who wish to make the full and complete Exercises. Ultimately, while it would be easier to adapt *parts* of the Exercises for Jews and Muslims than it would be for most members of other faith traditions, because of the Abrahamic faith traditions' shared belief in God and their shared scriptures and history, for these very same reasons other parts of the Exercises could possibly be *more* difficult to adapt than they would be for members of other faith traditions. For it is precisely *because* of their shared history that Judaism and Islam have explicit views concerning who Jesus was and who he was not. Much will depend, of course, on the particular orientation of the individual making the Exercises, and this is something I will discuss at length in the following chapters. Nevertheless, as a result of the extraordinary degree of complexity in understanding the different views found in Abrahamic faith traditions concerning Jesus and in considering how the Exercises might need to be adapted in light of them, I believe the particular challenges involved in adapting the Exercises for Jews and Muslims will be best addressed by those who specialize in Judaism and Islam, and also by those who have experience giving modified forms of the Exercises to Jews and Muslims (as well as by Jews and Muslims who have made the Exercises in any form). For this reason and for the other reasons discussed above, I do not attempt chapter-length discussions of these traditions. However, my general discussions of adapting the Exercises for other faith traditions in the first two chapters of this book—including a more in-depth examination of some of the issues I have just touched on—applies to Judaism and Islam as well the traditions I discuss in greater detail in later chapters.

In order to engage the Exercises in greater depth and in order to see how genuine interreligious understanding can be promoted through first-hand engagement with Christian spirituality, I will focus strictly on the prospect of giving the full and complete Exercises. By "full and complete" I mean first and foremost the content of the retreat, meaning all four weeks of the Exercises. But making the full and complete Exercises is not only a matter of content; it is also a qualitative—a matter of depth rather than just breadth.[10] I am interested in whether all four weeks of the Exercises can be adapted in a way that not only makes them accessible and fruitful for members of other faiths, but which also includes the depth (and not just the breadth) that is emblematic of the experience of the full and complete Exercises.

My decision to focus on the nineteenth and twentieth annotations and not on the eighteenth annotation is rooted in my conversations with Jesuits and others who have given the Exercises to members of other traditions during weekend or weeklong retreats, conversations that make clear that the Exercises *can* be adapted quite successfully in a partial form for members of other traditions. Two caveats are important here. First, what "successfully" means is complicated, and many of the pages

---

10. This means that one might pray through all four weeks of the Exercises without experiencing the full and complete Exercises, because there is a *magis—something more, deeper, or richer*—still awaiting. Much depends upon the extent to which the exercitant allows Christ to take them over more and more, over the course of the Exercises. This takes a keen sense of adventure for Christians, and even more so for members of other faiths. Thanks to Brian McDermott, SJ, for conversation on these points.

that follow explore how the aims and purposes of the Exercises are best understood in relation to other faith traditions. What I mean here is simply that the Exercises were adapted in a way that was meaningful for, and deepened the faith of, members of other traditions who made the Exercises in that form. Second, I fully recognize that simply because the Exercises *have* been adapted successfully for members of non-Christian faith traditions does not mean that this *should* be done. There are various arguments that can be (and have been) made against the practice of adapting the Exercises for members of other traditions. This is why the first chapter of this book is dedicated to examining the theological justifications for giving the Exercises to members of other faith traditions, and these justifications apply to giving the Exercises in whole or in part. It is, however, important to understand that it is much easier to give *parts* of the Exercises to members of other faith traditions (e.g., the first week) with significant adaptations (e.g., using only Hebrew scriptures) than it is to similarly adapt the full and complete Exercises for members of other traditions. For instance, if one attempted to adapt the full and complete Exercises so that they made use of only Hebrew scriptures, it is not clear what one would do in the second, third, and fourth weeks, since they center on the life, death, and resurrection of Jesus Christ presented in the gospels; indeed, given how dramatically removing the story of Jesus Christ would alter the content of the Exercises, it is difficult to see how they would still be the Spiritual Exercises. If one wished to construct a four-week retreat drawing wholly upon Hebrew scriptures, one would surely be better off turning to the contemplative traditions within Judaism and Islam. One might engage in a new creative project that would meld some key themes and approaches from the Ignatian Spiritual Exercises with contemplative practices in other traditions, but wouldn't this be to create some new set of spiritual exercises that are informed by the Ignatian tradition but nevertheless distinct from the Spiritual Exercises? The key questions this book explores are fully evident here: How much can the Exercises be adapted or changed before they are no longer the Exercises? How much can they be changed and still achieve their purposes or aims? What are those aims? What are the defining features of the Exercises, and what makes them distinctive when compared with the rich and diverse forms of contemplation, prayer, and meditation that one finds in other faith traditions? What are the various reasons that members of other traditions might be interested in making the Spiritual Exercises, and are those reasons faithful to the purposes of the Exercises?

In addition to clarifying the boundaries of what I am exploring in this book, I want to briefly clarify what type of work this is. Most importantly, this book is not primarily descriptive: it is not a survey of Christian spiritual practices nor is it a historical or social-scientific study of whether and to what extent Jesuits and others who are trained to give the Exercises have given or are giving them to members of different faith traditions around the world. There has been excellent work done by historians on the history of the Exercises, and, although I discuss some of this history, it is not possible to include a survey of it here, nor is a historical study my aim in this work.[11] The task of documenting what Jesuits and others who are trained to give the Exercises are currently doing with the Exercises is important and interesting, but it is also a monumental task that is best suited for those who are trained in sociology of religion and who have at their disposal the tools to conduct a careful (and very large, and international) ethnographic study.[12] Perhaps most importantly, historical and social-scientific projects differ from this one because they are primarily descriptive. Instead of attempting to document what Jesuits and others who give the Exercises are doing, as a philosopher and a theologian I am interested in offering a *normative* account—in exploring what *ought* to be done and where the key challenges lie. My account

11. See, for example, the historical work of John O'Malley, George Ganss, and John Padberg. Historians focused on particular countries and regions have done important work on the history of the Exercises in particular places. See for example Nicolas Standaert, "The Spiritual Exercises of Ignatius of Loyola in the China Mission of the 17th and 18th Centuries," *Archivum Historicum Societatis Iesu* 81 (2012): 73–124. Studies of particular Jesuit missionaries offer insights on these matters as well. See for example Anthony D'Costa, SJ, *The Call of the Orient: A Response by Jesuits in the Sixteenth Century* (Mumbai: Heras Institute of Indian History and Culture, 1999); and Jonathan Spence, *The Memory Palace of Matteo Ricci* (New York: Viking, 1984).

12. There are, of course, scattered reflections on this topic by Jesuits. Francis Clooney points out that some Indian Jesuits have written about how the Exercises are being read and used in India, citing a number of essays in *Ignis*, the Indian journal of Jesuit spirituality, from the 1970s to 2000, as well as comparative works on Hinduism and Christianity, such as those by Sebastian Painadath, Varghese Malpan, and Ignatius Hirudayam, and Michael Amaladoss's *Inigo in India* (Anand, India: Gujarat Sahitya Prakash, 1992). See Francis Clooney, SJ, "Learning to Learn Interreligiously: In Light of the *Spiritual Exercises* of St. Ignatius of Loyola," *Asian Christian Review* 2, no. 1 (2008): 75–78.

is also *practical*: while I examine the different kinds of theological justifications for adapting Exercises for members of other traditions, I am
most concerned to spell out how such an adaptation would work, what
the practical challenges would be, and how they might be addressed. In
order to do all of this, I draw upon my conversations with Jesuits around
the world who are giving and have given the Exercises—for any good
normative theory is informed by actual practice—but I do not attempt
to document or describe in detail what Jesuits and other trained directors in various places are doing. I believe the latter task should be undertaken not in a piecemeal sort of way but carefully, in a way that systematically documents what Jesuits around the world are doing, which
will require a substantial book-length study of its own. I also believe it
is important to distinguish between the tasks of describing what is being done and presenting an argument for what ought to be done. And as
readers will see, I think it is a mistake to move too quickly (and uncritically) from one to the other. That being said, I think it is worth noting
that I did not encounter any evidence that the practice of giving the full
and complete Exercises to members of other faith traditions is common
or widespread, though I talked with a number of Jesuits who found the
prospect intriguing.

Outline of Chapters

Chapter 1 begins by tackling the broader question of why the Exercises
should be given to *anyone*, and how the Exercises are close to the core of
Christian spirituality: What are the aims and purposes of the Exercises as
Ignatius originally envisioned them and as they have evolved over time?
How are these aims emblematic of Christian spirituality? In order to
give the Exercises to members of other religious traditions, would those
purposes need to be adapted? Why, and in what ways? What are the potential pitfalls of altering the purposes of the Exercises? The second part
of the chapter examines the Jesuit mission in relation to the possibility
of giving the Exercises to members of other traditions, including Father
Nicolás's discussion of Jesuit norms for choice of mission and the impact of the decrees issued by two Jesuit General Congregations (GC 34
and GC 35) on how the relationship with co-workers and companions

in mission should be understood. The final part of the chapter examines two different kinds of theological justifications for giving the Exercises to members of other faith traditions, and also examines and responds to arguments against this practice. Here I focus strongly on the larger relevance of this book: the prospect of interreligious understanding and exchange at the level of spirituality, and the reasons why the future of interreligious dialogue lies in this task.

Chapter 2 focuses on the general questions relating to how the exercises would best be adapted for members of other faith traditions, including a broad spectrum of possibilities, from heavier to lighter forms of adaptation. The chapter begins with an examination of some general questions relating to the Exercises and adaptation, including the question of who is a good candidate to make the full and complete Exercises, followed by an exploration of how or in what ways the Exercises are usually adapted for different individuals and why the process of adaptation is central to their aims and purposes. Here we will be able to see some of the reasons why Ignatian spirituality is eminently adaptable to different religious contexts. I then turn from a general examination of these questions to an exploration of why members of other faith traditions might be interested in making the Exercises and what might make members of other faiths (as opposed to Christians) good candidates to make the full and complete Exercises. Especially because the Exercises are not designed to be a tool for conversion to Christianity, I attend closely to how the aims and purposes of the Exercises would apply to members of other faiths. I go on to present an argument against heavier forms of adaptation for members of other traditions—where significant parts of the Exercises would be removed and replaced with sources from other traditions—for reasons relating to the motivations and needs of such individuals and based on some more general issues of advisability and feasibility, including some of the underlying theological assumptions of such views. Instead, I argue in favor of the approach to adaptation that is widely observed by Jesuits giving the Exercises to Christians today, with the addition of particular kinds of supplemental sources. The following chapters go on to explore what these kinds of supplemental sources might need to address for those making the Exercises who are from specific faith traditions.

In the chapters on Hinduism and Buddhism, I focus primarily on the question of how the full and complete Exercises should be adapted for members of these traditions.[13] However, I stress in these chapters the diversity of belief and practice that is a part of both Hinduism and Buddhism, which means that although I suggest texts, themes, and ideas from these traditions that are shared widely and that are therefore likely resources for adaptation, each individual will require her or his own adaptations; we must guard against the temptation to expect members of another faith tradition to be more alike than members of one's own faith tradition. Indeed, the chapter on Buddhism focuses on two different clusters or types of Buddhism: theistic Buddhism (which typically includes a belief in multiple deities and which describes a majority of Buddhists worldwide) and philosophical Buddhism (which is typically non-theistic and focuses strongly on contemplative practice, seen for instance in Zen Buddhism). In the chapters on Hinduism and Buddhism, I also stress the importance of guarding against an overly ambitious approach to adaptation; it is important to remember that adaptations are for the purpose of removing stumbling blocks that would prevent exercitants from being able to deepen their faith and to grow in various ways from the Exercises. If an exercitant is not stumbling, there is usually no need to work out an adaptation tied to her faith tradition. To this end, I highlight particular places and themes in the Exercises that might be common stumbling blocks for Hindus and Buddhists, and I suggest possible ways to address them, often using the resources of the Hindu and Buddhist traditions.

In the chapter focused on Confucianism, I turn from the task of outlining adaptations of the full and complete Exercises for members of other traditions to a different type of endeavor: I explore some of the other ways in which Ignatian spirituality might meaningfully inform the lives of those who identify with, or have been shaped by, other traditions: How might elements of the Exercises be "fruitfully appropriated" or "shared" by non-Christians, as Father Nicolás suggested, without their making the Exercises? How might members of other traditions make

13. For the sake of manageability and length, in this book I focus primarily on outlining adaptations for the four weeks of the Exercises in as much detail as possible, but I do not cover the Election, which is certainly worthy of its own treatment.

certain dynamics in the Exercises their own, outside of adapting the Exercises? What might those in Jesuit circles do to encourage and facilitate this process, and what can it help us to achieve, at the level of interreligious dialogue and cooperation? Since few people in the world today would describe themselves as Confucians but many are deeply influenced by this tradition culturally, it would make little sense to outline an adaptation for "Confucians," but Confucianism presents an excellent test case for how Ignatian spirituality might enrich the lives of members of other cultural traditions, without having individuals make the full and complete Exercises. I argue that one of the keys to preserving the integrity of the Exercises while adapting them for members of other traditions is to carefully distinguish between giving the Exercises and innovating new practices that are inspired by and perhaps even based on the Exercises. I discuss examples of the latter in relation to Confucianism, aiming to show how distinguishing between these tasks has the added benefit of encouraging us to do both intentionally. Both are worthy endeavors, and each one answers the call that Father Nicolás presented, but we must also understand that they are different tasks, each with its own distinctive aims and challenges.

The conclusion to this work discusses some of the practical challenges that the prospect of giving the full Exercises to members of other traditions might pose for those in Jesuit circles, such as the need for more individuals who are trained to give the Exercises, as well as the need for additional training and resources for those who would give the Exercises to members of other religious traditions. I also discuss the importance of these kinds of adaptations for Jesuit institutions, including schools and universities where students, faculty, and staff come from diverse religious backgrounds and yet all play an important role in preserving, expressing, and shaping the Jesuit identity of their institutions.

1

Why Should Ignatian
Spirituality Be Shared with
Other Religions?

W HILE MUCH has been written about the importance of interreligious dialogue, very little work has focused what interreligious
understanding might look like at the level of spiritual practice. Some
have suggested that we ought to share and exchange spiritual practices across faiths, but little has been done to work out the details of what
that might mean and how it might actually be done. Yet spirituality represents a unique opportunity for members of different religions to move
beyond dialogue *about* interreligious understanding to the actual practice
of interreligious understanding. The idea that Christian spirituality—or
the spirituality of any religion—might potentially enrich and enliven the
spiritual lives of members of other religions is grounded in the idea that
interreligious understanding should be more than simply understanding
and dialoguing about *what* members of other religions believe; the sort of
understanding that is promoted in such an exchange is accompanied by
firsthand insight into why others believe and practice as they do. It is accompanied also by a desire to share the spiritual riches of one's own tradition with others and to draw from theirs, not in order to leave one's own
tradition or to convert others, but with the aim of genuinely enriching the
spiritual lives of all.

Within the Christian tradition, Ignatian spirituality has unique resources to contribute to this sort of exchange, and there is a historical

precedent for it, as well. In *The First Jesuits*, John O'Malley writes that the idea of giving the Ignatian Spiritual Exercises to members of other faith traditions was not entirely foreign to the first Jesuits. In 1553, Jeronimo Nadal, in his *Apologia* for the Exercises against their detractors, "advanced his 'personal' opinion that at least up to a certain point they could be adapted to heretics and even to pagans. His justification for this viewpoint was that the *Exercises* essentially taught nothing more than that human beings were 'to love God above all things, with all their heart, all their mind, all their soul, and all their strength.'"[1] Perhaps this is not surprising, for the first Jesuits were going to places such as India, Japan, and China, where they encountered a rich variety of non-Christian religious traditions—including those that are the focus of this book. But, as Francis Clooney points out, "a long Jesuit tradition of interreligious encounter" does not easily inspire interreligious learning today: "We have little evidence (at least in the India context, with which I am most familiar) that the missionaries thought there were like-minded, like-practicing persons around them, as their religious peers."[2] Considering the examples of Matteo Ricci (late sixteenth century China) and Roberto de Nobili (early seventeenth century India), Clooney writes, "Despite their cultural creativity and determination to be open where possible, in the end, whatever they identify as 'pagan,' they reject."[3] The Exercises were not viewed as a tool for conversion; they were clearly designed for Catholics already grounded in their faith, so in China, for instance, Ricci gave them only to Catholics, as did Francis Xavier before him, in other parts of Asia.[4] So

---

1. John O'Malley, SJ, *The First Jesuits* (Cambridge, Mass.: Harvard University Press, 1993), 38–39. Ignatius entrusted the first promulgation of the *Constitutions* to Nadal, writing that he "altogether knows my mind and enjoys [for this task] the same authority as myself." Juan Alfonso de Polanco, who worked with Ignatius on the *Constitutions*, wrote of Nadal that "'He knows our father, Master Ignatius, well because he has had many dealings with him, and he seems to have understood his spirit and comprehended our Institute as well as anyone I know in the Society'" (quoted in O'Malley, *The First Jesuits*, 12).

2. Francis X. Clooney, SJ, "Learning to Learn Interreligiously: In Light of the *Spiritual Exercises* of St. Ignatius of Loyola," *Asian Christian Review* 2, no. 1 (2008), 74n14, 74.

3. Ibid., 74.

4. Ricci gave the first week of the Exercises to certain Chinese Catholics and also used Ignatian prayer methods with them. Jesuits in China during the seventeenth and eighteenth centuries gave the Exercises in a variety of forms to Christians. In letters to Ignatius, Xavier mentions a Catholic convert in Goa who was making the Exercises, as well as the need for more Jesuits to come "to preach and undertake the conversion of infidels," and others to "hear confessions and give the *Spiritual Exercises*." There is no evidence to suggest that they entertained the possibility of

while the Exercises were undoubtedly important in the lives of the early missionary Jesuits in Asia and elsewhere, they were not regarded as a resource for engaging members of other traditions. Indeed, giving them to other Christians was a rare and substantial challenge. O'Malley notes that while in the early days of the Society a few Protestants did make the Exercises, the sacramental confession of the sins of one's past life in the first week would be "among the many stumbling blocks that would deter heretics [Protestants], infidels [Muslims], and pagans [members of indigenous religions in places where Jesuits were missionaries] from entering upon the full *Exercises*."[5] The general confession that is a part of the first week, he writes, "does not itself require a Catholic sacrament to achieve its end, but the sacrament was the mode Ignatius had learned and himself practiced."[6]

O'Malley's remarks raise a number of interesting questions. To begin, he shows that the first Jesuits considered the possibility of adapting the Exercises to non-Catholics, and even non-Christians. Nadal advances an understanding of the purposes of the Exercises that sees them as teaching that humans are to love God—which means that there would be no reason to exclude non-Christians from making them. To the contrary, if the Exercises are an engaging way of sharing the Gospel, then perhaps they should be given widely, without hesitation. O'Malley, though, draws our attention to some of the specifics that made this difficult in the early days of the Jesuits, including the role of Catholic sacraments in the Exercises. This is worth considering, especially because over time Jesuits giving the Exercises have successfully adapted them for Protestants, which in part means that these sacraments are among the elements of the Exercises that are sometimes removed as part of an adaptation. While O'Malley is of course correct that the sacrament was the mode Ignatius practiced, he is also correct in noting that the general confession that is so central to the first week does not require a Catholic sacrament to achieve

---

giving the Exercises to non-Christians. On Ricci and Chinese missionaries, see Nicolas Standaert, "The Spiritual Exercises of Ignatius of Loyola in the China Mission of the 17th and 18th Centuries," *Archivum Historicum Societatis Iesu* 81 (2012): 73–124; for Xavier's letters, see M. Joseph Costelloe, SJ, trans., *The Letters and Instructions of Francis Xavier* (St. Louis, Mo.: Institute of Jesuit Sources, 1992), 219n18, 225.

5. O'Malley, *The First Jesuits*, 39.

6. Ibid.

its end. This is one of the reasons why many who give the Exercises to-day see the removal of the sacramental confession as acceptable. Another reason, however, is that one must weigh the gains against the losses. If a Christian does not believe in particular ritual obligations or does not find them meaningful, does this mean we should not give her the Exercises? Those who have given the Exercises to Christians who are not Catholic have not found it difficult to give the Exercises with sacraments such as this one removed, partly because the sacraments are a relatively minor part of the Exercises as Ignatius originally envisioned them.

Of course, much depends on what one deems "minor," and why, but those who give the Exercises are acutely aware of Ignatius's own insistence on the importance of adaptation. This means that he never intended for everyone to make the Exercises in the same way. Annotation 15 is one of the central reasons why adaptation is the modus operandi of the Exercises: God works directly with each person, and thus spiritual directors must be flexible, because each person is different and unique.[7] In the next chapter of this work, we will explore the different ways in which Ignatius recommends adapting the Exercises for each exercitant, taking into account a person's disposition, age, education, and ability, as well as the ways that different spirits affect them. Some people, he says, will work more diligently than others, while some "are more pushed back and forth and tested by different spirits" (SE 18, 4). The adaptations he suggests include lengthening or shortening different parts of the Exercises (SE 4), explaining the rules for recognizing the different kinds of spirits earlier in the retreat if necessary and warranted (SE 8, 9, 10), and having exercitants spend more time in contemplation in times of desolation (SE 13). He writes that "exercitants should be given, each one, as much as they are willing to dispose themselves to receive, for their greater help and progress," which suggests considerable flexibility (SE 18). O'Malley points out that Ignatius believed the Exercises needed to be adapted according to the situation and needs of the individual but writes that he "did not envision the possibility of omitting the basic elements of the first week for anybody who wanted to continue beyond it. If the purpose of that week was successfully achieved, the individuals had found a new

---

7. Ignatius says this from his own experience, including the experience, detailed in the *Autobiography*, in which God worked with him directly, as a teacher works with a pupil.

and happier orientation at the very core of their being and were thus set more firmly than before on the path to salvation."[8] Here again O'Malley's discussion raises some key questions for us. First, if we do not have evidence that Ignatius envisioned a particular adaptation, should we avoid it? Second, how are we to decide what the "basic elements" of the Exercises are? What is the basis for deciding that the sacramental confession is a basic element? Is it that Ignatius himself did not envision the possibility of omitting it? Most contemporary Jesuits giving and writing about the Exercises today do not seem to accept this type of view, for many reasons, one of which O'Malley's subsequent remarks about the *purpose* of the first week anticipate. In deciding how to adapt the Exercises for an exercitant, one's greatest responsibility seems to be to discern whether it is faithful to the purposes of the Exercises. In some cases, after all, the removal of particular elements might be the very thing that facilitates the achievement of the purposes of the Exercises.

It is only natural to begin this work with an examination of the purposes of the Exercises—which is in fact how Ignatius opens the text of the *Spiritual Exercises*—because this will tell us about the fundamental rationale for giving the Exercises to *anyone*. What are they designed to achieve? What ends do the Exercises aim to serve? In the first part of this chapter, I will examine what Ignatius says in the *Spiritual Exercises* concerning the aims and purposes of the Exercises, and how the purposes of the Exercises seem to have been understood by Jesuits giving the Exercises, beginning with the practices of Ignatius and his companions, and continuing with those who give the Exercises today. Then in the second part of the chapter, we will explore how the purposes of the Exercises should be understood in relation to the Jesuit sense of mission and, more broadly, in relation to Christian spirituality. We will examine closely the Jesuit mission as it is conceived both in the *Constitutions of the Society of Jesus* and in the more recent documents of the thirty-fourth and thirty-fifth Jesuit General Congregations, including how Jesuit mission relates to giving the Exercises. Finally, the third part of the chapter will consider two different theological justifications for the practice of having members of other religions make the Exercises, one of which is

8. O'Malley, *The First Jesuits*, 39–40.

inclusivistic (since it does not regard conversion to Christianity as necessary for salvation) and the other of which is exclusivistic (since it regards conversion to Christianity as necessary for salvation). Drawing upon the preceding discussions of the purposes of the Exercises and Jesuit mission, I will argue that both of these theological justifications have merit and provide reasonable arguments that it is acceptable to give the full and complete Exercises to certain (though not all) members of other religious traditions.

What Are the Aims and Purposes of the Exercises?

In the opening lines of *The Spiritual Exercises*, Ignatius clarifies what he means by the term "spiritual exercises": "every method of examination of conscience, meditation, contemplation, vocal or mental prayer, and other spiritual activities. . . . For, just as taking a walk, traveling on foot, and running are physical exercises, so is the name of spiritual exercises given to any means of preparing and disposing our soul to rid itself of all its disordered affections and then, after their removal, of seeking and finding God's will in the ordering of our life for the salvation of our soul" (SE 1). Although he will have more to say about the aims of the Exercises in the following pages, this is our first indication of how Ignatius understands them. He outlines a twofold process: (1) preparing and disposing one's soul for the removal of disordered affections, which are understood as "tendencies, attachments, etc., which are not ordered according to the principles in the Foundation" (meaning the kind of interior freedom described by "indifference" in the Principle and Foundation),[9] and (2) after the removal of disordered affections, seeking and finding God's will in the ordering of one's life for the salvation of one's soul. As Michael Ivens points out, the purpose of the Exercises is explained as a conversion of the heart, conceived as both a "turning to" and "turning from": "'Turning to' in the language of the Exercises consists in seeking and finding the will of God, while the correlative 'turning from' is the process of getting

9. George E. Ganss, trans., *The Spiritual Exercises of Saint Ignatius* (Saint Louis, Mo.: Institute of Jesuit Sources, 1992), 143n2.

free from the influence of 'disordered' drives and attachments that stifle love and impede integrity of intention."[10]

There are some important indicators in the text that understanding the aims and purposes of the Exercises is not as simple as it might seem at first glance. To begin, notice how closely Ignatius ties together the different parts of his text: the aims of the Exercises outlined in the opening lines of annotation 1 are explicated in the Principle and Foundation, which states,

Human beings are created to praise, reverence, and serve God our Lord, and by means of doing this to save their souls. The other things on the face of the earth are created for the human beings, to help them in the pursuit of the ends for which they are created. From this it follows that we ought to use these things to the extent that they help us toward our end, and free ourselves from them to the extent that they hinder us from it. To attain this it is necessary to make ourselves indifferent to all created things, in regard to everything which is left to our free will and is not forbidden. Consequently, on our own part we ought not to seek health rather than sickness, wealth rather than poverty, honor rather than dishonor, a long life rather than a short one, and so on in all other matters. Rather, we ought to desire and choose only that which is more conducive to the end for which we are created. (SE 23)

The shared emphasis that annotation 1 and the Principle and Foundation place on interior freedom and its role in our end and purpose helps to show that there are several interlocking parts of the Exercises that together specify their proper aims and purposes. In order to grasp what Ignatius means when he speaks, in annotation 1, of disordered affections and the ordering of one's life, one must have an understanding of the Principle and Foundation. This shows that it is important to consider the entirety of the text and not just particular parts of it—even those parts where Ignatius seems to formulate the aims of the Exercises concisely—in order to fully apprehend the purposes of the Exercises.

Additionally, such an integrated reading yields some interesting clues to the theological view that grounds the Exercises on matters that will be especially important for considering whether members of other

---

10. Michael Ivens, SJ, *Understanding the Spiritual Exercises* (Leominster, U.K.: Gracewing, 1998), 1–2.

traditions might make the Exercises in a way that would be faithful to the original aims and purposes of the Exercises. For one, Ignatius writes that the soul will *"rid itself* of all its disordered affections" (italics mine), emphasizing one's work upon oneself, or the role of self-cultivation, in this process.[11] Although scholars of non-Christian religions sometimes portray Christianity as marginalizing (or even wholly eliminating) the individual's role in the process of transformation in order to make room for God's role, in truth one finds a broad spectrum of views on this matter in the Christian tradition. Ignatius insists that the individual must leave room for grace while also reaching toward God (SE 5). His view holds these two in tension: the individual is not a passive recipient of divine action; when making the Exercises, she intentionally makes efforts to bring about change in herself, but she is not solely responsible for this change. We shall see that, for Ignatius, this is a "graced collaboration," as Ivens describes it, but in any real collaboration, each collaborator contributes actively. Most religious traditions—including Buddhism, Confucianism, Daoism, Hinduism, Islam, and Judaism—describe and advocate spiritual activities that involve an individual's intentional efforts to remove "disordered affections" in a broad sense—meaning that these activities seek to remove tendencies and attachments that are not conducive to a good life as it is envisioned in those particular traditions. This would appear to be a promising connection between the purposes of the Exercises as Ignatius understands them and other faith traditions, both because Ignatius clearly accords a key role to the individual in bringing about change in herself (as these other traditions do), and because that individual is engaged in a process of removing or turning away from disordered ways, and turning toward a properly ordered life.

There are indeed genuine resonances here, including the turn from a "disordered" to an "ordered" self. John Hick famously described this turn

11. Ivens translates this as "preparing and making ourselves ready to get rid of all disordered affections" (ibid., 1). This reading highlights the individual's role in preparing herself to be changed, but also leaves room for God's role in bringing about that change (i.e., actually getting rid of all disordered affections). I think this reading equally emphasizes the importance, in the Exercises, of self-cultivation, that is, of the individual's role in bringing about change in herself. Nevertheless, as I discuss below, Ivens also notes, "Liberation and redirection of heart is the work of the Spirit, in which our own action is a graced collaboration; it is not achieved simply by performing 'exercises.'" (ibid., 2). Indeed, a fundamental premise of the *Exercises* is the continuous action of God throughout the whole process.

in different religious traditions as different paths of salvation, understood as the transformation of human existence from self-centeredness
to a limitlessly better new orientation, because it is centered in the divine
Reality.[12] While the latter part of this—the "divine Reality" part—will not
come so easily for all religious traditions—the claim that they all offer
an account of an ethical turn from "disordered" to "ordered" is accurate.
Another important resonance is that, within each of these traditions,
some important relation or set of relationships is central to that process,
whether it is a relationship to or with the Real (whether it is conceived
as a supreme divine being(s) or not) or particular kinds of relationships
with other human beings and/or spirits. The fact that different religious
traditions share an emphasis on turning from a disordered life to an ordered life that is grounded in the right kind(s) of relationship(s) is not
insignificant, and I will return to these commonalities throughout this
book. Nevertheless, it is important to acknowledge the differences and
tensions that exist in the midst of these commonalities, for an open exploration of these tensions will be essential to any potential adaptation
of the Exercises for members of other faith traditions.

One of the biggest challenges lies in the fact that Ignatius—just like
major thinkers in other faith traditions—has a highly specific account
of what the terms "disordered" and "ordered" mean, and the apparent
shared theological ground with other traditions narrows here. He specifies that by disordered affections he means the kinds of tendencies and
attachments that are not ordered according to the principles in the Foundation, and as we shall see, it is not at all clear that other traditions hold
views that are compatible with seeking "indifference" in the sense in
which Ignatius describes it in the Principle and Foundation. Further, Ignatius explicitly describes a means of seeking God's will for the ultimate
end of salvation. So we are immediately presented with two theological
challenges relating to the purposes of the Exercises as they are described
in the first annotation: (1) Is the kind of indifference that is central to
the Exercises something that members of other religious traditions can
embrace? (2) Is the idea of seeking God's will for the ultimate end of salvation something that members of other traditions could affirm?

---

12. See John Hick, *An Interpretation of Religion* (New Haven, Conn.: Yale University Press, 1989).

Taking these two questions as our starting place, let us turn to the Principle and Foundation, which, as Ganss writes, "orients the retreatant for his or her work during the Exercises and for living after they are finished. It is both the starting point of the *Exercises* and a premise from which flow conclusions of the greatest importance for the spiritual life."[13] At the same time, it is important to remember that experience grounds the text of the *Exercises*: Ignatius spent many months exploring the Exercises with various individuals prior to using the text, and it is thought that he spent time helping them recall and re-experience God's unconditional love for them. This would later be called the "Principle and Foundation experience" (where the movement is from God to us), as distinguished from the Principle and Foundation text (where the movement is from us to God and thus is a response to God's prior initiative). The Principle and Foundation text is important not simply as a source for examining disordered affections—which is a key purpose of the Exercises as they are outlined in annotation 1—but also because "it sketches the worldview of Christian faith as the background against which everything else in the *Exercises* and in life should be viewed."[14] I want to linger on Ganss's words here because it is important to openly acknowledge just how deeply Christian the view that Ignatius presents is. For as much as making the Exercises is not about studying theology or developing an understanding of particular theological doctrines, the Principle and Foundation is imbued with thick theology. Nowhere is this clearer than in the opening lines: "Human beings are created to praise, reverence, and serve God our Lord, and by means of doing this to save their souls" (SE 23). Ignatius here specifies the meaning and end of human life, as well as a particular understanding of salvation and how it is achieved. As Ganss points out, Ignatius is quite clear on what it means "to save one's soul": "to save and perfect or develop one's whole self into the eternal life (John 17:3) of the beatific vision (1 Cor. 13:12; 1 John 3:21)."[15]

Also in the Principle and Foundation, we find the clearest account of the Ignatian concept of disordered affections. Ignatius describes what a proper ordering would look like, namely that "we ought to desire and

13. Ganss, *The Spiritual Exercises of Saint Ignatius*, 148n17.
14. Ibid.
15. Ibid., 150n19.

choose only that which is more conducive to the end for which we are created," namely the end of praising, reverencing, and serving God. He goes on to say that we should "make ourselves indifferent to all created things, in regard to everything which is left to our free will and is not forbidden." Ignatian indifference concerns neutral things—things neither good nor bad in themselves—and as Ganss explains, for Ignatius indifference means "undetermined to one thing or option rather than another; impartial; unbiased; with decision suspended until the reasons for a wise choice are learned; still undecided. In no way does it mean unconcerned or unimportant. It implies interior freedom from disordered inclinations."[16] For Ignatius, ridding oneself of disordered affections is not simply a matter of removing selfish desires or unhealthy attachments; rather, it means something much more specific and theologically loaded: when our affections are ordered and we become indifferent, we desire and choose what is most conducive to praising, reverencing, and serving God. Indifference, as Ivens puts it, is "an affective space within which the movements of the Spirit can be sensed and things seen in relation to the signs of God's will, an affective silence making possible an unconditional listening. The indifference of the Exercises is a stance before God, and what makes it possible—and also something quite other than either apathy or stoicism—is a positive desire for God and his will."[17]

All of this helps to make clear just how theocentric the aims and purposes of the Exercises are, at least as Ignatius describes them. This is important because, as we shall see, although there are broader aims that are a part of the Exercises, it is not the case that the aim of the Exercises is simply human freedom, understood broadly. Ignatius offers a specific account of interior freedom, and it is particularly important to come to terms with this if one hopes to adapt the Exercises for members of other faith traditions who may not share that view of freedom or even a belief in God. Ivens points out that the terms "praise," "reverence," and "serve" all express "an attitude of radical God-centeredness, a desire simply that God be God and that his purposes be realized." Ivens argues that on this view "God is praised not only by formal worship, but when we so live that in our heart and behaviour God is acknowledged to be God and his

16. Ibid., 151n20.
17. Ivens, *Understanding the Spiritual Exercises*, 31.

will is done in all things. Again, we give praise, reverence and service in becoming involved in God's 'project', which is simultaneously the ongoing conversion of our own lives and the establishment of his reign in the world."[18] So, if the purpose of the Exercises is, as Ignatius says in annotation 1, to rid ourselves of disordered affections and to seek and find God's will, and if freeing ourselves of disordered affections means coming to desire and choose what is most conducive to praising, reverencing, and serving God, what sorts of challenges might these aims and purposes pose for members of other faith traditions making the Exercises? Given that other parts of the Exercises have been adapted and changed, what sorts of adaptations might be acceptable when it comes to the purposes of the Exercises? The latter question raises larger questions about adaptation and the Exercises, including how far one can go in adapting the Exercises and still maintain the integrity of the Exercises—questions that will be explored more fully in the subsequent chapters of this book—but let us briefly consider the question of how the aims specified in annotation 1 might be compatible or incompatible with the commitments of members of other faiths.

As readers shall see in a moment, one's answer to these questions will depend heavily upon (1) which religious traditions, and which members of those traditions, one is speaking of, as well as (2) how broadly or narrowly one interprets certain key terms in the *Spiritual Exercises*. The most important of these are "God" and "God's will," and much of what follows is dedicated to this issue. In addition, much will depend on one's belief about how closely we should adhere to Ignatius's own understanding of these terms and his own theological view. As the best literature on the Exercises shows, Jesuits who give the Exercises and Christians (Catholic and non-Catholic alike) who have made the Exercises regularly bracket, modify, or reject various features of Ignatius's theological view. For instance, in the meditation on hell (SE 65–72), David Fleming, SJ, suggests that instead of contemplating Ignatius's very medieval images of hell (including fire, smoke, sulfur, and tears), modern exercitants might find it helpful to "try to experience the breadth and length and depth of hell—the despair of facing a cross with no one on it, the turning out

18. Ibid., 29–30.

upon a world which has no God, the total emptiness of living without purpose...."[19] Similar kinds of adaptations have been suggested for understanding good and evil spirits—another aspect of Ignatius's theological view that may seem foreign to modern exercitants—and for Ignatius's comparison of the evil spirit to a woman who quarrels with an adversary.[20] Such changes make the Exercises more accessible in a contemporary setting and help to prevent unnecessary obstacles in the course of the retreat, but without completely removing or changing the meaning of these parts of the Exercises. We have a historical consciousness in a way that Ignatius did not, an awareness of how belief needs to develop and even to change.[21] As we have seen, the Exercises lend themselves to adaptation, and adaptation was central to Ignatius's own vision of what the Exercises ought to be. So the question before us is whether there are some features of Ignatius's theological view as it is expressed in the purposes of the Exercises that should *not* be rejected or modified under any circumstances—or that *cannot* be rejected or modified substantially without undermining the integrity of the Exercises.

There is nothing about the purposes of the Exercises as they are presented in annotation 1 that should be problematic for monotheists such as Jews and Muslims. It is also quite possible that these purposes would not be problematic for certain other kinds of theists, including some Hindus, especially those who are comfortable talking about "God." The most serious challenge will be for non-theistic traditions and for theistic traditions that have nothing that is analogous to God. Confucianism, Daoism, and Zen Buddhism would all be potential examples, and although I will explore these traditions in greater depth later in this book, it will be helpful here to consider some of the basic challenges before us. Confucianism and Daoism would in most cases involve some sort of polytheism, seen in a belief in ancestral spirits or a large pantheon of

---

19. David L. Fleming, SJ, *Draw Me into Your Friendship: A Literal Translation and a Contemporary Reading of The Spiritual Exercises* (Saint Louis, Mo.: Institute of Jesuit Sources, 1996), 59.

20. See Kevin O'Brien, SJ, *The Ignatian Adventure: Experiencing the Spiritual Exercises of Saint Ignatius in Daily Life* (Chicago: Loyola Press, 2011), 116 (on good and evil spirits), and 191 (on the enemy's behavior). O'Brien follows Fleming in replacing the image of a quarreling woman with a spoiled child.

21. We owe much to John Henry Newman's views on this set of issues, seen especially in *An Essay on the Development of Christian Doctrine* (Notre Dame, Ind.: University of Notre Dame Press, 1994).

Daoist deities.[22] The multiplicity of spirits or deities presents a tension that cannot be eased or alleviated in the ways that one can potentially ease it in the case of Hinduism—where one can draw upon the spiritual monist view, internal to the Hindu tradition itself, in order to understand "the divine" as part of the same whole. Confucians and Daoists, however, are not dealing with different manifestations of the same deity or entity; they genuinely venerate and interact with different spirits or deities. Additionally, there is not a clear analogue to "God's will" for Confucians and Daoists. It would not make sense in either tradition to take as one's goal coming to desire and seek what is most conducive to praising, reverencing, and serving God, even if we modified this claim so that one was (in the case of Confucianism) desiring and seeking what is most conducive to praising, reverencing, and serving the ancestors, or (in the case of Daoism) desiring and seeking what is most pleasing to the gods. Traditional Confucians did not typically seek to *do the will of* their ancestors, although the Confucians developed many practices for cultivating filial piety and deepening one's commitment to ancestral sacrifices, and they certainly believed that one had a religious obligation to have children—which was one of the most important ways of serving one's ancestors. In the case of contemporary Daoism, one's relationship with the gods is much more transactional than relational; the gods are not believed to have a plan for one's life or to call one to a certain vocation. Their role is rather to provide assistance in times of need, and to ensure a certain measure of justice—punishing those who behave immorally and rewarding those who are good. In the case of both of these forms of theism, the spirits or deities in question are not analogues to God; they are more powerful members of this realm, but they are not omniscient, omnipotent, or omnibenevolent, and they do not have a plan or will that human beings need to discern and then follow.

The case of Zen Buddhism is perhaps even more difficult, although there is diversity of practice and belief in Zen Buddhism around the world today. In relation to the Exercises, the two most challenging as-

---

22. For now, I am setting aside the beliefs of classical Confucians and Daoists concerning *Tian* ("Heaven") and the Dao, respectively, which did, for these early thinkers, represent singular impersonal entities with which they interacted and which they sought to follow. This is something that changed over time; it is difficult to find contemporary Daoists or Confucians who hold these beliefs today. The chapter on Confucianism in this book will address these issues.

pects of Zen Buddhism are, first, the fact that it does not involve a commitment to any form of theism, and, second, the fact that it involves a commitment to eliminating desires *completely*—a fundamental Buddhist teaching that is emphasized throughout the history of the tradition. The latter is deeply at odds with Ignatian views, especially because Ignatius believed that God speaks to us through our desires, something that we see in Ignatius's insistence that the Exercises ought to cultivate certain kinds of desires in the exercitant. In contrast, the Buddhist tradition holds that suffering originates with desires, and that in order to overcome the former one must completely extinguish the latter. While some Buddhists are polytheists, most Zen Buddhists are not; there is no analogue to God in this tradition. Indeed, liberation depends on apprehending the fundamental emptiness of all things—including the fact that there is no such thing as the soul, and no such thing as God.

Even this very brief consideration of these traditions helps to show why the purposes of the Exercises might potentially need to be modified for at least some members of faith traditions that are not monotheistic. I qualify this statement, though, because much depends on the orientation of the particular individual making the Exercises and the ultimate aims of those who wish to give the Exercises to members of other traditions. Here we can see that giving the Exercises to members of other faith traditions involves some of the same challenges as giving them to Christians: one must always consider where that particular individual is, and how they can most benefit from the experience. As we have seen, this is something Ignatius makes abundantly clear in the text of the *Exercises*, and it is also why the role of a spiritual director is so important and requires significant training and experience. For instance, consider a Zen Buddhist who is interested in making the Exercises but who understands that the Exercises are very much about God. Perhaps she is, in Roger Haight's terms, a kind of "seeker": maybe she is dissatisfied with her own tradition on some level and has begun to suspect that her Christian, Jewish, and Muslim friends are having real religious experiences. In the case of such an individual, it would not seem necessary to adapt the purposes of the Exercises dramatically, because part of the reason she is interested in making the Exercises is, in fact, to open herself up to the possibility of encountering God. The principle of reversibility—whereby one imagines herself in another's position in order to better understand and respond to others—can also be of some assistance here. A Christian might imagine herself choosing to participate in a retreat that introduces her to Hindu or Buddhist meditative practices by having her engage in those practices. Would she expect or wish for the leaders of the retreat to adapt the purposes of these meditative practices for her so that they would be conducive to deepening her monotheistic faith? Would she expect or desire for them to change the practices in order to Christianize them for her? The answers to these questions will depend heavily on the individual's reasons for making a particular retreat. An individual who makes a retreat with the ultimate aim of deepening her appreciation for and understanding of another faith tradition would be unlikely to want particular contemplative practices to be adapted significantly for her, at least if her aim is to have an authentic experience with the practices of another tradition. Similarly, someone who makes a retreat because she is dissatisfied with her own tradition on some level and wishes to explore another tradition would probably not be looking for a heavily adapted retreat experience, either.

All of this highlights the fact that when we talk about adapting the Exercises for members of other traditions, we are in fact talking about a very specific sub-set of people from other faith traditions. We also must consider a spectrum with varying degrees of adaptation. I will take up these issues in chapter 2, but for now I want to stress that the subset of people from other faith traditions who would be in need of a specially adapted form of the Exercises are not the "seekers" Haight describes, nor are they those who wish to learn about other traditions by trying out their contemplative practices. While as we have seen, various kinds of adaptations are made in the course of the Exercises for any exercitant, and certainly would be for members of these groups, both of these types of individuals are being drawn to the Exercises because of their traditional aims and content. This is significant to note, because the truth is that when we talk about adapting the Exercises for members of other faith traditions, we are really talking about *members of other faith traditions who wish to use the Exercises as a tool for deepening their own faith.* This might be someone with Christian friends or family members who have made the Exercises, who has observed how meaningful the experience was for them, and who wishes to have a similarly deepening, enriching experience with their own faith. It might be a Buddhist or Hindu who has tried contemplative practices in his own tradition, but for whom they were not especially meaningful or effective. It might be a Muslim student at a Jesuit university who has learned about the Exercises and wishes to experience them firsthand in order to grow in her faith. Again, in chapter 2, I will more fully consider questions relating to the reasons that members of other faith traditions might wish to make the Exercises, but I want to acknowledge these issues now because if we keep in mind the kinds of individuals who would be interested in an adaptation of the Exercises that is designed for someone of another faith tradition, we will be better able to proceed in thinking about the degree to which the *purposes* of the Exercises might need to be shaped or adapted.

The aims of those who give the Exercises also matter greatly here. Of course, Ignatius makes clear that when a person is seeking God's will, "the one giving the Exercises ought not to lean or incline in either direction but rather, while standing by like a pointer of a scale in equilibrium, to allow the Creator to deal immediately with the creature and the creature with its Creator and Lord" (SE 15). But attempting to influence an exercitant when she is working to discern God's will—or having strong views about what she should choose—is different from hoping for certain kinds of outcomes. For instance, anyone who gives the Exercises hopes that the experience will deepen the exercitant's faith and help them to lead a better life—one that is richer, more fulfilling, and ethically better. Such hopes can help us to better understand the purposes of the Exercises not just in relation to Ignatius's aims, but also within the context of how the Exercises are given today, because they tell us about the aims of those who give the Exercises. For the vibrant tradition that springs from the *practice* of giving the Exercises—and not just from the text of the *Exercises*—it is important to remain grounded in practice. Indeed, a complete understanding of Ignatius's own views concerning the ultimate aims and purposes of the Exercises is based not only on what his text says, but also on what he *did* in giving the Exercises. Ganss points out that while Ignatius's text more strongly emphasizes the aim of facilitating a good election—helping people to make important decisions such as getting married or entering religious life—Ignatius himself gave the Exercises to individuals whose election was already made. His objective in these cases was to lead them toward unity with God: "He found the principles in the text leading to an election to be equally suitable for guiding the exercitant to lofty union with God; but he did not trouble himself to state this explicitly by stylistic revisions in the text itself. He left it to directors to adjust the text and its principles flexibly to the personalities and needs of each exercitant."[23] It is clear that while the Exercises often help individuals to make a momentous choice about a state of life—and this was certainly a part of their original aim—they often serve a much broader purpose that goes beyond deciding what to do: they help people decide how to live, which includes living the choices they have already made.

All of this helps to show why traditional commentators on the *Exercises* disagreed about whether the purposes of the Exercises revolve solely around making an election.[24] The text makes clear that one comes to determine God's will through a real encounter with God—which means that the Exercises aim to enable, facilitate, or prepare the ground for an encounter with God. Indeed, the fact that creating and sustaining a relationship with God is central to the Exercises gives us a broader picture of what they are meant to achieve. To be sure, in the opening paragraph Ignatius formulates the purposes of the Exercises as they relate to discerning God's will, and he reiterates this basic view in multiple places. At the beginning of the first week he writes that these Spiritual Exercises are "to overcome oneself and to order one's life, without reaching a decision through some disordered affection" (SE 21). In annotation 5 he writes that those who make the Exercises will "benefit greatly by entering upon them with great spirit and generosity toward their Creator and Lord, and by offering all their desires and freedom to him so that His Divine Majesty can make use of their persons and of all they possess in whatsoever way is in accord with his most holy will." But in addition to the overar-

---

23. Ganss, *The Spiritual Exercises of Saint Ignatius*, 147n14.

24. The fact that we find in the *Exercises* themselves a dual emphasis on discernment and on encountering God directly—which as we can see go hand in hand for Ignatius—helps to explain in part why, over time, different schools of thought emerged on the matter of what the essential ends or purposes of the Exercises are, with De Grandmaison maintaining in 1921 that the aim is to prepare one to make a wise choice of a state of life which will serve God best, and Peeters maintaining in 1931 that the aim is an intimate union with God. Joseph de Guibert unified these two views in 1953, arguing that the two ends are complementary.

ching emphasis on interior freedom and discernment, he also outlines more-specific aims for particular parts of the Exercises, such as, in the first week, finding contrition, sorrow, and tears for one's sins. And the instructions offered in annotation 15 to those giving the Exercises shed further light on how the purposes of the Exercises go beyond making elections, because he addresses *how* one will, ideally, come to discover God's will while making the Exercises: "during these Spiritual Exercises when a person is seeking God's will, it is more appropriate and far better that the Creator and Lord himself should communicate himself to the devout soul, embracing it in love and praise, and disposing it for the way which will enable the soul to serve him better in the future." This passage is particularly important because it highlights the fact that one of the primary aims of the Exercises is that a person encounter God directly; Ignatius here specifies that the purpose of the Exercises is not only to enable an individual to seek and find God's will, but to give her a direct experience of God through which she comes to understand God's will. But Ignatius clearly intends for this experience to enable a lifetime of decisions that will be grounded in interior freedom. This is a long-term goal, and it reflects the aim that the Exercises will facilitate a real change in the orientation of a person's life through a deepened personal relationship with God. Here we see that one of the aims of the Exercises is to give rise to a religious experience in the form of an encounter with God, which is not surprising given that Ignatius crafted the Exercises in part as a record of his own encounter with God.

All of this helps to show why contemporary works on the Exercises tend to describe their aims and purposes not solely or exclusively in terms of discernment, but more broadly. For instance, Carol Ann Smith and Eugene Merz write that the Exercises are "intended to occasion a conversion of the heart and mind so that a person may follow Jesus with greater faith, love, and freedom. Ignatius first discovered the reality of this conversion experience in his own life and later in the experience of his followers and friends."[25] Fleming, too, offers an account of the aims of the Exercises that moves beyond a sole focus on discernment, in his contemporary reading of the latter part of annotation 1: "what we call

25. Carol Ann Smith, SHCJ, and Eugene F. Merz, SJ, *Moment by Moment: A Retreat in Everyday Life* (Notre Dame, Ind.: Ave Maria Press, 2000), 10.

spiritual exercises are good for increasing openness to the movement
of the Holy Spirit, for helping to bring to light the darkness of sinfulness and sinful tendencies within ourselves, and for strengthening and
supporting us in the effort to respond ever more faithfully to the love
of God."[26] While he notes that the Exercises increase openness to the
movement of the Holy Spirit, Fleming frames this not in terms of making a particular election or in terms of discernment more broadly, but in
relation to bringing to light sinful tendencies and facilitating a faithful
response to the love of God. He is clearly grounded in Ignatius's vision of
the Exercises as it is specified in annotation 1, but his language also takes
into account the various specific aims that Ignatius outlines for different
parts of the Exercises, as well as the longer-term goal of bringing about a
certain sort of conversion in the individual. Similarly, Kevin O'Brien, SJ,
in his guide to the nineteenth-annotation retreat, writes that while, for
Ignatius and the Society of Jesus, the Exercises are the primary instrument to discern God's call, they do more than this, as well: "Through the
Exercises, we grow in faith, hope, and love. In them, we prepare for and
sustain ourselves in the service of God and others."[27] O'Brien contends
that the overarching purpose of the Exercises is "to grow in union with
God, who frees us to make good decisions about our lives and to 'help
souls.' Ignatius invites us into an intimate encounter with God, revealed
in Jesus Christ, so that we can learn to think and act more like Christ.
The Exercises help us grow in interior freedom from sin and disordered
loves so that we can respond more generously to God's call in our lives
(SE 2, 21)."[28]

Here we can see clearly how Ignatian spirituality reflects the very
heart of Christian spirituality, for it centers on what it means to follow
Christ. All of these contemporary interpreters remind us to avoid being
reductionistic about the aims of the Exercises, for they serve not just one
but a number of interlocking purposes that reflect fundamental Christian values. Yet all of these interpretations remain grounded in Ignatius's
understanding of the purposes of the Exercises, as well. In this way, their
accounts are clearly and recognizably Ignatian. The aims we have dis-

26. Fleming, *Draw Me into Your Friendship*, 5.
27. O'Brien, *The Ignatian Adventure*, 11.
28. Ibid., 14.

cussed relating to discernment are accounted for, but they are nestled in a broader set of aims—aims that are intimately bound up with the details of each individual's life. Fleming's contemporary reading of SE 21 is an example: "The structure of these exercises has the purpose of leading a person to a true spiritual freedom. We grow into this freedom by gradually bringing an order of values into our lives so that at the moment of choice or decision we are not swayed by any disordered love."[29] O'Brien writes that the Exercises help each of us to "become more aware of how God has guided me in the past, how God labors in my life in the present and calls me in the future. The Exercises do this by helping me become freer of all the interior clutter that gets in the way of reaching this graced awareness."[30] While Ignatius concludes the Principle and Foundation with the claim that "we ought to desire and choose only that which is more conducive to the end for which we are created" (SE 23), Fleming's contemporary reading is as follows: "Our only desire and our one choice should be this: I want and I choose what better leads to God's deepening life in me."[31] Fleming's language here emphasizes, among other things, the very personal nature of the Exercises: God's deepening life in each individual will look different. Indeed, as O'Brien points out, "The genius and beauty of the Exercises is that we learn to weave our own life narrative into the life story of Jesus Christ in such a way that both become more vivid and interconnected."[32] This feature of the Exercises has particular significance for the task of adapting the Exercises for members of other faith traditions, because it reminds us that the Exercises seek to connect each person's unique life story with that of Christ—which is of course why Ignatius insisted on adapting them to the needs and abilities of those who make them.

Those who know the Exercises well might see in the interpretations of Jesuits like Fleming and O'Brien little that departs significantly from Ignatius's original text, but for the purposes of this book it is important to note how their presentation of the aims of the Exercises differs from a narrower reading of the text of the *Exercises*. The fact that they use

29. Fleming, *Draw Me into Your Friendship*, 23.
30. O'Brien, *The Ignatian Adventure*, 4.
31. Fleming, *Draw Me into Your Friendship*, 27.
32. Ibid.

broader language and include the various aims and purposes that are a part of Ignatius's vision throughout the *Exercises*—and which were evident in his and his companions' practice of giving the Exercises—does in fact make the Exercises more accessible to members of other traditions, because it opens them up to those who may not have a firm sense of the need to discern "God's will." As we have seen, these commentators are clearly rooted in Ignatius's text and practice, yet they also move beyond it in articulating a broader set of purposes—and ways of understanding them—than one finds outlined by Ignatius in annotation 1.

It is, of course, possible to broaden the purposes of the Exercises even more, and an example of this is seen in Haight's work on adapting the Exercises for seekers. In his account of three "holistic frameworks" or "comprehensive views" of the Exercises, Haight presents three different interpretations of the purposes of the Exercises. He writes that these interpretations "work together," which seems to mean that they can be complementary, but Haight's account nevertheless makes clear that these are three quite different ways of understanding the Exercises, and he notes their different origins in the work of various thinkers.[33] The first interpretation, a "salvation history" view, is the most traditional. It focuses on the content of the Exercises, "their specifically Christian provenance, and the narrative that defines them. In this view the Spiritual Exercises provide a concentrated program that mirrors the Christian story and leads the people making them through the stages of the Christian narrative."[34] These include creation, sin, salvation, church, and the end times, all grounded in the scriptural story of Jesus. On this view, Haight writes, "The Exercises reproduce those New Testament stories of Jesus and through them draw people into the great plan of human history."[35] Haight quotes Gilles Cusson's view of the purposes of the Exercises based on annotation 1 in support of this first interpretation, which offers a reasonably straightforward, textually grounded presentation of the purposes of the Exercises.

The second interpretation Haight discusses is the "anthropological"

---

33. Roger Haight, *Christian Spirituality for Seekers: Reflections on the Spiritual Exercises of Ignatius Loyola* (Maryknoll, N.Y.: Orbis Books, 2012), 48.

34. Ibid., 47.

35. Ibid.

view, which "comes from a theological anthropology with deep roots in Augustine's appropriation of Neo-Platonism that in effect contains a Christian philosophy of religion."[36] However, the resonances with Christianity are not immediately apparent in Haight's description of this view. Haight writes that this interpretation entails the view that "[h]uman existence dynamically interacts with the world through knowledge, desire, and action. This ceaseless quest for the true and the good is driven by a base instinctual desire to know, will, possess, and *be* absolutely." While one *could* interpret this view through a Christian lens, it is important to note that there is nothing here that is specifically Christian or even theistic. On this view, Haight writes, "the Spiritual Exercises most fundamentally provide a program for decision making, for a taking possession of the self and directing it toward the highest imaginable goal, in order that, in the end, persons unite themselves with what they perceive to be absolute value."[37] The focus on decision-making here is recognizably Ignatian, but as we have seen, Ignatius offers a distinctive account of and approach to discernment in the Exercises, and the aim of directing oneself toward "the highest imaginable goal" or uniting oneself with "what one perceives to be absolute value" is a notable departure from Ignatian goals. The language Haight uses here is deeply informed by particular philosophical and theological views: one hears shades of Hegel and Tillich, but not Ignatius. But I want to stress that we are not just dealing with differences in language; this interpretation presents a view that departs from Ignatian views in some key ways.

Now, there are obvious ways in which this account departs from the Ignatian tradition—such as replacing "God" with "absolute value"—and it is important to note that there is substantial subjectivity here. On this sort of view, each individual can decide for herself what "the highest imaginable goal" is, as well as what she perceives to be "absolute value." The Ignatian tradition, of course, provides a specific account of what "the highest imaginable goal" is, and while we *could* describe union with God as union with "absolute value," there are plenty of other ways of understanding "absolute value" and "the highest imaginable goal" without God

---

36. Ibid.

37. Ibid. Haight cites Gaston Fessard, Edouard Pousset, James Connor, and John English as examples of this understanding.

or any sort of divine entity as part of the picture. But the ways in which this interpretation departs from the Ignatian tradition go beyond these more obvious issues. To begin, note the content of the claim that "persons *unite themselves* with *what they perceive to be* absolute value" (italics mine). This is not the "graced collaboration" that Ignatius describes: on this view, the individual does the uniting. This accounts for the fact that "absolute value" may not be a being or entity that is capable of relating to or interacting with the individual at all. Here we see two ways in which this view departs from Ignatian views: not only is the goal of "union" no longer union with God or the divine (e.g., perhaps one strives for union with—or strives to embody—certain values or virtues), but there is a singular emphasis on personal effort. Additionally, persons unite themselves with *what they perceive to be* absolute value. The individual's perception is at the center here, which suggests that one is *not* having a direct experience or encounter with absolute value, or God, or the Real; note the important difference between claiming that "the individual unites herself with absolute value" and claiming that "the individual unites herself with what she perceives to be absolute value." While Ignatius certainly accepted the view that we all see through a glass darkly, he also believed that we can have direct and real encounters with God—not just with what we perceive to be God. This is important because direct religious experience, as we have seen, is and always has been central to the Exercises.

The third interpretation Haight discusses is the "social,'historical view," which he says "works within the framework of" the first two interpretations. On this view, "The Spiritual Exercises appear as a program in which persons correlate their stories with the stories of Jesus of Nazareth in a dialogue of mutual exchange that enhances life before ultimate reality. The mutually critical fusion of narratives opens up new possibilities for freedom."[38] Haight acknowledges that this view takes inspiration from the philosophical hermeneutics of Gadamer and Ricoeur—something that is apparent in the language that is used. Like the second interpretation, though, note how the language refers to the broad, non-theistic, existentialist aims of "enhancing life before ultimate reality" and "opening

---

38. Haight, *Christian Spirituality for Seekers*, 48.

up new possibilities for freedom." Again, there is no mention of God, and while one could certainly interpret "ultimate reality" to mean God, it can mean many other things, as well—and historical examples are of course found readily. Note also the degree of emphasis placed, in true Gadamerian fashion, on the fact that it is a "dialogue" that enhances life before ultimate reality, and a "fusion of narratives" that opens up new possibilities for freedom. Once again, such a view does not require an entity or being that relates to the individual. Note the language that is used: "persons correlate their stories with the stories of Jesus of Nazareth." Each person does the "correlating" here—nothing else necessarily relates to them; so again, we find a view that departs from the "graced collaboration" that is so characteristic of Ignatian spirituality, and which distinguishes it from so many other approaches to self-cultivation. Of course, such language is open to virtually any interpretation one chooses. While one could interpret "freedom" as interior freedom, there are many other types of freedom, as well. This language *could* be used to re-describe Ignatius's original vision of the Exercises, but it could also be used to describe a person's experience on a wholly secular, self-help retreat.

One of the challenges that Haight's second and third interpretations present is that they have broadened the purposes of the Exercises so much that they could be used to describe the purposes of almost any type of self-help or self-cultivationist practice. They are not recognizably Ignatian in any way, and it isn't quite clear what is gained from re-interpreting the purposes of the Exercises in this manner, except that it makes them accessible to virtually anyone. Haight's second and third interpretations show clearly how one can revise the purposes of the Exercises so that they can be made to accommodate anyone, regardless of what they believe. The worry, however, is what might be lost in the course of such a dramatic change to the purposes of the Exercises. If one understands the purposes of the Exercises in these ways, for instance, then one ought to revise the Exercises themselves in order to bring them into line with these purposes. But what, then, would the Exercises look like? Surely, they would not be recognizable as Ignatian Spiritual Exercises any longer, and the worry here is that we will lose much of what is meaningful and transformative about the Exercises. Another worry is that there are many different kinds of contemplative practices and spiritual exercises in the world today, and if we depart from so much of what makes Ignatian Spiritual Exercises Ignatian, then we will lose the distinctive contributions that Ignatian Spiritual Exercises can make to people's lives. Here I think it is worth considering a pluralistic view of contemplative practices, which sees them as having different strengths, including the fact that some are better suited to the needs of some individuals than to others'. If we try to make them all the same by secularizing them or by revising their purposes and redesigning them in order to adapt them for as broad an audience as possible, we should worry about whether they will continue to be effective and meaningful in the same ways. In other words, the more theologically rich content of contemplative practices may be an integral part of how they serve particular spiritual needs.

Overall, it seems that we are looking to hit a mean when it comes to understanding the proper aims and purposes of the Exercises. Interpretations that are too broad or too narrow each have serious shortcomings. On the one hand, if we interpret the text of the *Exercises* so narrowly that a specific decision, or election, lies at the heart of the purposes of the Exercises, then we do not seem to be faithfully characterizing the purposes of the Exercises either as Ignatius understood them or as the dynamic tradition of giving the Exercises has presented them. On the other hand, the latter two interpretations offered by Haight allow us to see some of the challenges of broadening the purposes of the Exercises so much that they are no longer recognizably Ignatian. Indeed, these interpretations help us to zero in on some of the core features of what it means for the Exercises to be "Ignatian"—including the centrality of the possibility of a direct encounter with or experience of God or the divine. I stress the absence of not just God but any sort of entity or being who can bring itself into relation with persons in the latter two interpretations Haight offers, as well as the use of "ultimate reality," "highest imaginable goal," and "absolute value" in place of God, because these views lie at one end of a spectrum of views concerning the purposes of the Exercises. At the opposite end of the spectrum, we have a narrow reading of annotation 1 as presenting the sole purpose of the Exercises. In the middle of the spectrum, we have interpreters such as Fleming and O'Brien, who allow for a broader understanding of the aims of the Exercises while remaining grounded in Ignatius's text and the idea that a personal relationship with God lies at the heart of the Exercises. But the views Haight describes understand the purposes of the Exercises in exceptionally broad terms, including the directing of the self toward the "highest imaginable goal," uniting oneself with "what one perceives to be absolute value," or "enhancing life before ultimate reality." While one could explain how Ignatius's account of the purposes of the Exercises can be recognized in this language (e.g., "the highest imaginable goal" could be taken to mean following God's will; "absolute value" and "ultimate reality" could be taken to mean God), these views nevertheless depart from the Ignatian tradition in important ways. Indeed, if the purposes of the Exercises are understood in these ways, then there is little that is distinctive about them.

Yet surely there is something distinctive in the Ignatian tradition that is worth preserving when it comes to the aims and purposes of the Exercises, and this is precisely what we are invited to consider here. What is the point of adapting the Exercises for a broader audience, if the purposes of the Exercises are no longer recognizably Ignatian? There are interesting examples to consider from other traditions, here, including the popular practice of yoga. It is worth considering whether the Exercises should be broadened in the same way that yoga has been, so that it becomes a secular practice stripped of its specific religious content. This occurred with yoga partly because there were physical practices that could be adapted apart from the religious goals to which they were traditionally connected—although it is worth noting that the tradition in which those practices originated certainly never envisioned them being extricated in this way.[39] Note here that the *purposes* of these physical practices were dramatically changed: most people who take yoga classes in the United States today have the goal of increasing their physical health and appeal in some way, and many also seek greater "spiritual health" as well—but what that is, exactly, remains undefined, and that is part of the appeal of yoga. Religious teachings are not an explicit part of most

---

39. Some have questioned whether Christians ought to practice yoga because they doubt that yoga *can* be extricated from its original goals. See the Congregation for the Doctrine of Faith, "Letter to the Bishops of the Catholic Church on Some Aspects of Christian Meditation," October 15, 1989, http://www.vatican.va/roman_curia/congregations/cfaith/documents/rc_con_cfaith_doc _19891015_meditazione-cristiana_en.html, and Albert Mohler, "The Subtle Body—Should Christians Practice Yoga?," *Articles on Jesus and the Gospels* (blog), September 20, 2010, http://www.albert mohler.com/2010/09/20/the-subtle-body-should-christians-practice-yoga/.

yoga classes, and in these contexts, yoga has been stripped of its religious purposes. There are both descriptive and normative questions to consider here in relation to the Spiritual Exercises. First, the descriptive questions: Could the same thing happen with the Spiritual Exercises? Especially since they do not include physical practices, would they lend themselves to this degree of adaptation? What would such an adaptation even look like? Second, the normative question: should the Exercises be adapted to this degree? I am especially concerned here with the *purposes* of the Exercises. If we consider the example of how yoga was stripped of its religious purposes and replaced by purely (or primarily) physical purposes, it is important to note that the meaning of a practice changes when its purposes change. While yoga is undoubtedly beneficial to practitioners in a variety of ways, its benefits and aims differ quite dramatically from those that were traditionally a part of the branch of Hinduism from which it originates.

We are pressed hard, here, on the question of *why* we wish to give the Exercises to members of other traditions. If the reason that we wish to share the Exercises with those of other faiths is tied to the rich experience that we have had with the Exercises, then we ought to be hesitant to go too far down the spectrum in altering the purposes of the Exercises. When the purposes of contemplative practices change substantially, their outcomes typically change, as well. Yoga is a case in point. In addition, though, it would be difficult to see how one might go about the process of adapting the Exercises without a more specific set of aims or purposes. The purposes of the Exercises serve as a helpful guide in deciding how far to go in adaptation—what parts of the Exercises to change and what parts must remain, and so on. The point here is that without purposes that have some clear focus—and my contention here is that the second and third interpretations Haight discusses are so broad that they do *not* have a clear focus—one does not have any way of determining such matters. What would serve as a standard for whether an adaptation is faithful to the integrity of the Exercises, if the purposes of the Exercises are no longer recognizable as such?

My concerns about the second and third interpretations Haight discusses are raised not only by their indeterminate character—the language is so vague that, as we have noted, just about anything could count as "absolute value" or "ultimate reality"—but also by how far they are from Ignatius's text and practice. By no means am I advocating some sort of originalist position, wherein we attempt to recover or duplicate Ignatius's original purposes precisely; it is clear that the tradition surrounding the Exercises is exceptionally vibrant and dynamic, and that many adaptations have been made over the years that are faithful to the original vision of the Exercises, even though they go beyond it in a variety of ways. But the second and third interpretations Haight discusses offer purposes that bear very little resemblance to the aims that have been a part of the Exercises throughout their history. Of course, one could adopt these purposes only in word and proceed to give a traditional form of the Exercises, but it is not clear why one would do this. It seems to me that if one says one is giving spiritual exercises that aim to "enhance life before ultimate reality" or to unify exercitants with "what they perceive to be absolute value," then one should be doing something very different from a recognizable form of the Exercises. Frankly, one really should be offering a secular retreat, or at least something that looks more like the sorts of retreats given in secular settings. Why else would one use such language? Of course, one might use this language simply in order to avoid using language that suggests that God is not the divine mystery we take God to be. The latter is a valid concern and one that has been taken seriously in the theological literature of the past fifty years. But it is not clear that "ultimate reality" or "absolute value" are better terms than "God," for, as we have seen, they carry certain associations, as well. It seems that it would be better to take our cue from Ignatius here and not avoid the term God but instead specify that God exceeds our understanding—and take seriously what this means in prayer. Indeed, this is precisely what the Exercises invite us to do.

Interestingly, Haight presents a reasonably traditional account of the Exercises; his reflections on the Exercises speak of God and not of the "ultimate reality." He does not describe an adaptation that deviates from the basic framework of the Exercises, though he does discuss some of the questions that would arise for seekers who make the Exercises and offers suggestions about how to handle them. But interestingly, his suggestions themselves do not point toward talking or thinking about the "ultimate reality" or "absolute value" in place of God. For instance, he writes that "If a seeker is one who is not religious but agnostic toward religious beliefs in God, a personal colloquy with God represents fairly precisely where he or she cannot go.... How can seekers who have had no encounter with a personal God entertain such a colloquy?"[40] Haight writes that there is no answer that would be right for all seekers, but he suggests looking to the traditions of negative theology and apophatic mysticism in the Christian tradition, which stress that God transcends everything we know in this world and that "God cannot be any thing because every thing is limited. To conceive of God as something is not to grasp even the notion of god for God is nothing."[41] Haight goes on to write, "The seeker has a sense of some encompassing reality that appeals to the pure openness of the human quest. That quest implies a basic trust in being itself. Standing before the unknown in silence from within such an openness is a colloquy. The prayer of a seeker may be described as a prayer to an unknown God."[42] Here, Haight appropriates the same type of theological language seen in the second and third interpretations that he discusses, and it has a similar lack of clarity. Haight draws upon Christian apophatic theology here, which stresses that God is far beyond our understanding, as a way of trying to address the agnostic's uncertainty as to whether God exists. But Haight does not clarify what this colloquy might entail—other than silence—nor does he offer examples of precisely how one might advise agnostics to proceed when making the Exercises. His suggestions are theologically interesting, but it is not clear how one might apply them in practice. The looming difficulty with the proposal that Christian apophatic theology might be an asset here is the fundamental difference between (1) the belief that God is an ineffable or ultimately mysterious divine being or reality (one that might best be described using negative language) and (2) the belief that God is "nothing," which seems to presume that the concept of God has no reference to any kind of reality (much less an ultimate one). In the latter case, we seem to have an empty concept with no application to reality. In other words, there is a fundamental difference between the apophatic theologian, who doubts that

---

40. Haight, *Christian Spirituality for Seekers*, 95.

41. Ibid., 96. He cites Meister Eckhart, *Meister Eckhart: Teacher and Preacher*, ed. Bernard McGinn (New York: Paulist Press, 1986), sermon 71.

42. Haight, *Christian Spirituality for Seekers*, 96.

we can fully understand or describe God, and the kind of seeker who doubts that God exists at all.

What would happen if we tried to address the seeker's challenge not by drawing upon Christian theology that interprets religious language in terms of some abstract system of concepts, or by viewing the Exercises through the lens of Eckhart, Tillich, Rahner, Hegel, or Heidegger, but by going back to Ignatius himself? How might Ignatius advise the seeker? What would a characteristically Ignatian response look like? One thing that Ignatius consistently does throughout the Exercises is ask us to engage our imaginations. An Ignatian response might be to ask the seeker to imagine that God exists. What would he or she say to God? This type of approach avoids drawing unnecessarily on contemporary theology and instead seeks to follow the outlines of Ignatius's approach—but adapting it for a different audience than Ignatius envisioned. When one is working with those outside of the Christian tradition, one of the merits of this type of approach is that it avoids adding more Christian theology to the mix. While one approach sees the addition of certain kinds of theology as an asset—precisely because they move us away from being specific about God, for those who may not believe in God—another approach would aim to keep the theology as thin as possible. Another merit to avoiding the addition of contemporary Christian theology to the mix is that, as we have seen, these discussions tend not to clarify what or who God is, but to speak in terms that are intentionally vague: the ground of being, ultimate concern, absolute value. As the subsequent chapters of this book will show, when dealing with other faith traditions, it will be more helpful to be as clear as possible about what precisely our beliefs are, how they differ from other beliefs and how they are similar. If we use vague, general terms instead of the terms our own traditions use, it will, I think, become even more difficult to sort out where adaptation might be necessary.

So, instead of describing the purposes of the Exercises in very general, non-theistic terms such as "uniting oneself with what one perceives to be absolute value" or "enhancing life before ultimate reality," I suggest that we turn to the positions closer to the middle of the spectrum. If we understand the aims and purposes of the Exercises in the terms that contemporary commentators like Fleming and O'Brien do—to include not only growing in spiritual freedom so that we can respond to God's call (or to God's deepening life in us), but also to provide an opportunity to encounter God so that we can grow in union with God, and to weave our own life story into the life story of Jesus Christ—then it is certainly possible to remain faithful to the purposes of the Exercises if we give them to members of other faith traditions—*provided that those making the Exercises are open to encountering God.* The latter qualification is critical, because it is difficult to make sense of the purposes of the Exercises in the absence of God or the possibility of God—although God may certainly be understood in a variety of ways, and one of the gifts of the Exercises is that they open us up to new ways of encountering and understanding the divine mystery.

Jesuit Norms for Choice of Mission and the Exercises

In his 2009 address in which he urges us to explore how the Exercises can be appropriated by non-Christians, Father Adolfo Nicolás stresses a number of broader Jesuit aims. Among these are the norms for choice of mission outlined in chapter 7 of the *Constitutions of the Society of Jesus*, which guide Jesuits as they consider establishing or continuing work in particular areas, and which Nicolás paraphrases as follows:

(1) helping souls, that is, helping people; (2) the greater glory of God; (3) going where there is greatest need; (4) searching for the magis, that is, for what exceeds mediocrity and moves toward excellence, going beyond what has already been achieved; (5) taking on works, also, where no other workers are present or available; (6) moving sometimes to controversial frontiers of action or knowledge, even breaking settled boundaries; (7) undertaking works that promise a more universal good and a deeper reach of contact; and (8) creating or joining communities of solidarity in seeking justice.[43]

I would like to focus on these norms, because there are good reasons to think that a number of them are pertinent to the question of wheth-

---

43. Adolfo Nicolás, SJ, "Companions in Mission: Pluralism in Action." Mission Day Keynote Address, Loyola Marymount University, Los Angeles, California, February 2, 2009, http://www.gonzaga.edu/About/Mission/docs/LoyolaMarymountUniversityAddressAdolfoNicolasSJ.pdf, 82.

er the Exercises should be offered to members of other faith traditions. Accordingly, considered alongside the aims and purposes of the Exercises, they can serve as a helpful guide in sorting out whether this practice might be an appropriate part of the Jesuit mission today. To begin with (1), the potential of the Exercises for helping souls or helping people who are not Christians is worth considering. Much depends here on what we regard as "helping." If the Exercises deepen the faith of a Muslim, a Buddhist, or a Hindu, even though it is not Christian faith, does this constitute "helping souls"? It might be helpful to consider some specific examples. A Zen Buddhist might make the Exercises, perhaps in a heavily modified form, and believe that she has had a direct experience not of God or Jesus but of the ultimate emptiness of the universe—including the fact that there is no such thing as the soul. If this reaffirms her Buddhist faith and she is able to live out her faith by showing greater compassion to others as a result of making the Exercises, has her soul been helped? (And does it matter if she denies that she has a soul?) A Hindu might make the Exercises and believe that in the course of the Exercises he has encountered the Hindu deities Kali and Shiva; perhaps he also encountered Jesus but regards him as an avatar (or incarnation) of Vishnu. His Hindu faith is deepened and he discovers his vocation as a result of making the Exercises. Has his soul been helped?

There are good reasons to think that both Christian inclusivists and Christian exclusivists could agree that these *do* constitute cases of "helping souls," although their reasoning would differ. Inclusivists and exclusivists are among the most prominent twentieth-century approaches to the question of how Christian theology should view other religions. Christian exclusivists are united by their belief that God is revealed exclusively in Jesus Christ (*solus Christus*) and that only those who profess Christ—who hear the Gospel (*fides ex auditu*) and confess it in their hearts—can be saved.[44] In contrast, inclusivists hold that Christ is the normative revelation of God but that salvation is possible outside of the explicit Christian Church (including, for some inclusivists, through

---

44. Exclusivists hold a variety of different positions on issues such as whether God elected some for salvation and others for damnation, and on whether the opportunity to confess Christ must take place before death. For a helpful overview of these differences, see Gavin D'Costa, "Christian Theology of Religions," in *The Routledge Companion to Modern Christian Thought*, ed. Chad Meister and James Beilby (London: Routledge, 2013), 662.

other religions), although this salvation is always from Christ. In various forms of inclusivism, then, we find *solus Christus* without the *fides ex auditu*.[45] So a Christian inclusivist, who might for instance believe that non-Christians sometimes encounter God and experience Christ's love without knowing that it is Christ—and who maintains that there can be salvation outside of Christianity, even though this is always the work of Christ, even if the person is unaware of it—should have no trouble maintaining that giving the Exercises to these non-Christians *may be* a way to help souls. For the inclusivist, the Buddhist and the Hindu described above have both, in fact, experienced Christ's love through the Exercises, even though they are unaware that it is Christ. They misunderstand (and thus misdescribe) their experience, but the outcome is good: they both go on to lead better lives, both by the standards of their own religious tradition and by Christian standards, even though they did not convert to Christianity, and their religious views did not become more Christian. The inclusivist is content to consider their fruits, with fruits understood primarily in ethical terms: the kind of lives they are leading, the sort of people they are. These fruits might look precisely the same for a Christian who made the Exercises and found that her faith was deepened, and that she is more patient and caring toward others as a result. For the inclusivist, the difference is that the Christian knows that this is due to Christ.

On the other hand, a Christian exclusivist, who maintains that conversion is necessary for salvation, could also maintain that these souls have been helped, but the exclusivist will be less satisfied with purely ethical fruits. The exclusivist will also contend that they have been helped because through the Exercises the person has been exposed to the Gospel and has thus been moved closer to conversion. The exclusivist is not satisfied with the inclusivistic view that some people will experience Christ but call that experience by another name; the exclusivist's goal is for the person to recognize that she is having an encounter with God in Christ and to profess Christ. In this way, having correct beliefs

---

45. If one moves further down the theological spectrum from inclusivism, one finds pluralism, which jettisons the uniqueness of Christianity entirely. Pluralists hold that all religions are or can be paths to either the one divine reality or plural divine realities; Christ is one revelation among many different and equally important revelations. For an overview of different forms of pluralism and inclusivism, see ibid., 661–62.

matters a good deal more to the exclusivist than to the inclusivist, espe-cially correct beliefs concerning one's understanding of one's religious experiences. The exclusivist's concerns can help us to recognize a series of important questions about members of other faith traditions who might make the Exercises. First, in what ways and to what extent do the exercitant's beliefs about what she is doing matter? If one of the pur-poses of the Exercises is to deepen one's relationship with God, does it matter if one does not believe that has happened? Do we feel differently about giving the Exercises to the Zen Buddhist who does not believe in any God, and the Hindu, who does? While we might be comfortable say-ing that the Buddhist has in fact encountered God but that she mistak-enly understands this as "emptiness," would we be equally comfortable saying that she has deepened her relationship with God without know-ing it (and without even believing in God)? Is it possible for a person to deepen her relationship with God if she doesn't believe in God? Or must a person believe in God in order for us to speak meaningfully of her having a relationship with God? It is important for monotheists who are interested in other religions to understand that not all members of other religious traditions conceive of their religious experience in terms of a relationship; many Zen Buddhists, for instance, deny that their expe-rience of reality is of a relationship. Instead of experiencing a presence or having an encounter with the divine, they experience the true nature of reality as *empty*.

Overall, I think most inclusivists and exclusivists could agree that giv-ing the Exercises to members of other faith traditions such as the Bud-dhist and Hindu described above can be a way of "helping souls," because these individuals can become better people both by Christian standards and by the standards of their own traditions, and perhaps also—and this would be especially important for the exclusivist—because the experi-ence might move them toward a full recognition of God in Christ.

In addition to "helping souls," a number of the other norms for choice of mission in chapter 7 of the *Constitutions* are helpful for thinking about why giving the Exercises to members of other faith traditions may or may not be central to Jesuit works. For instance, "searching for the *magis*, that is, for what exceeds mediocrity and moves toward excellence, going be-yond what has already been achieved" is worth our consideration. The

Exercises have long been given to Catholics and now are widely given to other Christians as well; they are an extraordinarily powerful way of experiencing the Gospel, and this has proven to be true for Christians of many different theological orientations. In what way might Jesuits "go beyond" in giving the Exercises? One way of answering this question is to consider who else might find them meaningful, which is of course precisely what Father Nicolás asks us to do. Giving the Exercises to members of other faith traditions is one way of searching for the *magis*. The norms for choice of mission are remarkably clear, as well, that Jesuits should be "moving sometimes to controversial frontiers of action or knowledge, even breaking settled boundaries" and also "undertaking works that promise a more universal good and a deeper reach of contact." Giving the Exercises to members of other faith traditions is certainly a way of moving beyond settled boundaries and seeking a more universal good by bringing the Exercises to new communities.

These are themes that resonate deeply with the address of Pope Benedict XVI to the thirty-fifth General Congregation of the Society of Jesus in 2008, when Father Nicolás was elected Superior General. In his speech, Pope Benedict called upon Jesuits "to reach the geographical and spiritual places where others do not reach or find it difficult to reach. These words of Paul VI have remained engraved in your hearts: 'Wherever in the Church, even in the most difficult and extreme fields in the crossroads of ideologies, in the front line of social conflict, there has been and there is confrontation between the deepest desires of man and the perennial message of the Gospel, there also there have been, and there are, Jesuits.'"[46] Today's obstacles "are not so much the seas or the long distances as the frontiers that, due to a mistaken or superficial vision of God and of man, are raised between faith and human knowledge, faith and modern science, faith and the fight for justice."[47] He stressed that the Church is in urgent need of people

to stand on those frontiers in order to witness and help to understand that there is in fact profound harmony between faith and reason, between evangelical

---

46. Benedict XVI, *Address of His Holiness Benedict XVI to the Fathers of the General Congregation of the Society of Jesus*, February 21, 2008, https://w2.vatican.va/content/benedict-xvi/en/speeches/2008/february/documents/hf_ben-xvi_spe_20080221_gesuiti.html.

47. Ibid.

spirit, thirst for justice, and action for peace. Only thus will it be possible to make the face of the Lord known to so many for whom it remains hidden or unrecognizable. This must be the preferential task of the Society of Jesus. Faithful to its best tradition, it must continue to form its members with great care in science and virtue, not satisfied with mediocrity, because the task of facing and entering into a dialogue with very diverse social and cultural contexts and the different mentalities of today's world is one of the most difficult and demanding.[48]

Pope Benedict concluded by calling upon Jesuits to "reserve a specific attention to the ministry of the Spiritual Exercises," noting that they are "the fountain of your spirituality and the matrix of your Constitutions, but they are also a gift that the Spirit of the Lord has made to the entire Church: it is for you to continue to make it a precious and efficacious instrument for the spiritual growth of souls, for their initiation to prayer, to meditation, in this secularized world in which God seems to be absent." Pope Benedict notes, further, "In a time such as today, in which the confusion and multiplicity of messages, the speed of changes and situations, make particularly difficult for our contemporaries to put their lives in order and respond with joy to the call that the Lord makes to every one of us, the Spiritual Exercises represent a particularly precious method to seek and find God in us, around us, and in everything, to know his will and put it into practice."[49]

Pope Benedict's remarks about the importance of going to the frontiers, with all of their social and cultural diversity and all of their confusion, have been echoed not only by Father Nicolás but by Pope Francis, who extends this work to theologians: "Teaching and studying theology means living on a frontier, one in which the Gospel meets the needs of the people to whom it should be proclaimed in an understandable and meaningful way. We must guard against a theology that is exhausted in academic dispute or one that looks at humanity from a glass castle.... Let the theology that you elaborate therefore be rooted and based on Revelation, on Tradition, but also correspond with the cultural and social processes, in particular difficult transitions."[50] Careful theological reflec-

---

48. Ibid.

49. Ibid.

50. Francis, *Letter of His Holiness Pope Francis to the Grand Chancellor of the 'Pontifica Universidad Catolica Argentina' for the 100th Anniversary of the Founding of the Faculty of Theology*, March 3, 2015,

tion on the practice of giving the Exercises is an instance of theology that fits this sort of description, for the question of why and how we ought to give the Exercises to members of other religious traditions is not only very practical, but surely marks one of these "difficult transitions." Yet Pope Francis insists, "Your place for reflection is the frontier. Do not fall into the temptation to embellish, to add fragrance, to adjust [the conflicts] to some degree and domesticate them. Even good theologians, like good shepherds, have the odour of the people and of the street and, by their reflection, pour oil and wine onto the wounds of mankind."[51]

In order to achieve such ends, Father Nicolás has stressed the importance not only of Jesuits sponsoring works but of Jesuits becoming companions and co-workers in someone else's work: "Yet even when they are co-workers in someone else's mission, Jesuits (alone or in groups) choose it because of its resonance with their own deepest sense of mission."[52] Throughout Jesuit history, he argues, Jesuits saw themselves as co-workers and companions with non-Christians, "with all men and women of good will—men and women with a good heart." He goes on to point out:

While Jesuits bring their own distinctively Catholic, Christian identity to whatever work they join, they know that others' projects are not always conceived explicitly in Christian or even religious terms. They join such projects, with the identities that are their own, because they see deep consonance between the non-religious mission and their own criteria for mission. Similarly, they ask members of other religious traditions or simply men and women of good will to join in their own sponsored works without, in any way, asking of them that they deny or negate their own identities in the common work.[53]

I want to tease out a couple dimensions of what Father Nicolás is highlighting here. He contends that it is possible to be faithful to one's own religious identity and tradition—and even further the mission of one's faith—while engaged in projects that are not rooted in one's tradition. One looks for areas of agreement between missions, and as he goes on to point out, we should not see "mission" here as suggesting prosely-

http://w2.vatican.va/content/francesco/en/letters/2015/documents/papa-francesco_20150303_lettera-universita-cattolica-argentina.html.

51. Ibid.
52. Nicolás, "Companions in Mission: Pluralism in Action," 82–83.
53. Ibid., 83.

tism, but as "clarity about goals and the strategies to achieve them." He mentions that Jesuits have run schools (e.g., in Muslim countries) where they explicitly promised that they would not try to convert anyone. Father Nicolás goes on to discuss the decree promulgated at Jesuit General Congregation 34 (held in 1995), normative for the whole Society of Jesus, entitled "Cooperation with Laity in Mission," which called on Jesuits to "foster an attitude of readiness to cooperate, to listen attentively, and to learn from others," being "men for others" and "men *with* others."[54] He quotes Fr. Peter-Hans Kolvenbach's 2004 reaffirmation of the commitment enunciated at GC 34: "We Jesuits need to be not only friends and companions of the Lord and each other, we must be friends and companions of our partners in mission."[55] Indeed, Father Kolvenbach (Superior General of the Society of Jesus from 1983 until 2008) has made clear that this vision of human solidarity is grounded in the vision that is articulated at the Second Vatican Council:

One is the community of all people, one their origin, for God made the whole human race to live over the face of the earth. One also is their final goal, God. God's providence, manifestations of goodness, and saving design extend to all people, until that time when the elect will be united in the Holy City, the city ablaze with the glory of God, where the nations will walk in God's light.

The council continues:

[T]he Church therefore exhorts her sons and daughters, that through dialogue and collaboration with the followers of other religions, carried out with prudence and love and in witness to the Christian faith and life, they recognize, preserve and promote the good things, spiritual and moral, as well as the socio-cultural values found among these people.[56]

Kolvenbach highlights the four dialogues recommended by the Pontifical Council for Interreligious Dialogue and Congregation for the Evan-

---

54. Ibid., 84–85.

55. From Peter-Hans Kolvenbach, "Cooperating with Each Other in Mission," address at Creighton University, Omaha, Nebraska, October 7, 2004, http://onlineministries.creighton.edu/CollaborativeMinistry/Kolvenbach/Cooperating.html, quoted in Nicolás, "Companions in Mission: Pluralism in Action," 85.

56. Paul VI, *Nostra Aetate*, Declaration on the Relation of the Church to Non-Christian Religions, October 28, 1965, http://www.vatican.va/archive/hist_councils/ii_vatican_council/documents/vat-ii_decl_19651028_nostra-aetate_en.html.

gelization of People—which were adopted into the Society of Jesus' way of proceeding at GC 34—one of which is "The *dialogue of religious experience*, where persons, rooted in their own religious traditions, share their spiritual riches, for instance, with regard to prayer and contemplation, faith and ways of searching for God or the Absolute."[57] While this is labeled a "dialogue," the language here—which refers to the "sharing of spiritual riches" with regard to prayer and contemplation—suggests more than just describing how we pray, which is something Jesuits have already done throughout their history. Father Nicolás points out that GC 34 "stressed that ecumenism is a new and essential way to be Catholic today and that interreligious dialogue—between Christians and those of non-Christian religions or those of secular faith—should be made a Jesuit apostolic priority."[58] He goes on to discuss Decree 6, "Collaboration at the Heart of Mission," the follow-up document from GC 35, which states, "We are enriched by members of our own faith, but also by people from other religious traditions, those men and women of good will . . . with whom we labor in seeking a more just world."[59] Father Nicolás adds, "It should not cause surprise that Jesuits, whose originating charism dictates that they attempt to discern and find God present and laboring in all things, might also try to find that same God working in and present to all persons, whatever their identities, traditions, cultures or religions."[60] He stresses that GC 35's document on collaboration reflects the reality that Jesuits "engage with Buddhists, Jews, Hindus, Moslems or even agnostic co-workers in their own works," and he quotes the document's conclusion: "The Society desires strong relationships in mission with as many collaborators in the Lord's vineyard as possible."[61]

The allusion to Luke's Gospel is interesting to consider in light of the

---

57. *Documents of the 34th General Congregation of the Society of Jesus: The Decrees of General Congregation Thirty-Four, the Fifteenth of the Restored Society and the Accompanying Papal and Jesuit Document,* ed. John L. McCarthy, SJ (Saint Louis, Mo.: Institute of Jesuit Sources, 1995), Decree 5, "Our Mission and Interreligious Dialogue." Kolvenbach's views on these aspects of the vision articulated at the Second Vatican Council and on the Society of Jesus' way of proceeding can also be found in Peter-Hans Kolvenbach, "The Service of Faith in a Religiously Pluralistic World: The Challenge for Jesuit Higher Education," in *A Jesuit Education Reader,* ed. George W. Traub, SJ (Chicago: Loyola Press, 2008), 168–71.

58. Nicolás, "Companions in Mission: Pluralism in Action," 85.

59. Ibid., 86, quoting GC 35, d.6.3.

60. Ibid., 86.

61. Ibid., 87, quoting GC 35, d.6.24.

concerns of this book. Jesus sends the first seventy-two disciples out on mission saying, "The harvest is plentiful, but the laborers are few; therefore ask the Lord of the harvest to send out laborers into his harvest" (Lk 10:2). There is a strongly inclusivistic tone to Father Nicolás's use of this passage, and also in the way he weaves together and stresses the importance of particular documents from GC 34 and GC 35. He highlights the connection between ecumenism and interreligious dialogue, maintaining that Jesuits should partner not only with other Christians but with those of other faith traditions as well. He further stresses that the goal is not conversion but the achievement of our shared mission and values, and the deepening of our awareness of the way in which God works in and is present to all traditions, cultures, and religions. He argues that all of this is central to what the *Constitutions* say about how Jesuits should choose their missions. Given that this discussion precedes his remarks about the prospect of sharing the Exercises with non-Christians, it seems clear that this endeavor, for Father Nicolás, is a way of being faithful to the mission of the Jesuit order. Indeed, not only is it *possible* to share the Exercises with members of other faiths, in his view; it is essential to do so.

What Father Nicolás says about the Exercises in relation to other traditions leaves the door open to a number of possibilities. In his speech, he quotes Father Kolvenbach: "We Jesuits owe it to our partners to remain rooted in the graces of the Spiritual Exercises and to find ways to make this apostolic resource available to those with whom we cooperate in mission."[62] What does it mean "to make the Exercises available"? The most straightforward interpretation would seem to be that it means giving the Exercises to them, but whether this would mean giving the full and complete Exercises is unclear. Father Nicolás does not specify any of this in his subsequent remarks. Rather, he writes that "[w]hile the Spiritual Exercises of Ignatius Loyola are radically Christo-centric, centered on the core notion of discipleship and the Kingdom of God, experience and the testimony of non-Christians suggest that important elements of the Spiritual Exercises, especially those concerned with spiritual freedom, equipoise and discernment, can be fruitfully appropriated even by non-Christians."[63] Here he reaffirms the Christocentric

---

62. Ibid., 87, quoting Kolvenbach, "Cooperating with Each Other in Mission."

63. Nicolás, "Companions in Mission: Pluralism in Action," 87–88.

nature of the Exercises and does not seem to envision adapting them in ways that move beyond the "core notions" he mentions. His claim that "important elements" of the Exercises can be "fruitfully appropriated" by non-Christians may suggest something other than giving the full and complete Exercises to non-Christians: it might mean drawing out particular elements of the Exercises—especially those elements concerned with spiritual freedom and discernment—for non-Christians. This could be an eighteenth-annotation retreat or it could be something still different; precisely what he thinks might be done with those elements of the Exercises—*how* they might be "appropriated" by members of other faiths—isn't clear.

In his speech, he goes on to say that "the Spiritual Exercises can be shared by non-Christians. Even though Christ is at the heart of the full experience of the Exercises, it is also true that their structure involves a process of liberation—of opening to new horizons—that can benefit people who do not share our life of faith."[64] Again, his remarks here suggest that he may not have in mind the "full experience" of the Exercises for members of other faiths, since he contrasts this with the structure of the Exercises, a structure that he says *can* benefit those who do not share our faith. It is not clear what he means when he refers to the "structure" of the Exercises, though. He goes on to say that in Japan—where he taught systematic theology for more than thirty years and served as Provincial before becoming Moderator of the Jesuit Conference for East Asia—non-Christians would sometimes ask if they could make the Exercises, but he does not specify how he responded to this request; only that it "triggered a reflection, and it is one that we need to continue. What are the dynamics in the Exercises that non-believers might make their own to find wider horizons in life, a greater sense of spiritual freedom?"[65] When Father Nicolás refers to "dynamics" here, it is not entirely clear what he means. He may be referring to various movements or phases felt within a person who is praying through the Exercises, or to the different exercises or dimensions of the Exercises. Is Father Nicolás suggesting the possibility of giving *parts* of the Exercises to non-Christians? Or by "make their own" does he mean to suggest something broader, such as creating a new set of meditations

64. Ibid., 88.
65. Ibid.

or contemplations that are inspired by the Exercises but designed to help individuals to make choices grounded in their faith? Much rests on which "important elements" or "dynamics" one thinks could be helpful to members of other faiths, and what it means to "appropriate" the Exercises and "make them their own."

The lack of clarity on these matters makes it unsurprising that Father Nicolás's remarks have been cited not only by those who believe the Exercises should be given to members of other faiths (who understandably tend to read these remarks and ask, "What else could he mean other than giving them the Exercises?"), but also by those who argue *against* the view that the Exercises should be given to non-Christians. William Reiser, SJ, for instance, writes that "Fr. Nicolas' language is careful. He speaks of the 'Ignatian experience,' particularly with its emphasis on each person's being led by God; he does not refer to the determinate Christian experience that lies beneath the *Exercises*."[66] As Reiser points out, the LMU speech was not the first time that Father Nicolás spoke of these matters. About a year before being elected superior general, he gave an interview in which he noted that there has been some discussion of whether the Exercises could be presented to non-Christians and how this might occur, saying, "The question is how to give the Ignatian experience to a Buddhist. Not maybe formulated in Christian terms, which is what Ignatius asked, but to go to the core of the experience. What happens to a person that goes through a number of exercises that really turn a person inside-out. This is still for us a big challenge."[67] Again, the language here is unclear. What does it mean to "give the Ignatian experience" to someone? What is "the core of the experience"? Father Nicolás here seems to be raising the question of what is at the core of the Exercises or the transformative element—the element that "turns a person inside-out."

There have been a variety of thoughtful responses to these remarks. Francis Clooney, SJ, writes that "Fr. Nicolas' insights bring to mind my own experience in Kathmandu in the mid-1970s, when I was teaching at St. Xavier's High School, a boarding school in which almost all the stu-

66. William Reiser, SJ, "The *Spiritual Exercises* in a Religiously Pluralistic World," *Spiritus* 10 (2010), 135.
67. Michael McVeigh, "Profile: Father Adolfo Nicolas," *Province Express*, February 21, 2007, https://web.archive.org/web/20080122063407/http://www.express.org.au/article.aspx?aeid=2305.

dents were Hindu and Buddhist. It was the custom, as in Jesuit schools here in the United States, for the senior students to go away on weekend retreats, and even when the students were not Christian, the Exercises were still at the core of reflections on the world, sin, our responsibilities, and the power of making a choice for God in human life."[68] Clooney talks about drawing upon stories from the Hindu and Buddhist traditions during these retreats, noting that "in such stories lies a way to God, for God does not spurn the small openings that appear when we discover, in what we've long heard and seen, that God has already been with us." It is noteworthy that Clooney, like Father Nicolás, uses monotheistic language here; Father Nicolás says in the above-cited interview that "the Exercises are about letting God guide people." He gives no indication of the view that the Exercises should be adapted in the kind of non-theistic terms that we saw in Haight's discussion. Yet Clooney goes further than Nicolás in acknowledging precisely where the challenges lie:

The Spiritual Exercises turned out to be a key to a rich range of spiritual exercises, the choice for Christ shedding light on the supreme value of giving God first place in one's life and practice. I am sure that this kind of venture will be somewhat worrisome for some of us—for is not companionship with Jesus, contemplation on his life and a choice for him, at the very core of the Exercises? Surely yes, and there is not much value in recasting them as a generic form of self-reflection. . . . Yet it is also clear—from my brief experience, but more importantly as validated in the ministry of Jesuits throughout Asia—that the gift of the Exercises, like the gift of Jesus himself—can be given and received in multiple ways, with an abundance that cannot be restricted to the properly normative ways already well known in the Church and the Society of Jesus.[69]

Two Theological Justifications for Giving the Exercises to Members of Other Faiths

As we have seen, the idea that the Exercises could be given to members of other faith traditions is not without its critics. In "The *Spiritual Exercises* in a Religiously Pluralistic World," Reiser argues that the Spiritual Exer-

---

68. Francis X. Clooney, SJ, "Inside-Out with Fr. Nicolas," *America Magazine*, February 3, 2008, http://americamagazine.org/content/all-things/inside-out-fr-nicolas.
69. Ibid.

cises have "clear and pronounced Christological parameters, and pre-suppose a certain level of incorporation into the Christian community." He also aims to show that the Exercises "set into relief distinctive elements of a Christian's relationship with the divine mystery."[70] For our present purposes, what is most important here is Reiser's claim that the Exercises "presuppose a certain level of incorporation into the Christian community," which suggests that they should be given only to Christians—although he does not specify what he means by "a certain level of incorporation." In support of his view, he appeals to Father Nicolás's claim that we should explore how to give the "Ignatian experience" to members of other faith traditions, finding it significant that Father Nicolás "does not refer to the determinate Christian experience that lies beneath the *Exercises*."[71] Clearly, for Reiser, Father Nicolás is suggesting *not* that we give the Exercises to members of other faiths, but instead that Ignatian spirituality can be shared in other ways. This interpretation, however, is problematic; if we look at the context of Father Nicolás's remarks, we see that he is in fact responding to the question whether the Exercises might be given to non-Christians.

Reiser's basic argument seems to be that since the Exercises are Christological, they cannot be given to members of other faith traditions without removing much if not most of their content, which he understandably finds problematic. He does not specify what sort of adaptation he envisions here, but it seems clear that he imagines the Exercises being given to non-Christians with large portions removed. But because Reiser assumes that giving the Exercises to non-Christians would require us to remove or change the parts of the Exercises that deal with Christ, the evidence he presents does not support an argument against giving the Exercises to members of other faith traditions, but an argument against adapting the Exercises so much that Jesus is no longer central to them. The problem with this argument is that, as I will argue in the next chapter, this is not the only way to adapt the Exercises for members of other faiths, nor is it a particularly defensible adaptation. So one can agree with Reiser (and Father Nicolás) that the Exercises are Christocentric, and that Christ should remain central in any adaptation of the Exercises,

---

70. Reiser, "The *Spiritual Exercises* in a Religiously Pluralistic World," 138.
71. Ibid., 135.

and yet still defend the view that the Exercises can and should be adapted for members of other faith traditions.

To be clear, Reiser acknowledges that adaptation is absolutely central to the Exercises; his concern is with *what kinds* of adaptations are made: "The point is not that we might do a disservice to the book of the *Exercises*; adaptations, after all, are anticipated. The point, rather, is that we would run the risk of reinventing the Jefferson Bible—cutting and pasting scriptural texts in order to avoid an overtly Catholic way of reading the gospels themselves."[72] Despite what his remarks here suggest, Reiser does not seem to accept the view that the Exercises should be given only to Catholics. He writes that "Protestants share the narrative of faith in Jesus contained in our common Scripture, although they might not subscribe to the same ecclesial line within that narrative," and he goes on to suggest a number of the ways in which directors can adapt the Exercises for Protestants, noting for example that that "[t]he triple colloquy could run against the grain of some religious sensibilities and ought not to be considered essential to the way a Christian should pray."[73] He also enumerates ways in which the Exercises "call for some re-framing, not on account of the background and needs of individual retreatants (Ignatius anticipated this sort of adaptation), but because of the changed circumstances in which the church of today finds itself."[74] In all of these ways, Reiser shows an openness to adapting the Exercises in many different areas, including several that are beyond what Ignatius himself specified or could have imagined. But Reiser contends that adaptations should be made for Christians and not for those outside of Christianity, writing, "The Jesus to whom one prays is the ecclesial Christ. . . . The service one is called to render presupposes church. For Ignatius, the one who follows Jesus should never act outside the framework of a community of faith."[75]

In making his case against giving the Exercises to members of other faith traditions, Reiser writes "The central dynamic of the Exercises concerns the dynamics of discipleship, not the identity of Jesus as the Son of God. . . . What happens interiorly when Jesus calls disciples? What inner changes must take place before men and women achieve the freedom to

---

72. Ibid., 141.
73. Ibid.
74. Ibid., 147.
75. Ibid., 145.

follow him, and in what mission does he call them to join him?"[76] Apparently, for Reiser, these are aspects of the Exercises that would not be feasible for non-Christians. However, a curious feature of Reiser's essay is that he does not engage other traditions in any substantive way in his attempt to show that the Exercises highlight "the distinctively Christian way of knowing and relating to God."[77] He writes, "The *Exercises* direct our attention not to doctrines as such but to Christian religious experience and what makes it distinctive."[78] Yet Reiser does not discuss religious experiences in other traditions or their differences from Christian religious experiences. His apparent lack of familiarity with other traditions creates difficulties for his argument at a number of key points. For instance, I would argue that Reiser's remark that the Exercises essentially concern the dynamics of discipleship and not the identity of Jesus as the Son of God actually *undermines* his claim that the Exercises should not be given to non-Christians. If, contrary to what Reiser claims, the Exercises dealt more heavily with the identity of Jesus as the Son of God, this would surely be a barrier for Muslims and Jews. But members of other faiths can understand discipleship. They can understand what it means to model oneself after and follow Jesus. And Reiser reaffirms this view of the Exercises in multiple places. For instance, he writes that within the context of the Exercises salvation is not tied to a particular theological view, but rather, "Being saved, in the making of the Exercises, means imitating and actually being more like Jesus; it means poverty, ridicule, and to be considered foolish and crazy for Christ. To be saved means imitating and serving Our Lord."[79] Indeed, the thinner theology that Reiser describes here is actually helpful in facilitating a non-Christian's engagement with the Exercises, since one does not have to accept that Jesus died for our sins or that he was the son of God in order to believe that we should imitate him and follow him.

Now, Reiser is correct to point out that there are very real differences between different traditions and that we should take these seriously in thinking about whether the Exercises should be given to members of other faiths. He is correct to stress that "Jesus is not the Buddha—and

76. Ibid., 141.
77. Ibid., 147.
78. Ibid., 137.
79. Ibid., 146.

not Moses or Elijah or Adam or John the Baptist. No one else can be the Son of God the way he was."[80] While, as I have already noted, Reiser's argument for the distinctiveness of Christianity would be strengthened if he could talk about how, for instance, Jesus' teachings differ from those of major figures in other traditions, his point does have direct applications to the possibility of adapting the Exercises for members of other traditions. Specifically, there are good reasons to be hesitant about heavy-handed adaptations that seek to de-centralize Jesus or re-style him in the image of other religious figures. But the fact that Jesus and his teachings are highly distinctive hardly seems like a reason not to give the Exercises to members of other faiths; to the contrary, it sounds like a reason why we *should* give the Exercises to members of other faiths, and not in a heavily adapted form. For if Jesus is a truly distinctive individual with truly distinctive teachings, doesn't this suggest that members of other faith traditions will have much to learn from encountering him?

Reiser follows William Harmless, SJ, in critiquing the claim that "all religions are all the same at the top" and that "mystics are all experiencing the same thing"; as Harmless puts it, those who make such claims "have simply not done their homework."[81] He further criticizes the suggestion made by Thomas Michel, SJ, that "the divine mystery has, by intention or by design, revealed and communicated itself to the peoples of the world in diverse yet complementary ways" and Michel's claim, "It is the Divine Spirit that motivates their various acts of faith, it is the Spirit that communicates with them in the very act of their prayer."[82] Reiser rightly points out that ethical evidence of salvation is not sufficient for demonstrating such claims, since "[r]eligion is not coterminous with morality; the 'cash value' or spiritual measure of ascetical practice and contemplation is not simply higher ethical standards and noble, humanitarian actions."[83] Reiser goes on to write that "spirituality is ultimately about the human being's living more deeply in God and experiencing

---

80. Ibid., 151.

81. Ibid., 154n21. See William Harmless, *Mystics* (New York: Oxford University Press, 2008), 222–23.

82. Reiser, "The *Spiritual Exercises* in a Religiously Pluralistic World," 142. See also Thomas Michel, "Crossing the Frontiers of Faith: GC34 and Interreligious Dialogue," *Review of Ignatian Spirituality* 28-3, no. 83 (1996), 19–24.

83. Reiser, "The *Spiritual Exercises* in a Religiously Pluralistic World," 143.

divine life in our communities and our common humanity. While spiritual people are expected to be moral, spirituality touches first, not on morality, but on what happens as the mystery of God penetrates one's life. It is about relationship."[84] Surely there is something right about the general sentiment that spirituality is about more than becoming a better person ethically, but it is also worth noting that Reiser defines spirituality in monotheistic terms here. It is not clear to me whether he does this intentionally, but his language suggests an exclusivistic way of thinking about spirituality, where spirituality concerns one's relationship with God, which means that only monotheists really have a spirituality.

What Reiser does not seem to realize is that, just as the Christological center of the Exercises does not constitute a reason that the Exercises cannot or should not be adapted for members of other faith traditions (though as I have argued, it does suggest something about the kinds of adaptations that might be advisable), the matters that are raised by Harmless and Michel are not matters that we have to resolve in order to address whether the Spiritual Exercises should be adapted for members of other faiths. If one believes that God is at work in other faith traditions and that members of other faiths sometimes have real encounters with God, then one might argue that the Exercises are a way for them to deepen their faith—specifically through an encounter with Jesus Christ, who as Reiser argues is quite distinctive compared with other religious figures. If one rejects the view that members of different religious traditions are experiencing God, then one might argue that the Exercises are a way for them to encounter God. Reiser claims that "by no means are they an instrument for proselytizing. At their core the *Spiritual Exercises* are intended to take people deeper into the mystery of the life, death, and resurrection of Jesus."[85] But Reiser does not provide an argument for why the Exercises should not be an instrument for presenting Christianity to non-Christians, especially if one insists on *solus Christus*, as both Christian inclusivists and exclusivists do. Additionally, given the view that God works directly with each individual in the course of the Exercises, shouldn't we be open to the possibility that in dealing directly with the creature, God might lead her to become a Christian? And if we are

84. Ibid.
85. Ibid., 152.

comfortable with Christians deepening their faith through the Exercises—sometimes in such profound ways that it leads them to change their lives dramatically—why are we not comfortable with the possibility that one might be led to convert to Christianity as a result of making the Exercises? What about Protestants converting to Catholicism? What about Catholics rededicating their lives to God? Are these types of conversions really so different? Now, the negative connotations of the word "proselytizing" may be the problem here, but if we talk instead about the Exercises as an instrument for conversion, then on some level isn't this *always* a part of what we are doing when we give the Exercises? We are right to attend carefully to Ignatius's concerns about spiritual directors being too meddlesome and not allowing God to work directly in the life of the exercitant. But it is worth considering whether the Exercises are, in fact, always a tool for conversion. How could *anyone* really go deeper into the mystery of the life, death, and resurrection of Jesus without experiencing a conversion of the heart?

Here it is helpful to revisit the basic impulse behind the Jesuit order when it was founded, including the norms for mission that Father Nicolás emphasized in his speech at Loyola Marymount University. As John O'Malley points out, "The basic impulse behind the new order was missionary. They formulated for themselves a special fourth vow that obliged them to travel anywhere in the world where there was hope of God's greater service and the good of souls."[86] For the first Jesuits, "helping souls" was certainly bound up with sharing the Gospel, and this in turn was bound up with giving the Exercises. Indeed, as O'Malley points out, the order had another important impulse, which came directly from the Spiritual Exercises, namely "to interiority, that is, to heartfelt acceptance of God's action in one's life through cultivation of prayer and reception of personalized forms of guidance in matters pertaining to one's progress in spiritual motivation and in purity of conscience."[87] The Jesuits began because of their experience of God entering their lives, *de arriba*, "from above," because of the way this grace enabled them to find God in all things, and "because each of them sought peace of soul and a more

---

86. John O'Malley, SJ, "How the First Jesuits Became Involved in Education," in *A Jesuit Education Reader*, ed. George W. Traub, SJ (Chicago: Loyola Press, 2008), 47.
87. Ibid.

deeply interiorized sense of purpose that they hoped to share with others."[88] This mission was deeply personal for Ignatius, who "ever more explicitly and fully saw the Christian life as a call to be of help to others.... No expression appears more often in his correspondence—on practically every page—than 'the help of souls.' That is what he wanted the Society of Jesus to be all about."[89]

As we have seen in this chapter, the many ways in which the Exercises can be used to help souls are not limited to Christians; to restrict them in this way seems only to limit the possible ways in which God might work in the lives of different individuals. O'Malley reminds us of the basic missionary impulse behind the founding of the Jesuit order and the way in which it was tied to the difference Ignatius believed the Exercises could make in the lives of different individuals. Now, we do not have reason to believe that Ignatius envisioned the possibility of adapting the Exercises for members of other faith traditions, but his way of thinking about other faith traditions differed from how most Jesuits think about them today. There is no reason to doubt that Ignatius was a religious exclusivist or to think that he envisioned any other alternative, but today religious inclusivism informs the work of Jesuits and Catholic theologians alike. Interestingly, when we consider the purposes of the Exercises and the mission of the Jesuits, there are both inclusivist and exclusivist theological justifications for giving the Exercises to members of other faith traditions.

The first type of theological justification for giving the Exercises to members of other faiths is inclusivistic, and I believe this is the justification that most Jesuits who give the Exercises today would find most appealing. Since Christian inclusivists believe that salvation is possible outside of the explicit Christian Church, and some inclusivists believe that salvation is or may be available through other religions, an inclusivist would justify giving the Exercises to members of other religions on the grounds that it will deepen their faith, opening them up to a richer relationship with God. But since inclusivists also believe that salvation always comes from Christ, because Christ is the normative revelation of God, an inclusivist may also emphasize the significance of the opportu-

88. Ibid.
89. Ibid., 49.

nity that the Exercises provide to encounter Christ directly. Unlike the exclusivist, though, the inclusivist would not (or not necessarily) have conversion as an ultimate goal, for conversion to Christianity is not considered necessary for the person's salvation. But it is important to distinguish the religious inclusivist's position from that of the religious pluralist. Pluralists contend that all religions are, or can be, equal and valid paths to divine reality. Since for the pluralist Christ is just one revelation among many equally important revelations—pluralists accept neither *solus Christus* or *fides ex auditu*—there is nothing special about Christ or Christianity, and no reason why one should desire to share the experience of the gospels with others any more than we should desire to share any other story. This means that the inclusivist will likely have a stronger desire than a pluralist to give the Exercises to members of other faiths. Unlike pluralists, inclusivists and exclusivists typically have reasons for being a Christian that go beyond the accidents of their birth; their religious experiences often play an important role in leading them to believe that Christ is the normative revelation of God, much as Ignatius's experiences did for him, and it is natural to hope, as Ignatius did, that others will have such experiences, as well.

For Christian exclusivists who hold to both *solus Christus* and *fides ex auditu*, and sometimes to *sola ecclesia* (salvation through Christ solely via his Church), there is also a strong theological justification for giving the Exercises to members of other faiths. We should do so because it is a profound way of not just hearing the gospel but experiencing it in a deeply personal way. All of this, on the exclusivist view, is necessary for salvation; one must hear the gospel in order to profess Christ. An exclusivist who is in favor of offering the Exercises to members of other faiths for this reason might emphasize the need to move beyond archaic views concerning conversion and proselytizing. Even the first Jesuits believed this to be true; Juan Alfonso de Polanco, who worked closely with Ignatius on the *Constitutions*, "insisted that the *Exercises* were intended for every class of society and in fact helped every class—in ways that preaching, exhortation, and fear of damnation did not."[90] If we have a rich and meaningful way of presenting the gospel and inviting Christ into each

90. O'Malley, *The First Jesuits*, 130.

person's story, why would we not make it available to all? Indeed, anyone who accepts the view that God is revealed in Jesus Christ should be eager to give others the opportunity to weave their life stories into the story of Christ. For the Society of Jesus—an order that took the name of Jesus simply because the inspiration for its mission was knowing, loving, and serving Jesus Christ—the most powerful justification for this practice is surely found in the gospels, where Jesus does not turn anyone away, but calls all to follow him, whether they are rich or poor, old or young. It is appropriate for us to imagine, and carefully consider, how Jesus would respond to those of other faiths who wish to make the Exercises. Would he really turn them away because they are not members of his Church? If the purposes of the Exercises center on providing an opportunity for individuals to encounter God, and if, as Nadal believed, the Exercises essentially teach that human beings are to love God above all things, with all their heart, mind, soul, and strength, then surely Nadal was correct in claiming that they can be adapted for members of other faiths. What we see here, though, is that there are also good reasons to believe that they *should* be adapted for members of other faiths. It is not just that it is *permissible* to do so; there are good reasons to think that this is precisely what the gospels call us to do.

2

How Should Ignatian Spiritual Exercises Be Adapted for Members of Other Religions?

I F ONE ACCEPTS THE VIEW that there are good reasons to make Ignatian spirituality accessible to members of other faiths—and more specifically to adapt the Ignatian Spiritual Exercises for them, one is quickly faced with a series of even more challenging questions: Which members of other traditions should be chosen to make the Exercises? What should their motives and aims be? And *how* should the Exercises be given to them; that is, what kinds of adaptations should be made to the Exercises for members of other faiths? These questions are obviously interconnected; one cannot begin to address the question of how the Exercises might be adapted for members of other traditions unless one has a genuine sense of why they wish to make the Exercises and what their backgrounds are. But none of this is new to those who study and give the Exercises, for although the challenge of giving the Exercises to members of other faith traditions is unique in a number of key respects, it also requires us to ask some of the same questions we ask of Christians who wish to make the Exercises: How do we determine whether someone is ready to make the Exercises? What are the ideal qualities of this person? How or in what ways should spiritual directors adapt the Exercises for different individuals and why is the process of adaptation so important? Since Ignatius addressed these and related issues, I will begin by examining what he says on these matters with respect to Christians who make the Exercises, and then I will turn more explicitly to the question of how the Exercises should be adapted for members of other faith traditions.

Who Is Ready to Make the Spiritual Exercises?

What does the ideal exercitant look like? While Ignatius envisioned many different kinds of individuals making the Exercises and gaining much from them, and while the practice of giving the Exercises to diverse populations has been exemplified throughout Jesuit history, he nevertheless highlights particular qualities that are typically shared by those who benefit most from the Exercises. In annotation 5, Ignatius writes, "The persons who make the Exercises will benefit greatly by entering upon them with great spirit and generosity toward their Creator and Lord, and by offering all their desires and freedom to him so that His Divine Majesty can make use of their persons and of all they possess in whatsoever way is in accord with his most holy will" (SE 5). This tells us something important about the sort of person Ignatius envisions: one who is characterized by a spirit of generosity and openness toward God. There are at least two distinct components that need to be considered here: the extent to which a person possesses the virtue of generosity and the spirit of openness that Ignatius describes, and the fact that God should be the object of this generosity and openness. Thus in annotation 5 Ignatius highlights two central characteristics of the person who "benefits greatly" from the Exercises: she is generous and open, and, to put things in the broadest possible terms, she feels that she is answerable to something beyond herself and is open to encountering it. In noting that individuals should offer "all of their desires and freedom" to God, we can see clearly that Ignatius does not intend for the Exercises to be simply a way of learning more about the Christian faith, or about how to pray. Rather, he expects a willingness on the part of the individual to surrender herself to God through this experience. However, as Ivens notes, Ignatius does not expect the individual who is poised to begin the Exercises to have already attained what, for instance, the Contemplation to Attain Love is designed to achieve (namely, a willingness to offer one's liberty and all one possesses to be disposed of according to God's will).[1] "At the end the exercitant may be graced with a transformed vision of reality and a quality of élan and spontaneity in his or her self-giving which are not presupposed at the outset. But a person can be possessed of generosity at various levels, and at the very beginning Ignatius asks the exercitant to bring to God all the resources of generosity they have—and in a candidate for the Exercises he presumes these to be already considerable."[2]

Here we see that the Exercises serve a dual function: they are not only designed to *cultivate* particular dispositions and traits of character such as generosity; the Exercises also provide an opportunity to *express* these traits.[3] So an individual who "benefits greatly" from the Exercises is one who is already possessed of, and clearly expresses, virtues such as generosity, and the possession of these virtues is visible from the outset; but Ignatius shows an understanding of the fact that the possession of particular virtues is not an "all-or-nothing" matter. As Ivens notes, one can be possessed of virtues such as generosity at various levels; in order to benefit from the Exercises one must already be generous with God, but the Exercises are designed to deepen that virtue in the individual. Here we see that while the aims and purposes of the Exercises, as we saw in chapter 1, revolve around the individual's relationship with God, this relationship is not disconnected from her character. A person who benefits greatly from the Exercises already possesses certain virtues, and those virtues ought to develop in her in new ways over the course of the Exercises, alongside the development of her relationship with God. There are complex, related, and parallel courses of development here. As a result, the *object* of the spirit of openness and virtue of generosity that Ignatius describes is important to consider: a potential exercitant might be open and generous with her family and friends but not with God, and this

---

1. It is worth noting that for Aquinas faith is a theological virtue because it comes from God and is orientated toward God—it is not something that we simply cultivate in ourselves. Ignatius, too, clearly affirms God's role in instilling certain virtues in us.

2. Michael Ivens, SJ, *Understanding the Spiritual Exercises* (Leominster, U.K.: Gracewing, 1998), 7.

3. This dual function is how early Confucians understood ritual: on their view, rituals serve as an opportunity both to express and develop the virtues. For a discussion of this issue, see Philip J. Ivanhoe, *Confucian Moral Self Cultivation*, 2nd ed. (Indianapolis: Hackett, 2000). For a discussion of the virtues that are central to the Exercises, see Gerald M. Fagin, SJ, *Putting On the Heart of Christ: How the Spiritual Exercises Invite Us to a Virtuous Life* (Chicago: Loyola Press, 2010). I explore these virtues in relation to other religious traditions in the subsequent chapters of this book.

would pose a problem. Here we see that it is not simply moral virtues that characterize the ideal exercitant; because the Exercises are designed to cultivate a relationship, the exercitant must be open and generous toward God. There is, then, a close relationship between virtue and faith here: on Ignatius's view, one must at the very least be open to encountering God, even if one is uncertain about one's beliefs concerning God.

In addition to the virtue of generosity and the spirit of openness toward God that Ignatius describes, it is clear that Ignatius assumes that those who make the full and complete Exercises will be highly self-disciplined. One must be not just willing but able to spend considerable dedicated time in reflection and prayer. The fact that this takes self-discipline is made clear at several points, including those places in the text of the Exercises where Ignatius mentions the importance of spending the full amount of time in prayer each day (SE 12, 13). He specifies that the Exercises should be adapted to the age, education, and ability of those who wish to make them, and that "[i]n this way someone who is uneducated or has a weak constitution will not be given things he or she cannot well bear or profit from without fatigue" (SE 18). Indeed, he warns that "if the one giving the Exercises sees that the one making them is a person poorly qualified or of little natural ability from whom much fruit is not to be expected," it is preferable to give them lighter exercises instead of pushing ahead. "This is especially the case when there are others with whom greater results can be achieved. There is not sufficient time to do everything" (SE 18). Along these lines, the Official Directory of 1599 states that while the Exercises are for everyone, since all people in the world need God's grace, "the full and complete Exercises" should be given "only to a select few who appear fit for greater things."[4] While these remarks may appear oriented toward the aim of selecting a spiritual elite, they offer a frank statement about the practicalities of offering the Exercises.[5] There is a certain reality to the general point that is being made: the full and complete Exercises require a substantial commit-

---

4. Martin E. Palmer, ed., *On Giving the Spiritual Exercises: The Early Jesuit Manuscript Directories and Official Directory of 1599* (Saint Louis, Mo.: Institute of Jesuit Sources, 1996), 293–94.

5. That is not to deny that Ignatius sometimes expresses views that may not appeal to our democratic sensibilities. There certainly are places in the text of the Exercises where Ignatius makes clear that he believes that certain ways of making the Exercises are superior to others (SE 20) and that certain vocations are superior to others (SE 15, 135, 356, 357).

ment—and not just on the part of exercitants but spiritual directors, as well. Partly because it is in no one's best interest to experience a sense of failure when it comes to the Exercises (or in his or her spiritual life generally), it is important to try to ensure that individuals are well-suited to the experience, and if they are not, to help them find other ways of experiencing the Exercises that are a better fit.

It is clear that Ignatius believes that those making the Exercises, in addition to being self-disciplined, must be open and honest with, and willing to take direction from, those who give them the Exercises. For instance, Ignatius notes, "It is very advantageous that the one who is giving the Exercises, without wishing to ask about or know the exercitant's personal thoughts or sins, should be faithfully informed about the various agitations and thoughts which the different spirits stir up in the retreatant" (SE 17). The only way the director could be informed about these matters without asking, of course, is if the exercitant volunteers this information. If the exercitant is consistently open with her director in this way, and if the director is attentive and perceptive, then the director will develop an understanding of the exercitant and how God works with her that will, at least much of the time, allow the director to be "faithfully informed" in the ways Ignatius envisions. But the director cannot develop that sort of understanding if the exercitant is not open and forthcoming about her experience. So the director and exercitant will ideally cultivate a relationship that is characterized by trust and openness on both of their parts. Thus a willingness to be open and forthcoming with one's director would seem essential for the most fruitful retreat, but Ignatius also makes clear that the director at times may need to take a firmer hand, questioning the exercitant about what she is doing (SE 6), and insisting that she spend the full amount of time in prayer (SE 12). Ignatius is highlighting separate but equally important qualities here: one might be good at sharing openly with her director but not as good at taking direction. It is important not to take the latter for granted; a willingness to receive direction may seem natural, especially to Catholics for whom the sacramental life depends heavily upon one's reliance on and trust in religious authorities, but, especially in contemporary Western settings where independence and self-reliance are highly valued, not all potential exercitants will be good at taking direction. There are clearly traits of character that one needs to possess; just as one must be generous with God from the outset, one must also have a sense of deference and humility, and be willing to follow the guidance of a wise spiritual director. This, too, is a trait that making the Exercises ought to nurture, especially as one finds that the guidance one's spiritual director offers is helpful and that the relationship is a constructive part of the experience of making the Exercises. But one needs a significant measure of this character trait to begin with. Accordingly, those who are interested in making the Exercises need to understand that one of the distinctive features of the Exercises, and one of the reasons why they are so effective, is that they are grounded in the recognition that we need help bringing about change in ourselves and can benefit greatly from the direction of others. Of course, as Ignatius makes clear, a delicate balance must be struck between the exercitant's willingness to receive direction and the spiritual director's sense of when and how to offer it. In order for this relationship to work as Ignatius envisioned it, the exercitant should be open but not overly eager to receive guidance, and the director should be generous in listening and offering direction but also attuned to allowing God to serve as the real director (SE 15, 22). To this end, the director should model God's faithfulness and generosity to the exercitant.

While we can see from Ignatius's text that the ideal exercitant is generous and open toward God, self-disciplined, and good at being open with and taking direction from a spiritual director—and no doubt possesses a variety of other virtues, as well—this still does not give us a good sense of what he believed the ideal motivations or reasons for wishing to make the Exercises should be. But if we look to the purposes of the Exercises we can find some measure of guidance on what kinds of motivations and aims are appropriate. Ignatius and subsequent Jesuits who have studied and given the Exercises clearly viewed the Exercises not simply as an intellectual exercise—a way of learning about, for instance, scripture. As Kevin O'Brien points out, "In the Exercises, we pray with Scripture; we do not study it."[6] One learns much in the course of making the Exercises, but one's aim in making the Exercises should not be primarily intellectual or educational, but experiential. As a school of prayer, the Exercises engage

---

6. Kevin O'Brien, SJ, *The Ignatian Adventure: Experiencing the Spiritual Exercises of Saint Ignatius in Daily Life* (Chicago: Loyola Press, 2011), 15.

our intellect, emotions, memory, and will, and they provide an opportunity for us to encounter God directly. The Exercises clearly aim to give rise to a particular sort of experience, in which one becomes aware of God's presence in one's personal history and learns to recognize God's ongoing presence in one's life and work.

This is particularly important as we consider the motivations that members of other faith traditions might have for wanting to make the Exercises, because some non-Christians have expressed a desire to make the Exercises as a way to learn more about Christianity in order to better understand Christians. In this sort of case, the Exercises are being perceived as a course of study, perhaps with the more ultimate aim of promoting interreligious dialogue and its ends: greater cross-cultural understanding, respect, and tolerance. Of course, these are worthy goals, to which Jesuits are committed, but there are reasonable questions we ought to raise here about whether the Exercises are the best way to achieve these particular ends, since the Exercises are not a course in Christianity and their aims are not to deepen one's understanding of and appreciation for Christianity—even though this may indeed be one of the outcomes for many exercitants. One reason why the full and complete Exercises should not be given to those who simply wish to use them as a way of learning more about Christianity is very practical: the Exercises are not the best way to learn more about Christianity; they do not explicate Christian doctrines or introduce individuals to the different branches of Christianity or its history. Not even the text of the *Exercises* does this; as John O'Malley points out,

in itself it was not meant to convey any special theological viewpoint. Its origins lay not in a scholar's study, an academic disputation, an inquisitorial courtroom, or an ecclesiastical council. It was not a counterstatement to Luther, Erasmus, or the *alumbrados*. It originated in religious experience, first the author's and then others'. Its basic elements were well in place before the author had any theological education. It is not, therefore, a book of dogma, but a dogmatic book—that is, it assumes that its basic message is the common Christian heritage and that that message, therefore, need not be argued. What was needed was personal appropriation, a clinging to the message with all one's heart and then a translation of it with all one's heart into one's life.[7]

---

7. John O'Malley, SJ, *The First Jesuits* (Cambridge, Mass.: Harvard University Press, 1993), 42.

As O'Malley's remarks suggest, a second reason why the Exercises should not be given to those who see them simply as a tool for learning about Christianity is that the Exercises are and always have been intended to serve as *spiritual* exercises—not as intellectual exercises. Accordingly, if we give the Exercises to those who have the sole or primary aim of better *understanding* Christianity, the Exercises become a form of intellectual exercise rather than spiritual exercise. It is difficult to see how this is being faithful to the aims and purposes of the Exercises, even when they are construed broadly. It is certainly the case that participating in a tradition's customs or rituals, or experiencing them firsthand, can be a highly effective way of learning deeply about a tradition. However, we must always be sensitive to which religious practices are appropriate venues for such participation, and learning about other religious traditions involves working to understand and appreciate such matters. For instance, while members of other faith traditions are certainly welcome to attend a Catholic Mass and to participate in such activities as the singing of hymns, they are not welcome to receive Communion. While I am arguing that the Exercises differ importantly from sacraments and should not be subject to the same ritual exclusions—which is why it is permissible in some cases to give the Exercises to members of other faith traditions—I do not think they should be offered to any and all members of other faith traditions. One should have motives and aims that are in line with the purposes of the Exercises. Thus I think it is fair to say that someone who wishes to make the Exercises solely or even primarily for educational or intellectual reasons (i.e., because one wishes to learn more about and come to understand Christianity more fully) is not a good candidate to make the Exercises.

At this point it may be helpful to distinguish between primary and secondary motivations. Most of us have a mixture of motivations and aims that are a part of any given desire or choice. So it would be rare to find someone—Christian or non-Christian—who wished to make the Exercises for only one reason. However, in many if not most cases we have primary and secondary aims. So an individual might, for instance, desire to deepen her faith, and this might be the primary thing that draws her to the Exercises, but she might also desire to become more fully acquainted with the story of Jesus as it is told in the Gospels. This is true for many Catholics who make the Exercises, and it might also be true of non-Christians who are interested in making the Exercises. A part of the process of helping an individual to consider the possibility of making the full and complete Exercises is helping her to discern her own motives, and sort out primary and secondary motivations. What is really driving her interest in the Exercises? Why does she see it as worthwhile to make such a significant commitment of time and energy? Such questions are important for Christians to consider before embarking on a nineteenth- or twentieth-annotation retreat, but they will be even more important for non-Christians, who are likely to have a wider range of motivations for wishing to make the Exercises.

What, then, are appropriate primary motivations for wanting to make the Exercises? To use the broadest, most inclusive language possible, an individual should wish to make the Exercises primarily out of a desire to deepen her faith. But as we saw in the first chapter, the aims and purposes of the Exercises dig a bit deeper than that, theologically, for they are ultimately theistic in character. As a result, it is appropriate to add that an individual should be open to encountering God. In arguing for this view I am attempting to be faithful to the middle position that I discussed in chapter 1, which I think is most faithful to the purposes of the Exercises. We ought not to interpret the purposes of the Exercises in excessively narrow terms, but we also should be honest about what their purposes and shape really are. On the one hand, many Catholics who make the Exercises do so because they hope to reignite their faith; it is by no means the case that those who "benefit greatly" from making the Exercises (to use Ignatius's words) always begin the Exercises feeling absolutely certain about their Christian faith, or feeling fully at home in the Christian tradition. Since the Exercises so often serve as an effective tool for reigniting and deepening the faith of such individuals, we have good reasons not to make certitude about the truth of Christianity, or one's commitment to it, a standard for choosing exercitants. On the other hand, if we genuinely care about a person's spiritual progress, we will want them to make the full and complete Exercises only if it seems like they will realistically benefit from them. As we have seen in this chapter, that means that they should possess certain traits of character, but it also means that they should be open to encountering God and exploring who

Jesus Christ is—for these are the things that make the Exercises what they are, and that distinguish them from all manner of other spiritual exercises and self-help practices, both religious and secular.

The truth is that it is hard to imagine someone who wasn't open to encountering God and exploring the life and teachings of Jesus desiring to make the full and complete Exercises. Jews who are uncomfortable with, or uninterested in, meditating on Jesus Christ would not be drawn to the Exercises unless they were uninformed or misinformed about what the Exercises are. Some Zen Buddhists have become interested in the Exercises because they believe them to be alternative forms of meditation, and indeed such individuals might potentially benefit from the Exercises, but it would first be important for them to understand the content of the Exercises and the way in which the aims differ from those aims that are at the heart of Zen.[8] As I will argue in the chapter on Buddhism, they would have to desire to pursue some different ends than they are pursuing through Zen meditation, and this is something that many Zen Buddhists who express an initial interest in the Exercises might not realize. Indeed, if the Exercises are opened up more widely to non-Christians, then there may be non-Christians who initially express interest in them without fully understanding what they involve. This is why it will be important to educate members of other faith traditions about what the Exercises are, including information about their content, in order to help them decide whether they are good candidates for making the full and complete Exercises. Indeed, for precisely this reason, it would be good to introduce them to various parts of the Exercises, perhaps through an eighteenth-annotation retreat, prior to having them make the full and complete Exercises. Ensuring that individuals know what the full and complete Exercises involve—at least as much as possible—before they begin can help to prevent individuals from having negative experiences with the Exercises (and Christianity), and can also ensure that spiritual directors are able to give their time to those exercitants who are most likely to benefit greatly from the Exercises.

8. There has been much written on the continuities between (especially Zen) Buddhism and various aspects of Christianity and even Ignatian spirituality in particular. I discuss this literature in the chapter on Buddhism, but one worry is the tendency to minimize or gloss over important differences in favor of highlighting similarities.

How Are the Exercises Best Adapted for
Members of Other Faiths?

Exploring the qualities and motivations of someone who is well-suited to make the full and complete Exercises helps to remind us that when we talk about adapting the Exercises for members of other faith traditions, we are not talking about *all* members of other faiths, but a particular sub-set of people: members of other faith traditions who wish to use the Exercises as a tool for deepening their own faith. This should have a bearing on how we adapt the Exercises for them. I argued in chapter 1 that it is not advisable to offer a heavily adapted form of the Exercises to such individuals. I will offer a fuller argument for that position here, but I want to begin by examining the various kinds of adaptations one might consider for members of other faiths and evaluating their benefits and drawbacks. In order to do this I will start out by exploring the different ways in which the Exercises have been adapted for and given to Christians throughout their history, for this will give us a sense of what the precedents are concerning adaptation.

There are many different ways of making the Exercises and many different kinds of adaptations. We might describe these as layers, each of which tells us more about the way in which a person experienced the Exercises and how they were given to her. The first layer concerns what sort of retreat one makes (eighteenth-, nineteenth-, or twentieth-annotation; preached or individually directed); the second layer concerns the adaptations that are made for the exercitant based on such things as her background and temperament; the third layer concerns adaptations that are primarily historical and cultural (parts of the Exercises that are modified in order to update them for a contemporary setting). In fact, each of these three represents not a single adaptation but a cluster of adaptations, for a number of different things are a part of each layer. So what we have is appropriately illustrated not by a layer cake, but by multiple layer cakes stacked upon each other. I want to distinguish between and examine each of these layers, because an appreciation of the various layers will help us to recognize that no one who gives the Exercises today gives them in what we might call an "originalist" form—precisely how Ignatius gave them, following his instructions to the letter. This is because the very existence of some single original form of the Exercises is a myth: as we have seen, Ignatius always intended for the Exercises to be adapted, and he and his companions gave them in many different forms. So if one attempts to give the Exercises in some single standard, original form, then one is in fact rejecting much of what Ignatius argued about the Exercises. Now, that is not to say that there are not some ways of making the Exercises that are more or less traditional or programmatic; we can certainly outline a spectrum with varying degrees of adaptation in a variety of different areas, and some retreats will involve more modifications or amendments than others. All of this is important because in order to evaluate what kinds of adaptations are advisable for members of other faith traditions who make the Exercises, we will first need to come to terms with the many kinds of adaptation that are already a part of how the Exercises are given to Christians.

To begin with the first layer (which we might call the "retreat" layer), as we saw in the previous chapter, Ignatius envisioned at least three different forms of the Exercises, each of which has considerable room for adaptation. In the eighteenth annotation, Ignatius describes cases in which individuals experience parts of the Exercises; today this form of the Exercises is often seen in weekend or week-long retreats, and there are many different kinds of eighteenth-annotation retreats, each drawing on different parts of the Exercises to greater or lesser degrees. The nineteenth and twentieth annotations describe different ways of making the full and complete Exercises. The nineteenth annotation describes how the Exercises may be made without a withdrawal from the world but through a "retreat in daily life" conducted over an extended period of time—usually several months—during which one sets aside time each day to make the Exercises. The twentieth annotation, on the other hand, describes a traditional retreat in which one removes oneself completely from ordinary life for thirty or more consecutive days, usually in a retreat house setting. There is, however, considerable diversity within each of these three kinds of retreats, for even if we just consider the history of the thirty-day retreat—which would seem to be the most rigid of the three, since it has a more precise length and setting than the other two—we find that the Exercises have been given in exceptionally diverse ways throughout their long history. Perhaps the most striking example of this is seen in the contrast between the individually directed retreat, which characterized the way that Ignatius and his companions gave the Exercises, and the preached retreat, which became a widespread practice through the founding of retreat houses around 1660. The latter continued to be the norm until after the Second Vatican Council, when the Society of Jesus rediscovered that its founder had given the Exercises to individuals, not to groups. It began to recover the practice of the individually directed retreat—which was almost unheard of (and had been unheard of for more than a century) prior to 1965.[9] But the retrieval of this practice involved such a dramatic departure from the preached retreat that training programs and courses had to be established in order for Jesuits and others to begin to learn how to give the Exercises to individuals. This fact underscores just how much the preached retreat departed from the individually directed retreat: so much so that in order to return to the practice of offering individually directed retreats, it was necessary to completely retrain those who were giving the Exercises. So if we are honest about the history of how the Exercises have been given, then we need to acknowledge that they have been given in dramatically different ways, and they have had an enormous impact in each of these different forms. If the preached retreat is understood as an adaptation, then it is certainly the case that Jesuits have heavily adapted the Exercises, giving them in ways that Ignatius never imagined and that changed the experience substantially.

The individually directed retreat allows for considerably more adaptation than retreats where the Exercises are preached to large groups of people; since directors are working one-on-one with individuals instead of with groups, they can select and adapt what is likely to be most helpful to each particular person. As we saw in chapter 1, this is faithful to what Ignatius originally envisioned. He contends that with each of the three forms of the Exercises—eighteenth-, nineteenth-, and twentieth-annotation retreats—adaptations should be made based on a person's disposi-

---

9. The individually directed retreat was an important part of the return to the sources, traditions, and symbols of the early Church that occurred after Vatican II. Between the two sessions of GC 31, the Vatican II document *Perfectae Caritatis* was published, and it is quoted in Degree 2 of GC 31: "... they [members of Religious orders] are to be renewed by a continuous return to the sources of all Christian life, to the spirit of the founder, and to the originating inspiration of the Institute." (*Perfectae Caritatis* 2, Quoted in *Documents of GC 31*, 73n3). This return to the sources helped to enable the recovery the individually directed retreat, for which formal permission is given to the Society in Decree 8 of GC 31.

tion, age, education, and ability, as well as the ways that different spirits affect them. We might call this the second layer (the "personal adaptation" layer), for two people might both be making an individually-directed nineteenth-annotation retreat but doing some different things; they are making the same *kind* of retreat, but in fact no two retreats are alike, because of the adaptations that are made based on each individual's disposition and background. According to the text of the *Exercises*, these adaptations include lengthening or shortening different parts of the Exercises (SE 4), explaining the rules for recognizing the different kinds of spirits earlier in the retreat if necessary and warranted (SE 8, 9, 10), and having exercitants spend more time in contemplation in times of desolation (SE 13). But the adaptations that are made for each individual certainly extend beyond those that Ignatius outlined explicitly in the *Exercises*. Today, those who give the Exercises sometimes give exercitants different readings to accompany the Exercises, and make a wide range of individualized suggestions throughout the retreat based on each particular person's situation and needs. This can engender highly personalized processes, especially given that each person's relationship with God, way of viewing God, personal history, and moral character is distinctive. Some exercitants will be advised to pause at certain times or to spend more or less time on certain parts of the Exercises than others. All of these adaptations are tied to the individual's own personal needs and disposition. It is also worth noting that, in addition to being highly individualized for the exercitant, the Exercises are given by spiritual directors in highly individualized ways, as well; no two spiritual directors give the Exercises in exactly the same way, and no two spiritual directors would be likely to make precisely the same adaptations for any one individual. So in addition to tailoring the Exercises based on the needs of the exercitant, different spiritual directors have different styles and tendencies when giving the Exercises, which adds to the diversity of ways in which the Exercises are given.

A third layer, which is less personalized but which nevertheless represents a distinctive third set of adaptations, is the adaptations that are made for historical or cultural reasons. I noted a few of these in chapter 1, but they are worth revisiting here so that we can see how they differ from the first two layers we have examined. Some parts of the Exercises reflect Ignatius's own cultural and historical place in ways that stand in tension with modern sensibilities. For instance, the meditation on hell (SE 65–72) presents very literal and very medieval images of hell, including fire, smoke, sulfur, and tears—images that do not reflect more sophisticated contemporary theological views of hell. Similarly, he understands good and evil spirits in quite literal terms—another aspect of his theological view that may seem foreign to modern exercitants. In the rules for discernment, Ignatius compares the evil spirit to a woman who quarrels with an adversary and then to a man who seduces a woman and then tries to hide the affair—analogies that are offensive to many people today. These are all examples of passages in the Exercises that have been amended for a contemporary audience by those who write about and give the Exercises today.[10] Other adaptations that fall into this category include the amount of time that is spent in prayer each day for the nineteenth-annotation retreat; Ignatius recommends an hour and a half in the text of the *Exercises*, but today retreats sometimes ask for less.[11] Such changes make the Exercises more accessible and more feasible in a contemporary setting, and represent adaptations that are often just as important for contemporary retreatants as those that are tailored to their own temperaments and backgrounds. It is worth noting that there is quite widespread agreement in Jesuit circles, even among some more conservative interpreters of the Exercises, on the need for these kinds of historical/cultural adaptations. William Reiser, who as we saw in chapter 1 opposes the idea of adapting the Exercises for members of other faiths, argues in favor of adapting the Exercises in a variety of ways "because of the changed circumstances in which the church of today finds itself."[12]

All of this helps to show the many ways in which Jesuits have adapted the Exercises significantly throughout history—as the emergence of

10. See David L. Fleming, SJ, *Draw Me into Your Friendship: A Literal Translation and a Contemporary Reading of The Spiritual Exercises* (Saint Louis, Mo.: Institute of Jesuit Sources, 1996), and O'Brien, *The Ignatian Adventure*, for excellent examples of adaptations that address each of these places in the Exercises and make them more suitable for modern exercitants. Indeed, it is worth noting that Fleming's translation is an example of an adaptation for the modern retreatant.

11. For instance, John Veltri, SJ, includes three different possibilities, ranging from thirty- to sixty-minute prayer periods, depending upon the individual exercitant's situation. See John Veltri, *Orientations*, vol. 2, *A Manual to Aid Beginning Directors of the Spiritual Exercises According to Annotation 19* (Guelph, Ontario, Canada: Loyola House, 1981), 2–3.

12. William Reiser, "The *Spiritual Exercises* in a Religiously Pluralistic World," *Spiritus* 10 (2010): 147. Reiser outlines five different areas where adaptation is needed (147–50).

the preached retreat and the recovery of the individually-directed retreat shows—and how contemporary Jesuits continue to adapt the Exercises today in different ways, including everything from the presentation of the meditation on hell to the length of time that exercitants spend in prayer each day to the supplemental readings that are suggested to exercitants. The various kinds of adaptations that are widely accepted in Jesuit circles—whether they concern the type of retreat or stem from personal or historical/cultural matters—all have a couple of important things in common. First, they all seek to remove stumbling blocks that might prevent exercitants from successfully completing or getting as much as possible out of the Exercises. For instance, if someone who does not share Ignatius's particular view of hell is not offered an alternative way of completing the meditation on hell, it may be very difficult for the exercitant to gain anything from that meditation. This would be a significant loss in itself, but it could also have profound implications for her experience with the Exercises as a whole. Not only is there much to be gained from each meditation, but the meditations are interconnected, and a bad experience with one meditation can sometimes color an exercitant's overall perception of the Exercises, leading her to doubt whether the Exercises are really applicable to her life. Indeed, she might be better off skipping this meditation entirely. But it is important to note that none of the historical/cultural adaptations that we have examined *remove* elements from the Exercises entirely, or dramatically change the form or content of the Exercises. Rather, they all update Ignatius's images and examples. This is the second thing that the widely accepted kinds of adaptations that we have examined have in common: they remove impediments to individuals making the Exercises without removing whole parts of the Exercises; they involve relatively minor changes that make a big difference, but they are not dramatic overhauls of the Exercises. This is a very important clue for us as we begin to consider how the Exercises might be adapted for members of other faith traditions, because one of the keys to successful adaptation for Christians has clearly been a focus on identifying impediments and working to remove them with the least amount of tampering possible. This serves to preserve the original design of the Exercises—indeed, it preserves those features of the Exercises that have made them effective for so many people around the world, throughout their history—while also making them more accessible, with changes made on an as-needed basis. I want to underscore this point, because if the purpose of giving the Exercises to members of other faith traditions is that we wish to share our "spiritual riches," then we must be careful not to adapt the Exercises so much that we remove the very things that make the Exercises a part of these riches, that is, the things that make them so effective and meaningful.

In deciding which kinds of adaptations are acceptable, a spiritual director cannot take the text of the *Exercises* as an absolute guide, for many of the adaptations I discuss above depart from what Ignatius specifies in the text, and yet spiritual directors have found them to be quite effective and at times even essential. As Mark Rotsaert points out, the *Spiritual Exercises* is not like a cookbook: "In the book of Ignatius, you don't find recipes that have to be carefully followed. The book of the Spiritual Exercises is more a map that helps the guide to see where the person is."[13] The question is just how far one ought to go in adapting the Exercises, and this is a more general question and not one that is confined to how the Exercises might be adapted for members of other faith traditions. How much should one depart from the outline that is offered in the text of the *Exercises*, especially considering that it was never intended as a manual to be followed strictly, and what should our standards be for determining whether certain adaptations are permissible?

In working to decipher how far one can go in adapting the Exercises, it is important to recognize from the outset that it is difficult if not impossible to specify a single defining feature that makes them Ignatian. As Rotsaert points out, "Most of the individual elements of Ignatius' Spiritual Exercises are not specifically Ignatian; Ignatius uses the spiritual items of his time. But the way he puts it all together is very Ignatian!"[14] But what are the defining features of "the way he puts it all together"? What features are so essential to the Exercises that they can properly be called central or defining features? Put another way, what features of the Exercises must remain intact in order for them to still be regarded as the full and complete Ignatian Spiritual Exercises?

13. Mark Rotsaert, "When Are Spiritual Exercises Ignatian Spiritual Exercises?" *Review of Ignatian Spirituality* 98 (2001): 36–37.

14. Ibid., 32.

Rotsaert proposes an answer to this question that focuses on what he regards as the most distinctive features of the Exercises, and which draws upon both the form and method of the Exercises: "To propose a process of four weeks—one of conversion and three weeks to contemplate the life of Christ—to come to a good choice on how to manage your life, this is the originality of the Spiritual Exercises."[15] He adds that there are also important aspects of the method that are important in calling a retreat "Ignatian," including the centrality of the role that Christ's life plays in contemplation and the importance of reflection *after* meditation, which encourages one to reflect on the inner movements one had during contemplation. Rotsaert writes that this kind of reflection is "perhaps the most Ignatian part of the method of the spiritual Exercises," and the central importance of it rests not just on the fact that it helps one to improve one's way of praying, but that it helps one to discern God's presence in one's prayer.[16] This, he writes, is very Ignatian, and we find that Ignatius has the same purpose in the Examen: "The most important aspect of the examen of conscience is not to see how I can improve in living the Gospel—even if this aspect is very present—but to see how God is present in all things. And this presence will help me to improve my life."[17] Rotsaert's proposal raises some interesting questions for us: why should we take some features or elements of the Exercises to be more central than others? He does not offer an argument for why the particular elements he highlights ought to be regarded as those that make the Exercises Ignatian. He is surely right to argue that both form and method ought to be taken into account, but what is less clear is *which* elements of the form and method of the Exercises are our proper focus. Rotsaert's claim that the structure and general content of the four weeks are essential seems reasonable, although there are further questions here: must all elements of each of the four weeks remain intact? At what point has too much been taken out of a week in order for it still to retain its fundamental character or integrity? Rotsaert's suggestion that reflection after meditation or prayer should be viewed as the most central part of the Ignatian method raises further questions. This method is certainly Igna-

15. Ibid.
16. Ibid., 33–34.
17. Ibid., 34.

tian, but is it more important than other aspects of the method of the Exercises? And if so, why?

There are at least three things worth noting here. First, in order to defend a specific view concerning how much adaptation can occur before the Exercises are not really the Exercises anymore, one must offer a detailed analysis of the structure and content of the Exercises, for one must present an argument concerning what can be removed or modified (and to what degree) and what cannot, and why. Such a task involves making point-by-point determinations about which parts are absolutely essential to each of the four weeks and why. Second, in order to argue that certain parts of or methods from the Exercises are essential and should not be removed (or modified significantly), one must be able to offer reasons for privileging certain parts of or methods from the Exercises over others. But this is a highly subjective task. Different Jesuits, each with many years of experience giving the Exercises, are likely to have different views on these matters. Indeed, different individuals who have made the Exercises likely feel that particular parts of the Exercises are more central than others, because they were more central to their own experience. This brings me to my third point: one of the defining features of the Exercises is that they are meant to be adapted for each individual. This means that it will be difficult to specify *for everyone making the Exercises* which elements must remain intact or unchanged. To make such generalized statements is to neglect the very nature of the Exercises as Ignatius envisioned them.

How, then, are we to find guidance on the matter of what the limits of adaptation should be? Instead of focusing on the question of which elements of the Exercises represent essential or defining features, perhaps we will need to focus on a different question altogether: How does one determine when it is appropriate to adapt the Exercises in a certain way? And how does one determine what kind of adaptation is called for? We have already seen that the widely accepted adaptations that are made for Christians making the Exercises are a helpful starting place: these adaptations are typically made in order to remove stumbling blocks and they typically involve the least amount of change or adaptation necessary to allow the exercitant to proceed. The combination of these two features of adaptations that are widely practiced in Jesuit circles is most significant, because these features remind us that we are not trying to invent something new when we adapt the Exercises for retreatants. Rather, we are attempting to facilitate a meaningful experience with the Exercises. The entire point of adaptation is to allow individuals to experience the Spiritual Exercises of Ignatius of Loyola—the same Exercises that have guided and transformed the lives of so many individuals, from so many different cultures and times throughout history. We must be mindful of this, because the last thing we will want to do in any adaptation is undermine the effectiveness of the Exercises—which is a gift from God, but a gift that is given through the design, structure, and content of the Exercises.

Having discussed the different kinds of layers of adaptation that we find in Jesuit circles, it is also important to note the different *degrees* of adaptation. I have referred many times now to heavier or more minimal kinds of adaptation. To be more specific, adaptation can involve amending some element of the Exercises, such as a particular meditation or contemplation, or it might involve removing it completely. For instance, when giving the Exercises to a Protestant who is uncomfortable with praying to Mary and who thus struggles with the triple colloquy of the first week, one might make a number of different adaptations. One could offer the exercitant some additional readings on Mary or images of her, and encourage the exercitant to try it again but with some additional suggestions on how to go about it. One could turn the triple colloquy into a double colloquy. One could even choose to remove the triple colloquy altogether. One could also ask the exercitant what she would like to do: skip the part of the colloquy that includes Mary, or try it again with some supporting suggestions or resources. Removing the triple colloquy altogether would be a heavier adaptation, but there might potentially be some exercitants who would be in need of such an adaptation. Here we can see just how well a spiritual director must know the exercitant in order to proceed in the most effective way. In this case, much depends upon the denominational background of the Protestant to whom one is giving the Exercises. I heard of one spiritual director who, when giving the Exercises to a Pentecostal Christian, suggested praying to the Holy Spirit instead of Mary—a quite brilliant adaptation because it draws upon the centrality of the Holy Spirit for Pentecostal Christians while remaining faithful to the structure of the triple colloquy and the Trinitarian character of the Exercises. It is also significant that the spiritual director made this suggestion only after the individual had attempted the triple colloquy and had found praying to Mary to be a genuine obstacle; he did not decide *for* the exercitant, from the outset, that this adaptation should be made.

In cases that seem to require heavier forms of adaptation, spiritual directors must work to ascertain as much as possible that the exercitant would benefit more from the complete removal of a particular element than from a less heavy-handed adaptation; while one ought to work to remove stumbling blocks, one also must take care not to remove potential opportunities for growth. It is important not to underestimate what is at stake here: various parts of the Exercises, including the triple colloquy, are designed to open the individual up to direct religious experiences, including encounters with Jesus and Mary. In the example above, the triple colloquy, when adapted in the right way for the right exercitant, opened the person up to an encounter with the Holy Spirit. The last thing a spiritual director will want to do is too quickly move the exercitant away from something that may, in fact, turn out to be a transformative encounter. Along similar lines, while turning the triple colloquy into a double colloquy might be most expedient and might indeed be most appropriate for some exercitants—and this is something that only a spiritual director who knows the exercitant very well could determine—it also might be on the heavy-handed side. In a way, the option that seems the most Ignatian is the one that involves asking the exercitant what she would like to do, for this might be an opportunity to attend to different interior movements. But even this depends upon the particular exercitant and her degree of readiness, and the director would still need to present some options from which she would choose.

In any case, one thing that this type of example makes clear is that it seems most advisable, by Ignatian standards, to avoid heavy-handed or unnecessary adaptations. Here we see a basic principle of adaptation emerge. Since the goal, as Ignatius puts it, is to help the exercitant get what she is seeking, one must not only avoid giving an overly rigid form of the Exercises, but an overly adapted form, as well. In addition, it is worth noting that, as much as the spiritual director must work to get himself out of the way so that God can work directly with the individual, he is, in fact, in a very important role. In order to make the best decisions about adaptation, the director must know the exercitant very well. The importance of the latter cannot be underestimated. While God is the real director, the Exercises at critical junctures still rest upon the personal relationships between those who give the Exercises and those who make them.

Where does this leave us? My argument is that we should not attempt to define the limits of adaptation based on an argument concerning which elements of the Exercises are absolutely essential and which are not; there would be a range of defensible views on this matter, and I doubt that one could demonstrate conclusively that certain elements are indeed absolutely essential while others are not. In addition, to declare some elements "in" and others "out" when it comes to permissible adaptations seems to violate Ignatius's insistence on adapting the Exercises for each individual. We should expect, as Ignatius did, that different kinds of adaptations will be required for each individual. I think we can say, though, that all other things being equal, it is best to trust the Exercises, their framework and different methods and elements. Thus I think it is advisable to operate with a certain degree of caution; no one should rush from the outset to make adaptations—especially heavier ones. Being overly eager about adapting the Exercises would seem to be an example of the sort of thing that Ignatius warns us about when he states that spiritual directors should "allow the Creator to deal immediately with the creature and the creature with its Creator and Lord" (SE 15). One way of remaining faithful to the spirit of the Exercises here is for the director to *discern* the adaptation. Like any discernment, it must begin with experience—the retreatant's experience in this case—and from there discern movements to wholeness and integrity, and movements to disintegration and falsehood. There is clearly a more general principle here: *nothing* should be heavy-handed or aggressive on the part of those who give the Exercises. So, adaptations should be made on a case-by-case basis as stumbling blocks arise, and when adaptation is necessary, heavier forms of adaptation should generally be avoided; the first line of defense, so to speak, ought to be more modest amendments, but all of this should be done with discernment. For the most part, I think this type of approach describes what those in Jesuit circles are currently doing, and my argument is that there would be no reason to change this practice when giving the Exercises to members of other faith traditions.

Indeed, my argument is that heavier forms of adaptation—as in the removal and replacement of large portions, elements, or entire weeks of the Exercises—would not be called for in the particular group of individuals from other faith traditions with whom I am concerned. I have argued thus far that, based on the purposes of the Exercises, those members of other traditions who would be well-suited to make the Exercises are those who wish to deepen their faith through the Exercises and who are open to encountering God. Why would there be no reason to heavily adapt the Exercises for these individuals? First, it is fair to assume that they are interested in making the Exercises because they have heard about them and want to benefit from them; I have argued that potential exercitants should have a good understanding of what the Exercises are prior to making them, and this is even more important in the case of members of other faith traditions, who might initially expect to be presented with alternative forms of meditation that resemble those from their own tradition. Provided that members of other faiths who wish to make the Exercises have a solid understanding of what they are, it is important to honor the fact that there is something about the Exercises that is attracting them. I think most of these individuals would be disappointed if someone changed the Exercises dramatically for them when they had hoped to experience the Exercises. As I argued in chapter 1, the principle of reversibility is helpful here: as a Christian, if I am interested in trying Buddhist meditation, would I want a Buddhist teacher to Christianize the meditation practices for me? No. If I want to experience Christian meditation, or some form of Buddhist meditation that has been Christianized, I would seek out (or request) another alternative.[18] Out of respect for those who make the Exercises, it is important not to deprive them of the very experience to which they are drawn.

Another reason to avoid heavier adaptations of the Exercises is that

---

18. Indeed, some who give the Exercises have been involved in shaping such practices. See, for example, James Skeehan's discussion of "Christian Insight Meditation," which is adapted from Buddhist Insight Meditation practice, in his *Place Me with Your Son: Ignatian Spirituality in Everyday Life* (Washington, D.C.: Georgetown University Press, 1991), 11. Since there are Christianized forms of Buddhist meditative practices, one question is whether it would be productive to create analogous alternatives for those who might wish to experience a Buddhist or Hindu version of the Exercises. I think it is important to distinguish such practices from adaptations of the Exercises. Just as Christian Insight Meditation is not Buddhist meditation (though it is inspired by and partially based on it), one can imagine any number of practices that might be inspired by and partially based on the Exercises—though they would not be adaptations of the Exercises. I explore some potential practices of this sort in later chapters of this book.

such adaptations might inadvertently strip the Exercises of their effectiveness. Given their remarkable historical track record in different times,
cultures, and places, we have good reasons to trust the Exercises and the
adaptability that is already built into them. If we wish to help members
of other traditions to deepen their faith by making the Exercises, then we
are, in fact, assuming from the outset that there is something about the
Exercises that can be fruitful for those of other traditions. If we believed
the fruits of the Exercises to be identical to the fruits of contemplative
practices in these individuals' home traditions, there would be no reason
to give them the Exercises. That is not to say that we must think our own
traditions and practices superior to others in order to justify this practice. It does, though, push us to be honest about the distinctive value of
the Exercises. One can believe, as many inclusivists do, that Christians
can sometimes enrich their own life of faith by encountering contemplative practices from other traditions, and similarly maintain that those of
other faiths can sometimes benefit greatly from the Exercises. My sense
is that some Jesuits, wanting to avoid any suggestion of superiority, have
been hesitant to claim that the Exercises have distinctive value for people of faith, but it's not a matter of superiority and inferiority. While one
set of contemplative practices might have distinctive value in a particular arena, other contemplative practices might have other values.

This brings me to another reason why the Exercises should not be
adapted in a heavy-handed way for members of other faith traditions.
To do this seems to turn the Exercises into contemplative practices that
belong to other traditions. Yet to do this is to fail to recognize and acknowledge that other traditions have rich and meaningful contemplative practices, too. Indeed, traditions such as Buddhism and Hinduism
have a much wider range of contemplative practices and a much longer
history of systematically developing those practices than does Christianity. Now, that is not to deny that it might be fruitful to combine practices
from some of these traditions, or to take, for instance, certain Ignatian
methods and reshape them so that they can be used to achieve Zen Buddhist aims. To do this, however, is not to adapt the Exercises for members
of other traditions; to do this is to invent new kinds of contemplative
practices—and highly syncretic ones at that. Asian traditions already
have a rich history when it comes to the development of syncretic prac-

tices. When Buddhism entered China, it was forever changed as a result of the influence of Confucianism and Daoism; and East Asian forms of Buddhism, including Buddhist meditative practices, show the influence of these other traditions and look very different in many respects from South Asian forms of Buddhism. Indeed, syncretism—seen especially in the blending of beliefs and practices from Confucianism, Daoism, and Buddhism—is a characteristic feature of Chinese religion. For this reason it is not at all surprising that members of East Asian cultures are often eager to draw upon the practices of other traditions and blend them with their own. I will discuss the potential of the Exercises for such engagement in subsequent chapters, but I do think it is important to acknowledge that this process of inventing or imagining new syncretic practices that draw upon the Exercises is very different from adapting the Exercises for members of other faiths.

A final reason to be hesitant about heavier forms of adaptation concerns their feasibility, from a practical standpoint. If one removes large parts of the Exercises, what are they to be replaced with? Or does one simply shorten the retreat? Either way, there are important questions about whether one is really offering the full and complete Exercises in such a scenario. Is someone who engages in such a heavy-handed adaptation really adapting the Exercises, or is he inventing new practices that are Ignatian-informed? If one intended to do this not just with an eighteenth-annotation retreat, but with a nineteenth- or twentieth-annotation retreat (which is the concern of this book), one would have to be extraordinarily resourceful and creative, and while some individuals would certainly be capable of doing it, many would not. If one were to engage in such an adaptation with members of other faith traditions, replacing Christian scriptures, themes, meditations, and contemplations with those of other traditions, one would also need to have a robust understanding of and familiarity with the sacred texts and practices of those traditions. As a specialist in other traditions, I am doubtful that this task would be easy even for those who have dedicated their lives to working with those canons. So there is a question about the very feasibility of heavier adaptations; I think there would be a very small number of people who could do this well. I also think most of those people would rightly raise the question of why they are engaged in this difficult task, when they could simply encourage these individuals to seek out the rich range of contemplative practices that are already available in their own traditions. Here again, we see that there are good reasons to trust the Exercises, their distinctive content, form, and method, and the more modest levels of adaptation (the retreat layer, the personal adaptation layer, and the historical/cultural adaptation layer) that are already built into them.

To be clear, I am not arguing that there are *no* cases in which heavier adaptations might be defensible. I am arguing, though, that these should be handled on a case-by-case basis, and that when the adaptation is for members of other faith traditions, spiritual directors must be aware of how demanding such a heavy adaptation would be. I am arguing also that we should be aware of the distinction between adapting the Exercises and creating a new set of practices that are inspired by, or partially based on, the Exercises. How do we determine when this line has been crossed? I think very practical measures can be used here. If you described the "adapted" retreat to someone who is familiar with the Exercises, what would they say? Would their response be that your retreat reminds them of the Exercises? Or would they remark on what an interesting adaptation of the Exercises you are offering? Would they have to ask if you are giving the Exercises? These are all very practical indicators of how far one has gone on the spectrum that runs from lighter adaptations to heavier adaptations to inventing new contemplative practices.

So what are we to do when we give the Exercises to members of other faith traditions? The argument I will present here and in subsequent chapters is that we ought to offer the Exercises in a reasonably traditional format, with at least most of their content intact, but with additional content incorporated as needed. The qualification I add here—that *most* of their content should remain intact—does not differ from how the Exercises are given to Christians. In some cases, it is advisable for those giving the Exercises to make adaptations, and this may include the removal of certain elements of the Exercises. But when it comes to giving the Exercises to members of non-Christian religions, excisions should not be done any more frequently or in any different way than one would do it for anyone else who makes the Exercises. Supplemental resources drawn from other religious traditions can, however, be helpful, and I think it would be advisable to include such sources intentionally. My proposal is that adding resources from other faith traditions has certain benefits that are not achieved when one uses these resources as a *replacement*. Indeed, all of the challenges I mention above can be addressed by adding resources, but not by necessarily or programmatically removing elements of the Exercises. This is because as they make the Exercises, members of other faith traditions will make inevitable comparisons between aspects of their own tradition and the ideas, themes, and experiences that they encounter through the Exercises. However, we ought to help them to engage in that process of comparison in an informed, careful manner, so that it can serve as a real opportunity for growth. Comparative theologians can help to provide resources that would facilitate this, and, while spiritual directors will have to proceed on a case-by-case basis, we can certainly anticipate some of the comparisons and challenges that are likely to arise in the case of different traditions. The subsequent chapters of this book are designed to provide introductory remarks on these issues for specific traditions. In what follows, however, I offer some general remarks that will apply across different traditions.

Adaptation through Comparative Theology

Before discussing the reasons why presenting a reasonably traditional form of the Exercises with supplemental material from other religious traditions would be the best way to adapt the Exercises for members of other faiths, I want to begin by discussing a hidden assumption that supports the alternative of a heavier adaptation for members of other faith traditions. Again, when I talk about a heavy adaptation of the Exercises, I am talking about the possibility of removing a significant amount of the content of the Exercises—potentially including scriptures, meditations, contemplations, or even entire weeks—and replacing them with scriptures and alternative meditations and contemplations that are drawn from or inspired by the exercitant's own faith tradition. I have argued that this is neither advisable nor practically feasible for a number of reasons, and in a moment I will argue that the alternative I am presenting—where the traditional content of the Exercises remains intact with additional sources from other faiths added—does not fall prey to those same problems. But first it is worth noting that anyone who advocates for a heavy adaptation of the Exercises for members of other faiths is assuming that all faith traditions attend to the same themes, and thus that we can expect to find "replacement" resources in other faith traditions. In addition, since not only certain religious *themes* but also a *person*—Jesus Christ—is central to the Exercises, one who advocates such an adaptation appears to be assuming that there are similar or analogous people in other traditions. These are hefty theological assumptions. As I will argue in subsequent chapters, I do not think these are defensible views and I think there is an abundance of evidence to the contrary, but this can be demonstrated only through a careful examination of the resources that are found in other traditions on the themes that are central to the Exercises and individuals who appear to be comparable in various ways to Jesus. We cannot operate accurately on generalizations here: some traditions offer an account of some of the themes that are central to the Exercises, but not others; there are considerable differences within traditions, as well—especially traditions, such as Buddhism, that are exceptionally diverse in belief and practice. But I do not think that one can find all of the themes that are central to the Exercises in the scriptures of other faith traditions, nor can one find sages, prophets, or messiahs that resemble Jesus closely enough to stand in effectively for him in a heavily adapted version of the Exercises. That is not to deny that there are *any* similarities between the major figures in different traditions; it is, though, to deny that one can consistently find analogues or replacements that would achieve the same ends that the Exercises are designed to achieve. One cannot, then, expect to pick up "replacement" scriptures or figures from other faith traditions for the entirety of the Exercises. In some traditions, one would find more scriptures that would be appropriate for the task, and in others one would find fewer. While I think one could find *some* "replacement" scriptures or sacred texts in Buddhism, Confucianism, Daoism, Hinduism, Islam, and Judaism, I do not think one could find all or even most of the needed texts in any of them. For all that different religious traditions share—and I think they do share a number of important features and even specific values—there remain deep and important differences between them. Their sacred texts do not simply say the same things in different ways. They say some of the same things—sometimes stated in the same way, and sometimes stated differently—but they also say some very different things. Some themes that are central to Christianity as Ignatius presents it in the Exercises are not found in other faith traditions. Some features of Jesus' life and teachings are genuinely unique when we compare him with important figures from other traditions. What we can say specifically about these matters differs in the case of each tradition (and also *within* each tradition, since different schools or branches of each tradition hold remarkably different views and in some cases have different canons). I will explore these differences and similarities in the chapters that follow. But for now I want to stress that this is another reason why it would not actually be feasible to engage in a "heavy" form of adaptation of this sort—unless one willfully read Christianity into these other traditions, so that one consistently saw Christian themes when one looked at the texts of other faith traditions. The temptation and tendency to do this when reading texts and encountering practices from another tradition—especially a tradition that one admires and values and for which one wishes to show respect—is substantial, and in a moment I will argue that this is one of the reasons why careful comparative work is an irreplaceable resource for us in adapting the Exercises for members of other faith traditions.

Before turning to the topic of comparative theology, though, I want to entertain one final issue. As we have seen, a heavy adaptation of the Exercises for members of other faiths is not *feasible* because the themes and person that are central to the Exercises are not all found in the sacred texts and practices of other traditions; but is such a "replacement" adaptation *advisable*? Even if one *could* find analogous themes in other traditions, it is important to ask ourselves what the point of replacing Christian scriptures with other scriptures or sacred texts would be. If they are essentially the same in every significant way other than in name, then I assume the reason for doing this would be to help the exercitant to more easily connect with the theme or topic, by giving them something that is more familiar. Faith-based familiarity, then, would be offered as an additional "layer" of adaptation: on the view I am critiquing, one would make adaptations by replacing Christian themes and stories with themes and stories from other traditions. But there are challenging assumptions embedded here, as well. If this is *necessary* in order to enable the exercitant's progress—or even if it is simply *better* for the exercitant's progress—then there are very real questions about whether she should be making the Exercises, or whether a retreat that is grounded in her own faith tradition would be a better choice. Those who give the Exercises and who are eager to share their spiritual riches with members of other faith traditions need to be honest here about a couple of things. First, there are quite robust contemplative practices and resources in other faith traditions. It is not as though the Exercises are the only extant set of spiritual exercises. If people are simply more likely to benefit from engaging with the scriptures or sacred texts of their own tradition, then it seems reasonable to assume that they might benefit more from making a retreat that is rooted in their own tradition, instead of the Ignatian tradition. Second, to defend the view that a heavy adaptation of the Exercises for members of other faiths is advisable is to reject the view that Jesuits ought to "bring their own distinctively Catholic, Christian identity to whatever work they enjoin."[19] I also worry that a heavy adaptation results in a genuine *failure* to share one's spiritual riches. Despite the fact that such an adaptation is clearly motivated by the desire to make the Exercises more accessible to members of other faiths, such a heavy adaptation does not really share the things that Ignatius shared with us.

An alternative approach lies in a form of adaptation that, first, follows the usual practices of adaptation—which of course occasionally involves amending or removing elements of the Exercises based on the three "layers" of adaptation we have already discussed. The second part of this adaptation—the "other faiths" layer—would add material to the Exercises that relates to the individual's own faith tradition, including work that explicitly engages in comparison between the exercitant's tradition and Christianity. This might involve developing—with the help of comparative theologians, philosophers, and scholars of religion—works that are short and accessible and that engage some of the key themes from the Exercises in relation to other faith traditions. The aim of such works would be to explore both similarities and differences in an attempt to help exercitants of other faiths (and their spiritual directors) to

19. Adolfo Nicolás, "Companions in Mission: Pluralism in Action," Mission Day Keynote Address, Loyola Marymount University, Los Angeles, California, February 2, 2009, http://www.gonzaga.edu/About/Mission/docs/LoyolaMarymountUniversityAddressAdolfoNicolasSJ.pdf, 83.

work carefully through the inevitable comparisons between their own tradition and Christianity. It would be essential to keep these "companion" works short, since one could not reasonably add a great deal of material to the full and complete Exercises and still have the time needed to make the Exercises. This is one of the reasons it would not be advisable to point exercitants to existing works in comparative theology, religious studies, or philosophy, which are quite long and challenging; indeed, another reason is that such works typically are specialized and not easily accessible to a wider audience. Since the goals of comparative studies vary widely, these comparative "companion" works would need to be oriented toward the goal of helping those of other faiths to deepen their faith as they make the Exercises. Of course, it would be impossible to anticipate all of the issues that might arise for each individual, but there are nevertheless a range of common themes and issues that would be particularly likely to arise in the case of each faith tradition. The subsequent chapters of this book discuss what some of those are for Asian religions, and seek to begin the task of writing such "companion" works.

While we have already examined the reasons why a heavy adaptation of the Exercises is neither feasible nor advisable, it is equally important to note the reasons in favor of the specific approach to adaptation that I am recommending. Adding an additional layer to the Exercises through comparative "companion" works is advisable for a number of reasons. First, it meets the needs of members of other faiths who wish to make *the Ignatian Spiritual Exercises* in particular—which means that they wish to engage the Christian content of the Exercises, and not a dramatically amended version of the Exercises. Again, we need only apply the principle of reversibility here to see why this is advisable. If we wish to respond to the spiritual needs of others, then we must respect the fact that something has drawn them to the Exercises in particular, as opposed to Buddhist, Daoist, or Hindu contemplative practices. Second, we ought to take care not to strip the Exercises of the features that have made them effective in the lives of so many diverse persons around the world. Adding supplemental material does not carry the same risks in this regard as removing significant parts of the Exercises. Third, the practice of adding supplemental material that explicitly works through similarities and differences between other faith traditions and Christianity—with a particular focus on the themes and stories that are central to the Exercises—has an advantage over simply *replacing* material from the Exercises with material from other traditions, because such a practice openly engages and seeks to address the exercitant's questions about and inevitable comparisons between her own tradition and that of Ignatius. There is tremendous potential for growth in such an exercise, and there is no reason why this task should be left to the exercitant alone. Careful comparative work can be an excellent resource here, for it provides signposts or markers that are designed to help exercitants of other faiths to better understand their own tradition as well as Christianity, and in the process, to deepen their faith.

In referring here to "careful comparative work," I am intentionally suggesting that exercitants and spiritual directors will need the guidance of those who are trained to work across traditions in order to undertake this task, and this, I think, makes the prospect of adapting the full and complete Exercises for members of other faith traditions a unique undertaking which can bring work in comparative theology and comparative religious studies together with the practice of giving the Exercises. This is not something to pass over too quickly, for comparative work and contemplative practice are often regarded—and sometimes with good reason—as separate domains. I am arguing, though, that we ought to see two of the "dialogues" developed by the Pontifical Council for Interreligious Dialogue and Congregation for the Evangelization of People and incorporated into the Society of Jesus' way of proceeding in 1995 as essentially interrelated when it comes to giving the Exercises. The first of these, which we have already examined, is the *dialogue of religious experience*, "where persons, rooted in their own religious traditions, share their spiritual riches, for instance, with regard to prayer and contemplation, faith and ways of searching for God or the Absolute."[20] As I have argued, what is needed here is more than a "dialogue" in the standard sense; the sharing of the Exercises should involve actual practice, and not just discussing practices and beliefs. The second is the *dialogue of theological exchange*, "where specialists

20. *Documents of the 34th General Congregation of the Society of Jesus: The Decrees of General Congregation Thirty-Four, the Fifteenth of the Restored Society and the Accompanying Papal and Jesuit Document*, ed. John L. McCarthy, SJ (Saint Louis, Mo.: Institute of Jesuit Sources, 1995), Decree 5, "Our Mission and Interreligious Dialogue."

seek to deepen their understanding of their respective religious heritages, and to appreciate each other's spiritual values." One of the reasons why these two areas—with their separate emphases on sharing contemplative practices and drawing upon the work of specialists in particular religious traditions—ought to be united when we adapt the Exercises for members of other faiths is that careful comparative work is incredibly difficult, and there are particular pitfalls that are likely to be especially problematic for those giving and making the Exercises.

Comparison by its very nature seems to draw humans like magnets toward one of two ends of a spectrum: complete sameness (as opposed to similarity) or complete difference. These two views lie at opposite ends of a spectrum, and when we compare religious traditions, the tendency to be drawn toward the conclusion that two religions are at bottom saying or doing the same thing, or that they are radically different and share nothing substantive in common, is a serious vice, because it both stems from and results in inaccurate representations of the two traditions under study.[21] Seldom if ever is it accurate to describe two religious traditions as completely different or completely same. Unfortunately, however, the magnetic tendency toward one of these two extremes characterizes two prominent approaches to the study of different religions.

In theology, and more specifically among many who are interested in Catholic inter-religious dialogue and religious pluralism—and I think this view is also the preferred view of many Jesuits who have an interest in other religious traditions—there has been a dominant trend toward various forms of inclusivism or pluralism that emphasize the similarities between different traditions. Such claims seek to reject older, exclusivistic "missionary-minded" ways of viewing other traditions, and this is a good thing: they accept and respect the value of religions other than Christianity. The claim that all religious traditions are, at bottom, doing the same thing or expressing the same yearning (for God, the Ultimate, or the Real) is fleshed out in different ways, but in these circles it is typically rooted in a desire not to condemn others. However, among Christian theologians who are inclusivists the move toward such condemnation is typically avoided by claiming that the spirit of Christ animates or

---

21. The noted scholar of religion Wayne Proudfoot refers to this vice as "descriptive reductionism." See Wayne Proudfoot, *Religious Experience* (Berkeley: University of California Press, 1985).

is in some way already present in other religions. There is an aspect of this position that might prompt a "thanks, but no thanks" response on the part of members of other faith traditions. On the one hand, it is good to move beyond simplistic claims of Christian superiority and blanket condemnation of other traditions. On the other hand, though, the reason why this is possible is the belief that Jesus Christ is already present in these traditions; they are *just like us*, and that is why we need not condemn them. There is something that is at once progressive and archaic about this view: it involves moving beyond the more traditional theological claims of Christian exclusivism and seeks to be less Christocentric, but it also typically involves simplistic, outdated claims such as the claim that all religious traditions involve a belief in God, even if God is called by another name. There are some very clear reasons why these claims persist: those who argue for such claims are not usually trained as specialists in any tradition other than Christianity, and even Catholic theologians from other cultures who argue for these types of views do not typically have scholarly training in religious traditions other than Christianity. Of course, there is something genuinely admirable about this sort of view, as it aims to recognize our common humanity, but this desire often leads to extreme claims of sameness. The tendency is to obscure the theological details of different views, claiming that they are *really* saying the same thing, at bottom, and that thing is not the Hindu or Buddhist view of reality, but the Christian view.

In the discipline of religious studies, there has been a dominant trend in the opposite direction, toward emphasizing the differences between traditions. There are a number of reasons for this, including the fact that scholars in religious studies who do comparative work or who respond critically to comparative work are typically specialists in particular religious traditions, having dedicated their lives to understanding those traditions. As a result of this training, the tendency of theologians (and some others) to misrepresent these traditions by portraying them as completely or essentially the same as other traditions—most notably Christianity—is offensive; it both stems from and gives rise to misunderstandings and neglect of what particular religious traditions have to say and of their long and complex histories. Scholars of religion who specialize in particular religious traditions find these types of misrepresentations troubling for understandable reasons: one does not want to see the traditions one knows well portrayed inaccurately, nor does one want their distinctive qualities to be watered down or neglected. But in addition to one's sense of scholarly responsibility, there are reasons relating to disciplinary history as well. In religious studies the sensitivity to this sort of work is especially acute because the study of religion in the academy originally focused on Christianity, and the discipline has progressed to a place where this is no longer the case. Religious studies is of course not unlike most other disciplines in the humanities in this regard: disciplines such as History and Literature are no longer Eurocentric in the ways they used to be and include the study of racially, ethnically, and culturally diverse peoples from around the world. In addition to these historical reasons, additional trends and movements in the discipline of religious studies have also led scholars to emphasize difference more strongly and indeed to doubt our reasons for calling them all "traditions" or "religious." The focus is sometimes on *radical* difference, including the influence of postcolonialism, postmodernism, and various (and often related) forms of anti-essentialism, which have led scholars to doubt that different religious traditions have *anything* in common. It is important to note that such claims place one firmly at one extreme end of the spectrum I have been describing, for the strongest versions of these views deny that any religious traditions really have anything in common—sometimes by denying that we have good reasons to call them all "religious traditions."[22]

As someone who does comparative work, I want to note that neither of these positions is rooted in the careful study and comparison of two traditions. They are not conclusions that result from the careful examination of two (or more) religious traditions, but rather they result from prior theoretical commitments. Those in theology who view different traditions as essentially saying or doing the same things are in many cases driven by a religious belief: that God is at work in all cultures and traditions, even if God is called by another name and described in different terms. This view can lead to the willful neglect of differences and to the tendency to dismiss

---

22. This "difference-mongering" sometimes even extends to claims about particular religious traditions, as seen in the recent trend in religious studies of using plural forms like "Christianities" or "Judaisms," as opposed to singular forms like "Christianity" or "Judaism."

differences that are revealed through the careful study of different traditions. Those in religious studies who view different traditions as radically different (sometimes to the point of being incomparable or incommensurable) are often in the grip of disciplinary trends, and therefore uninterested in what the evidence gained from careful comparative work might tell us. Interestingly, theologians and scholars of religion who occupy opposite ends of this spectrum often dismiss comparative work that engages both differences and similarities, because they believe it is impossible that the evidence could tell us such things. Theologians of a certain stripe tend to find a way to interpret the evidence as supporting their view; religious studies scholars of the opposite stripe maintain that any attempt to compare traditions falls into some sort of essentialistic trap.

I believe that the best comparative work avoids beginning with a conclusion that one wishes to prove, or believes that one will inevitably prove, by examining two traditions. I have never seen the careful study of different religious traditions deliver us to one or the other end of the spectrum—to the conclusion that two traditions are exactly the same at bottom, or to the conclusion that they are radically different to the point of having nothing in common. Of course, either of these possibilities is theoretically possible. But in reality, the careful study of different traditions shows us repeatedly that there are varying degrees of similarity and difference, and that to dismiss the similarities or the differences, or to attempt to explain them away, is to misrepresent the traditions under study. Comparativists therefore have good reasons to expect to operate in various places along the middle of the spectrum—though sometimes further to one side than the other, since some traditions have more in common than others, or have similarities that run deeper or are less superficial than others.

I want to establish all of this up front because I believe the vice of seeing too much similarity or complete sameness will tend to plague those who give the Exercises to members of other traditions and those members of other traditions who make the Exercises, and I think this vice could seriously undermine the richness of the Exercises for these individuals. Given the desire to share the Exercises with members of non-Christian faiths, and given the eagerness of members of other traditions to make the Exercises, I think the inclination on the part of both those who give the Exercises and those members of other faiths who make them will be to see more similarity—indeed, even identity—where it does not really exist. Why should this be viewed as a vice in giving or making the Exercises? Why not simply allow exercitants to conclude that what Jesus is saying is precisely what the Buddha, Krishna, Confucius, or Laozi taught as well? I think the answer to this question is twofold.

First, it is simply not the truth. Just as Jesuits and others who give the Exercises have an obligation to present the gospels accurately, if they wish to give the Exercises to members of non-Christian faiths and therefore to include sources and themes from other traditions, they have an obligation to present those accurately, as well. Indeed, if we believe that we have good reasons to give the Exercises to members of other faith traditions, then we must seize the opportunity to really learn about other faith traditions, and this will be necessary if we are to adapt the Exercises for members of other faiths. In addition to being honest about and respectful toward other traditions by not misrepresenting them, we gain more by having exercitants openly grapple with both the similarities and differences between their own traditions and that of Ignatius (as opposed to encouraging them to conclude that it is all "really the same"). There is a greater potential for growth, because this is a much more challenging endeavor, but there is also a greater potential for exercitants to have a different sort of religious experience or encounter than they would have within the context of their own tradition.

This brings me to the second part of my answer. If the purpose of giving the Exercises to members of other faith traditions is to help them to deepen their faith, then they will have to grapple with what they really believe and how it differs from other alternatives. If the engagement with Christian sources and themes simply gives them a mirror image of their own tradition, and allows them to learn nothing new or different from what their own tradition teaches, then there would be no point to making Christian spiritual exercises. Since those in Jesuit circles who are interested in giving the Exercises to members of other traditions are often inclined toward emphasizing similarity or sameness, I want to be especially clear on this point: if all traditions are really doing the same things, then there is no reason to adapt the Exercises for members of other traditions. The very acknowledgment of the need for adaptations that are specifically oriented toward the needs of members of other faiths requires the acknowledgment of real differences between traditions. This is not something we should fear or seek to avoid. In giving the Exercises, both inclusivists and exclusivists ought to openly engage the differences between Christianity and the exercitant's own tradition in order to give her the opportunity to more fully appreciate the role that God and Jesus Christ can play in a life of faith, and this involves both reflective and experiential elements; it is a matter of understanding and feeling as well as experiencing or encountering. If the exercitant wishes to make the Exercises in order to deepen her faith, the role of God and Jesus Christ would seem to be the obvious elements that Ignatian spirituality can bring, particularly given that such a rich range of spiritual exercises exist in the home traditions of exercitants. For this reason especially, we should not attempt to lessen the distinctive elements of Ignatian spirituality for exercitants from other traditions.

3

Hindu Adaptations of the Spiritual Exercises

THIS CHAPTER WILL FOCUS on how the full and complete Ignatian Spiritual Exercises might be adapted for members of the Hindu tradition, but it will first be helpful to remember that this adaptation is designed for Hindus who wish to deepen their faith through the Exercises, and who are open to encountering Jesus Christ and the God of biblical faith. Hinduism, like most religions, is large and diverse. What it means to be a Hindu and what Hindus believe vary considerably, and so it is especially important to remember that we are concerned with only those who, as outlined in the first two chapters of this work, would be good candidates for making the Exercises; this chapter by no means aims to outline an adaptation for *all* Hindus. As we have seen in the preceding chapters, not all members of other religions would be interested in making the Exercises, and of those who might express interest, not all would be adequately prepared. Since this adaptation is designed for Hindus who wish to deepen their faith through the Exercises and who are open to encountering God and Jesus Christ, most of the content of the Exercises will remain intact and supplemental texts from Hinduism will be added. As I argued in the previous chapter, there are good reasons to avoid heavier forms of adaptation—including the removal of large portions or entire weeks of the Exercises and the attempt to replace them with texts from other religions. One of those reasons is that other religions do not have analogues or correlates to all of the movements of the Exercises—

even though there are important resonances with some movements. Indeed, this chapter highlights some of the reasons why we cannot find all of the themes that are central to the Exercises in the sacred texts of Hinduism, nor can we find sages, prophets, or messiahs that resemble Jesus enough to stand in effectively for him in the Exercises. Similarly, we cannot find all of the themes that are central to Hindu contemplative practices in Christian scriptures, nor can Jesus serve as an effective replacement for important Hindu religious figures. This chapter will highlight some of the specific reasons why this is true. But this is one of the reasons why the Exercises ought to be shared with members of other faiths, and more broadly, why we ought to exchange with each other on the level of spirituality: Ignatian spirituality has a distinctive gift to bring. It is in virtue of our differences that we are able to be enriched by one another's spiritual traditions. If our religions were all the same, there would be no point in having such an exchange or working on such an adaptation.

The goal of the adaptation I outline in this chapter is to remove stumbling blocks that might prevent a Hindu exercitant from being able to benefit from the Exercises, and to do so in a way that involves the least amount of change or adaptation necessary in order to allow the person to proceed. I will focus primarily on the addition of texts and practices from Hinduism that would help Hindus to grapple with the tensions and resonances between their tradition and that of Ignatius. Hindus making the Exercises will inevitably make comparisons between aspects of their tradition and the ideas, themes, and experiences that they encounter through the Exercises. Our goal will be to provide signposts or markers to help them to better understand their own tradition, as well as Christianity, without either denying important differences or exaggerating them. Most of all, our goal is to help exercitants to deepen their faith and to lead lives grounded in their faith. As I have argued, this endeavor results in a distinctive adaptation of the Exercises, for it includes the ideas and practices of another religion. This adaptation seeks to open up the possibility of a different sort of religious experience for Hindu exercitants (since it is Ignatian) while also deepening their roots in and understanding of Hinduism (since it incorporates elements of Hinduism).

A Brief Overview of Hinduism

Of the religions that are the primary focus of this book, Hinduism is arguably the religion that most lends itself to an adaptation of the Exercises. Indeed, a case could be made that Hinduism is the best candidate for adaptation even when compared with the other Abrahamic faiths, since Muslims and Jews must wrestle with the question of who Jesus is according to their traditions, compared with the very different view that is central to the Exercises. That is not to say, however, that adapting the Exercises for Hindus is an easy task. But in beginning this dialogue with Hindus, we can begin with a common belief in and comfort level discussing God—even if God is understood in different terms.

The term Hindu, meaning "of India," literally refers to an entire culture that originated in India, but its more common usage refers to the philosophical and religious tradition beginning with the indigenous religions of India and arising from the *Vedas* (from 1500 BCE), the *Upanishads* (after 1000 BCE), and an accompanying array of rituals, texts, and social structures. Both India and Hinduism are astonishingly diverse. By one estimate, 325 languages and 2,000 dialects are spoken in India today, with 25 scripts in use and 80,000 subcultures. Hinduism as a religion is similarly diffuse, and not just because of its size—one of every six people on earth considers her- or himself a Hindu, including roughly 82 percent of India's population (of 1.1 billion people). Francis Clooney, SJ, writes that, while it is very hard to define Hinduism, "[i]n its unity-in-difference—seemingly infinite variety that seems often enough to point to a deeper oneness—it differs from Buddhism and other religions east and west."[1] Nevertheless, Clooney's description affirms the diversity and complexity of Hinduism in the midst of that oneness, for it is a tradition that

combines the complex indigenous and Vedic heritage, Brahminical orthodoxy, and ascetical extensions and alternatives; epics such as the Ramayana and Mahabharata plus other important texts and practices; devotion to new, popular Gods such as Shiva, Vishnu, Rama, Krishna; leading to the formulation (particularly in Brahminical discourses) of major theistic traditions, plus an array of

---

1. Francis X. Clooney, SJ, "Learning Our Way: Some Reflections on the Catholic-Hindu Encounter," in *Catholicism and Interreligious Dialogue*, ed. James L. Heft, SM (New York: Oxford University Press, 2012), 90.

holy places, images, pilgrimages, and so forth, connected with devotion—some traditions being dedicated to one supreme Deity or Reality, and all of this flourishes as a complex Hinduism constantly and continually enriched and challenged.[2]

The story of the deep origins of Hinduism, and the heart of this tradition, can be told in many ways. One is to begin with the Sanskrit root of the term *veda*: *vid*, meaning "to know." *Veda* is knowledge of truth—God-given truth, Truth given by the ultimate reality or supreme power of the universe, or supreme knowledge, divinely inspired. *Veda* is Truth itself, as opposed to the ordinary truths of daily experience. For all of its diversity of belief and practice, the Hindu tradition is ultimately grounded in the view that our goal as humans is to come to know *veda*, the Truth, and to live our lives in a way that reflects our understanding of that Truth. Our salvation ultimately rests on that understanding: what humans need, on this view, is a saving insight into the True nature of the world. The earliest concrete expressions of veda, the Truth, are found in sacred hymns and ritual chants known as the *Vedas*, which date to about 1500 BCE. Composed by an elite group of priests, the *Vedas* began as and remained an oral tradition, even though in time they were written down. The question of Vedic authorship points us toward some important aspects of Hinduism. The *Vedas* were not scripture, for the latter term comes from the Latin root for "scribe," implying written religious expression. Rather, the term *śruti*, "that which has been heard," is used in reference to the *Vedas*, as in *hearing* divine revelation. Brāhmin priests were understood as mediators between the humans and the gods, and an elite group of brāhmin priests known as *rishis* ("see-ers") composed the *Vedas*. The term *rishi* is significant here: these individuals were believed to have *seen* the true structure and nature of the universe and transformed it, when they composed the *Vedas,* into a form that could be heard by others (*śruti*), thus taking us from *veda* (Truth) to a very specific set of compositions: the *Vedas*. On one view of authorship, the *Vedas* are revealed hymns of which God is the true author. On another view, they are authorless, with no human or divine composer, no mind behind them; they are simply the universe's structure and nature revealed to us.

2. Ibid., 91.

In the *Vedas* we find the seeds of the Hindu tradition, but as we have already noted, this is a tradition that finds expression through a diverse set of texts and practices throughout its long history. The Vedic tradition of ancient India—including the *Upanishads*, which might be compared to first flowers that grow from the seeds of the *Vedas*—offers a clear introduction to a number of fundamental Hindu beliefs. The Vedic tradition consists not only of these early texts but of an array of rituals, social structures, and theoretical developments such as *Vedānta* theology, which interprets the *Upanishads* comprehensively. Vedanta, one of six orthodox schools of philosophy in the Hindu tradition (all of which defended the infallibility of the *Vedas*) contends that the *Upanishads* make a series of claims about the fundamental nature of the universe, including its basic characteristics. First among these is *multiplicity*: we have a seemingly infinite number of things around us. Second, the world is characterized by *change*: all matter is constantly changing. Third, *transformation*: all matter is constantly becoming something else. Fourth, *order*: the change and transformation we see is orderly; there are patterns and laws that characterize nature. Fifth, the activity of *causation*: everything is the result of something else, the "doing" of something else; things are active, and causes and effects are constantly in play. Against this backdrop, a number of fundamental Hindu ideas emerge. First and foremost, *Brahman*, which is ultimately ineffable, is the underlying reality of everything, the ultimate inner essence of everything, the fact of existence (pure existence), the root cause of everything or the root of existence from which the world grows, and pure consciousness or spirit. *Brahman* plays the universe like an instrument—dynamic and creative, ever the great musician. *Dharma*, in this analogy, is like the musician's score. It is the order or pattern of the universe, the law that upholds the universe and creates harmony throughout it. *Prakriti* is the primal material essence, cosmic dust, matter, or brute stuff of which all things are made. *Māyā* is the world of temporary, changing forms or shapes (which are made of *prakriti*): the appearance of the many out of one. *Ātman*, from the Sanskrit root "to breathe," as in "to breathe life into something," is the core of all sentient (conscious) beings, the inner self, the conscious essence.

With these concepts in view, we can begin to appreciate the insight that is at the very core of Hinduism, specified in the doctrine of *Brahman-Ātman*: *Ātman* is *Brahman*. You and I are not distinct selves or souls; we are, in fact, continuous. We are one with everything. As *Mandukya Upanishad* puts it, "Brahman is all and ātman is brahman."[3] This truth finds expression throughout the *Upanishads* in a variety of metaphors, such as that of rivers or waves in an ocean, seen in this passage from *Prasna Upanishad*: "As when rivers flowing toward the ocean find final peace, their name and form disappear, and people speak only of the ocean" (74). We are not just ourselves, for we are not separate but continuous with the rest of creation, and our destiny is to understand that fundamental truth. "Far spreading before and behind and right and left, and above and below, is brahman, the spirit eternal. In truth brahman is all" (*Mundaka Upanishad*, 79). The appearance of separateness is just that—an appearance, or more precisely, an illusion. The fundamental problem with human beings is that we mistakenly think that we are distinct from other beings, when in fact we are all part of the same whole. In each of our cases, the atman—our essential self or soul—misidentifies itself with the ego it assumes. We come to believe that we are truly distinct selves, just as each of us has a body and a distinct set of roles define us throughout the course of our lives. Even though our bodies and our roles change—for they are part of maya, the world of changing, temporary forms—they nevertheless create the appearance that we are separate and distinct from others. This illusion of separateness is called *avidyā*, and, according to the Hindu tradition, it is the root of all suffering. Until we awaken from the dream-like state of *avidyā*, in which we are trapped in the illusion that we are separate and distinct individuals, our atman—our conscious essence or soul—will continue to be reborn. *Samsāra* is the term for this cycle of rebirth—the belief in reincarnation that is a part of the Hindu tradition that specifies that the atman will be reborn over and over until it awakens to its *brahman* identity. The fundamental goal of human existence is to break free of the illusion that we are separate individuals and awaken to our true identity with the realization that we are one with everything. Atman's awakening to its *brahman* identity is called *moksha*, and it represents salvation, and liberation from

---

3. Juan Mascaro, trans., *The Upanishads* (New York: Penguin, 1965), 83. Hereafter cited parenthetically with page number.

the wheel of samsara. Much of the Hindu tradition is dedicated to specifying how we attain *moksha*.

This fundamental insight concerning the *oneness* of all things lies at the heart of Hinduism, but there are a diversity of texts and practices concerning how humans might be led to this insight and how they can live in a way that reflects the most important truth of existence: we are not just ourselves—we are not separate, but continuous with the rest of creation. As Clooney points out, the insights originating with the Vedic tradition of ancient India and regularized as the brahminical heritage in the theory and practice of orthodoxy—the dharma—is "a heritage that proves to be enormously resourceful, elastic, and inclusive for millenia."[4] Over time, Hinduism came to involve devotion to popular gods such as Shiva, Vishnu, Rama, and Krishna, as well as goddesses such as Sarasvati, Lakshmi, Devi, and Kali. In practice, these deities are worshipped as many; theologically, they are all part of the same whole, just as we are one with all of creation. It is important to recognize that these deities are not simply saints in service of one supreme God; there are multiple supreme, gracious gods and goddesses, and the Hindu belief in oneness does not amount to monotheism here. As Clooney puts it, "These deities have a substantive reality for most Hindus, and should not be condescendingly termed 'representations of the One.'" This is partly because it is not simply deities that are one; we are *all* one. Living beings "are always already one with God, Ultimate Reality, and indeed are materially and spiritually generated from that Being."[5] Here we see a striking difference from the Ignatian view that will be explored throughout this chapter, namely that while, in the Christian tradition, the Father, Son, and Holy Spirit are all one in substance and nature, humans and the rest of creation are not one with them and each other. The kind of oneness that is a part of Ignatian spirituality—including being in a relationship with Christ and imitating his way of living—differs in important ways from the Hindu sense of oneness.

The *Bhāgavad-Gītā*, one of the most important religious texts in the Hindu tradition and one that has long been used for devotional purposes by Hindus, can help us to understand how theistic belief and devotion to

---

4. Clooney, "Learning Our Way: Some Reflections on the Catholic-Hindu Encounter," 91.
5. Ibid., 98.

deities is integrated with foundational Hindu teachings about oneness. The *Gītā* is a small part of a much larger text, the *Mahābhārata*, which comes from the Epic period, with origins in the sixth century BCE. The *Mahābhārata* is one of the two great Sanskrit epics, the other being the *Rāmāyana*. It is impressive for its size: it is over one hundred thousand verses in length, roughly eight times the size of the Iliad and the Odyssey. The *Bhāgavad-Gītā* is only seven hundred verses, and purportedly is based on events from the tenth century BCE. Set "in the fields of righteousness," of truth, of sacred duty, sometimes also rendered "the battlefield of life," the text contains a dialogue between the young warrior Arjuna and his charioteer, Krishna, who is the deity Vishnu incarnate. It offers a synthesis of Vedic and Upanishadic teachings as well as Hindu ethical teachings through the telling of Arjuna's story. Arjuna, paralyzed by fear on the battlefield and convinced that he cannot simultaneously fulfill his duties as a warrior and his duties to his family, is trapped in the illusory state of *avidyā*, bound up in his ego attachments and devoid of a sense of his true identity. Krishna, representing the true nature of the atman—the essential self that recognizes that it is one with all and is not trapped in the illusion of separateness—urges Arjuna to fight, a metaphor for doing battle against his ego attachments. He instructs Arjuna in ethical action, which means fulfilling his duties as a warrior and acting without the desire for a result. Here, desires are problematic because they are an expression of our ego attachments, which betray the illusion that we are separate beings. The view that desires are fundamentally problematic is a central part of Hinduism and marks another area in which we will see some tensions between Ignatian spirituality and Hinduism.

However, for the present purposes the *Gītā* is particularly important for the way it communicates the Hindu belief in gracious gods that come to the aid of humans, who even sometimes walk beside them in human form, patiently and lovingly offering comfort and guidance. In one of the most arresting scenes from the *Gītā*, Arjuna asks Krishna to show him his true form—his true oneness with all things—and Krishna reveals himself in his totality, in all of his glory, to Arjuna, who sees *everything* in this magnificent vision. Here we see the unity of the Hindu belief in particular deities and Hindu teachings concerning oneness. While Krishna is the incarnation of a particular deity, Vishnu, when he reveals his true nature, he reveals the entirety of the whole universe—including other deities and all of creation, unified in his body. But this does not make him any less of a personal deity to Arjuna. Rather, the vision of Krishna's totality is a part of his teachings to Arjuna, all of which are designed to help him in a particular time and place, but also to help him on the way to salvation or liberation by teaching him his true identity with all things.

What does contemporary Hindu devotional practice look like? To begin, it is theistic—it involves belief in and devotion to a god or gods. It is important to remember that although theism is often equated with traditional forms of monotheism, theism in fact does not denote belief in the existence of a single omnipotent, omniscient, eternal, supremely good being who created the world, but rather belief in the existence of some sort of divine being or divine reality. Many Hindus freely talk about "God" conversationally, which suggests a kind of monotheism, but as we have seen, there is a diversity of practice; many Hindus worship and petition multiple deities. Clooney points out that these types of differences between theists do not necessarily prevent interreligious understanding at an experiential level:

just as the ideas and great texts of the Hindu tradition are interesting and impressive, so too the lived devotion is real and persuasive, the practices most often inviting. I have learned too that to recognize connections and decipher their meaning also requires us to reflect on what we learn in practice, with a vulnerable openness that makes learning possible.[6]

It is this same openness that we will be seeking as we turn to the potential the Ignatian Spiritual Exercises might have for Hindus.

An Adaptation of the Ignatian Spiritual Exercises for Hindus: The First Week

The dynamics of the Exercises are driven by the graces or gifts sought—not by a text. In the Christian tradition, grace takes on a variety of meanings. In the Exercises, grace is essentially the active, laboring, loving presence of God in one's life. More colloquially, grace is often translated

6. Ibid., 90.

as a gift of God, but it means more than the gift we receive from a loved one. Grace as a gift does not simply remind us of the giver of the gift, but mediates or reveals in some way the divine presence. This is key in the Spiritual Exercises, because their whole point is to lead us to a direct encounter with the Giver of all good gifts. Thus Ignatius asks us throughout the Exercises to pray for certain graces. These are like signposts on the way to God, or building blocks of a relationship. The spiritual director is not confined to following the spiritual exercises, one after the other, as laid out by Ignatius. Better, the director listens attentively and discerns the graces that the retreatant is praying for and which she experiences in particular exercises. Having discerned them, they then follow the grace to the next one. For instance, an experience of God's unconditional love prepares one to consider the reality of sin—of not returning love for love—in the first week; or having a felt experience of God's mercy, one desires to extend that mercy to others in the second week.

As we shall see, these graces are not exclusively Christian, but are needed by all human beings; they can be sought and appreciated by those of exceptionally diverse backgrounds, and this makes them an excellent point of focus for members of other religious traditions who make the Exercises. For this reason, the adaptation I will outline for those coming from different religious traditions—in this chapter, the Hindu tradition—will focus on these graces as a way of understanding the movements of the Exercises. At each stage of the Exercises, a traditional way of making the Exercises should be laid out for the person—something that can be facilitated by using an accessible guide to the Exercises such as O'Brien's *The Ignatian Adventure* or Tetlow's *Choosing Christ in the World*. The exercitant has an opportunity, then, to see what each movement in the Exercises is about, but with a special focus on the gift one is looking for at that point in the Exercises (e.g., the gift of gratitude for the gift of one's own life). The exercitant must help to identify for herself the grace or gift she is seeking at each stage by praying for that grace or by naming what she desires, because Ignatius believes God speaks to us through our desires. But this occurs in the context of relationship; in conversation, a spiritual director offers her own presence and describes the gifts of the Exercises for her and for others she has directed. This helps to facilitate a deeper understanding of the graces of the Exercises for the exercitant and ideally will help her to discern the ways she is being invited to grow.

Once the exercitant has a sense of the gift she is seeking and the traditional movements of the Exercises at a particular stage, she can be invited to look to the texts and practices of her own tradition as a source of further reflection. In this adaptation, I will suggest readings from the Hindu tradition that aim to deepen the experience of the Exercises for Hindus, while also highlighting those parts of the Exercises that might contain stumbling blocks and suggesting possible ways around them, but in order to be faithful to the Ignatian model, the exercitant should always be encouraged to see what texts she is drawn to and which stories capture her imagination, especially in relation to the gift she is seeking.[7] While I will suggest potential sources and themes from other faith traditions in the adaptations I outline in this book, it should always be remembered that the appropriate adaptation can be found only in the relationship and conversation between the exercitant and the director.

In the early stages of making the full and complete Exercises, the question of whether the Exercises will be helpful and whether the person is ready ought to be considered. For members of other religions, it will be especially important to consider a couple of unique questions in addition to the things that other exercitants normally consider. One of these questions is whether the Exercises will be helpful, given that they are grounded in Christianity. The Hindu exercitant must consider whether a retreat or contemplative practices that are grounded in the Hindu tradition would be more helpful (if such options are available), and whether she will feel fully comfortable contemplating the life of Jesus as it is understood in the Christian tradition in such an in-depth way, for a considerable period of time. Indeed, she should not just be *comfortable* with this; she must be someone who is searching for something along these lines. Does she believe that an Ignatian retreat will help her to grow in her faith in ways that she is being called to grow? In a way, this is something that the Hindu exercitant can fully answer only after begin-

---

7. I will draw primarily from the *Vedas*, *Upanishads*, and *Bhāgavad-Gītā*, which are widely known and accepted by all Hindus. Given the diversity of the Hindu tradition, individual Hindu exercitants will have additional texts that are important to them, depending upon their specific backgrounds.

ning the retreat; only then will she get a clear picture of what it will demand of her and how she feels about it. Despite the fact that adaptations will be made that take into account her Hindu faith, she will nevertheless be making the Ignatian Spiritual Exercises, and the adaptation that I am outlining here is, after all, an *adaptation*, which means that the core of the Exercises will remain intact. Making the Exercises—even in a form that is adapted for Hindus in particular—demands more of the exercitant than making a syncretic set of spiritual exercises, because they require her as a Hindu to engage in much greater depth with Christianity.

The preparatory days that precede the beginning of the first week of the Exercises are critical for any exercitant. During this time, one asks for the experience of unconditional love that is at the very heart of the Exercises, reflecting on God's faithful, unconditional love for each person. During this preparatory period, the Principle and Foundation and the Examen are helpful introductions to the reality of what the purposes of the Exercises are, the extent to which they are grounded in Christian beliefs, and the kind of prayer that will be involved in making the Exercises. The Examen requires a very active way of praying, which will give Hindu exercitants a chance to experience firsthand how Ignatian prayer differs from less active religious practices, including certain forms of Hindu meditation. A Hindu praying the Examen may also begin to experience some of the specific ways in which the Exercises might deepen her Hindu faith—through Christian practices. One of the purposes of the Examen is to help us to find God in all things and discern how God is calling us in both large and small ways: to reflect back on a period of time and attend carefully to what was happening in and around us, and then to look ahead to see how we might act in a way that is worthy of our vocation. A Hindu making the Exercises should not have difficulty addressing God in prayer or considering how God is calling her; she may or may not feel a need to consider which of the gods of the Hindu pantheon she is praying to.[8] Likewise, naming one's blessings and express-

---

8. Some of the adaptations that I suggest in this chapter and in the chapter on Buddhism allow for Hindus and Buddhists to address deities from their own traditions in prayer, typically in cases where exercitants encounter stumbling blocks when trying to address Mary, Jesus, and God the Father, especially early in the Exercises, when they are still getting acquainted with these figures. These adaptations are never recommended as a replacement for encountering (or praying to) Jesus or God the Father; as I have argued, one of the points of adapting the Exercises, on my

ing gratitude for them, attending to one's "interior movements"—including feelings, emotions, desires, attractions, repulsions, and moods—and considering whether they drew one closer to God or led one away from God, are all things that a Hindu should be comfortable with. Hindus making the Exercises will need to be open to the idea that not *all* desires are problematic, since the view that God speaks to us through some of our desires is fundamental to the Exercises; but most Hindus, in practice, acknowledge that some desires, such as a desire for a sense of oneness with God or knowledge of God, are acceptable. Thanking God, seeking forgiveness from God, and asking for God's help should not pose special challenges for most Hindus, either. Finding God in all things, from a Hindu perspective, invites consideration of foundational Hindu teachings about oneness. For Ignatius and for Christians, God is separate from but at work in the things of the world, whereas for Hindus, God is ultimately one with them all. Here, a Hindu understanding of what it means for God to be in all things may differ, but the exercise of finding God in all things, even the most mundane things, by praying the Examen can be done in the same way. Just as a Christian might be led to recognize God's presence with her at each moment, which in turn cultivates in her a desire for a closer relationship with God, a Hindu might be led to recognize that she is part of the seamless whole of creation, which might have the effect of making her feel less isolated, nurturing in her a desire to serve others more, and to discover how she can partner with God in this task. Indeed, as we shall see in this chapter, Hindu conceptions of oneness frequently resonate in fruitful ways with the senses and values of oneness as they are understood in Ignatian spirituality, and the Examen serves as a helpful starting point for this.

The Principle and Foundation, too, resonates in interesting and fruit-

---

view, is to provide members of other faiths with the opportunity to encounter Jesus and God. So, when other deities are included, it is always a preparatory step to help move the exercitant closer to Ignatian ways of praying. I recognize that for some spiritual directors (and some readers), this will be a bridge too far. Some may worry, for instance, about the first commandment. But it is important to remember that the exercitants discussed here are not Jews or Christians, who would recognize the force of such commandments. Put another way, Hindus and Buddhists do not understand themselves to be worshipping the God who gave the Ten Commandments, which distinguishes them from the ancient Hebrews who were worshipping Yahweh alongside other deities. Even if one believes the Ten Commandments apply to all people, their authority for a given individual stems from that person's belief that they are issued by God.

ful ways with Hindu beliefs, as it invites us to experience how we are related to God and all of God's creation. The Hindu tradition is filled with dynamic images of creation. Texts, prayers, and images relating to the seamless whole of creation in Hinduism will be helpful supplements as Hindus consider the Principle and Foundation. Consider, for instance, the following passage from the *Upanishads*:

The Spirit thought: "In whose going out shall I go out, and in whose staying shall I stay?" And he created life, and from life faith and space and air, light, water, and earth, the senses and the mind. He created food and from food strength, austerity, sacred poems, holy actions, and even the worlds.... Even as a spider sends forth and draws in its thread, even as plants arise from the earth and hairs from the body of man, even so the whole creation arises from the Eternal (*Prasna Upanishad*, 74; *Mundaka Upanishad*, 75).

Some of the traditional images and descriptions of Hindu sages may also be helpful as Hindu exercitants consider the grace of indifference that we seek with the Principle and Foundation, which urges us to hold all gifts reverently and gratefully, treating them as gifts from God, while holding them also loosely, ready to either embrace them or let them go depending upon how God calls us. As O'Brien points out, "Indifference is another way of describing spiritual freedom. It is a stance of openness to God: we look for God in any person, any situation, and any moment. Indifference means we are free to love and serve as God desires" (63). Texts such as the *Bhāgavad-Gītā* offer vivid descriptions of sages who withdraw their senses from the world, centered in the oneness that is the most fundamental truth of creation: "The higher self of a tranquil man whose self is mastered is perfectly poised in cold or heat, joy or suffering, honor or contempt. Self-contented in knowledge and judgment, his senses are subdued, on the summit of existence, impartial to clay, stone, or gold, the man of discipline is disciplined. He is set apart by his disinterest toward comrades, allies, enemies, neutrals, nonpartisans, foes, friends, good and even evil men."[9]

There is an opportunity here for the Hindu exercitant to compare and contrast the ideal sage in Hindu texts such as the *Gītā* with the ide-

9. Barbara Stoler Miller, trans., *The Bhagavad-Gita* (New York: Bantam, 1986), 64. Hereafter cited parenthetically with page number.

al of indifference that is found in the Exercises. Unlike Ignatian indifference, the Hindu ideal here is one of thoroughgoing detachment, but both call the believer to a life of faith that does not involve disordered attachments to the things of this world. Ignatian indifference hinges on openness to God and properly ordered desires and attachments, while the detachment of the Hindu sage hinges on a sense of oneness with the rest of creation and a thoroughgoing rejection of personal desires. The Spiritual Exercises are not about running away from all desire, but about tapping into our deepest and therefore holiest desires, that is, those that are God-given and that direct us to the Giver of the gifts we are asking for. Detachment in Ignatian terms is only from disordered attachment; we detach or are indifferent in order to discern which desires lead us to God and which do not, then we "reattach" or remain attached to the holy desires. In both cases, though, we find a warning against some of the dangers of our desires. Such an exercise should deepen a Hindu's sense of her own tradition and its distinctive ideals while also inviting her to consider how the Ignatian grace of indifference might enrich her own life of faith. Ultimately, the Principle and Foundation is an invitation "to experience more deeply how intimately related you are to God and to all of God's creation (including persons, other creatures, and the natural world)," and the graces sought include an awareness of and willingness to embrace one's fundamental vocation to praise, love, and serve God and others.[10] Given the emphasis Hinduism places on oneness, this invitation should resonate with Hindu exercitants, and a rich variety of Hindu texts address these themes, making this an excellent opportunity to invite the exercitant to bring texts from her own devotional life into her experience of the Exercises. Here we can see how the Examen and the Principle and Foundation can serve as a helpful preparation for members of other faiths before they embark on the first week of the Exercises.

Much of the first week focuses on our experience of sin as "an inescapable reality of the human condition; we abuse the freedom God gives us and make choices that hurt God, others, and ourselves. God does not punish us for our sins; instead, we suffer the natural consequences that flow from our sinful choices and the sinful choices of others. We see the

---

10. Kevin O'Brien, SJ, *The Ignatian Adventure: Experiencing the Spiritual Exercises of Saint Ignatius in Daily Life* (Chicago: Loyola Press, 2011), 64.

effects of sin in the disorder of our individual lives and in social struc-tures that dehumanize, marginalize, oppress, and hurt people."[11] The graces we pray for include a healthy sense of shame and confusion as we consider the effects of sin in our lives and in the lives of others. The exer-citant asks herself, "Where in my life have I not cherished the gift of my life or even abused it?" For Hindus, recognizing and confronting the re-ality of sin should not be a unique barrier. Fundamental to Hinduism is the recognition that, as a result of our own sinful choices, we are caught in the wheel of samsara, destined to be reborn again and again until we awaken to our true identity. The illusion of separateness (*avidyā*) is the root of all suffering, and it frequently leads us to act selfishly and sinful-ly—and not in a way that reflects an understanding of our deep unity with others and with God. As we shall see, the movements of the first week are all quite accessible for Hindus. Indeed, in some ways, Ignatius's view of sin resonates deeply with Hindu views of sin. As Gerald Fagin, SJ, points out, "Ignatius sees sin as ingratitude and irreverence. . . . When we cease to see everything as gift that connects us to the Giver, we take things for grant-ed and claim them as our own. We no longer acknowledge that we have received everything from the hands of a loving God. We consume rather than cherish and misuse rather than share."[12] Here, sin is alienation from God, from others, and from the world: "It is rooted in possessiveness and a sense of self-sufficiency that leads to an inability and unwillingness to respond to the call of discipleship."[13] Sin includes such omissions as our failure to reconcile with others and to reach out to those in need, which leads James Keenan, SJ, to describe it as "the failure to bother to love."[14] All of this is in line with the Hindu view that a false sense of separation from others is at the root of our problem as humans. Even the covenantal dimension of sin in the Christian tradition emphasizes the way in which sin undermines our sense of oneness with God and others; as Richard Gula puts it, sin is a failure "to respect the *worth* of ourselves and others as constituted by God's love; to live in *solidarity* with creation and with

---

11. Ibid., 90.

12. Gerald Fagin, SJ, *Putting On the Heart of Christ: How the Spiritual Exercises Invite Us to a Vir-tuous Life* (Chicago: Loyola Press, 2010), 54.

13. Ibid., 56.

14. James Keenan, SJ, *Moral Wisdom: Lessons and Texts from the Catholic Tradition* (Lanham, Md.: Rowman and Littlefield, 2010), 39.

one another as covenantal partners."[15] While the metaphysical understanding of what this means differs in Hinduism, there remains an important resonance here: sin is rooted in the failure to recognize the way in which we are one with others and with God, which results in the kind of alienation that Ignatius describes.

For the first exercise of the first week, Ignatius proposes three meditations: on the sin of the angels, the sin of Adam and Eve, and the sin of one person who chooses to separate herself from God through an act of rebellion. These meditations are followed by a colloquy with Jesus on the cross. In this way, Ignatius highlights how our sin is not an isolated act in human history, but a fundamental part of the human condition. Hindus agree with this general claim. So while the story of the sin of the angels and the sin of Adam and Eve may be new to Hindus, insofar as the stories serve as examples of how evil works in human lives, and so long as they serve to help the exercitant recall her own rebellious and sinful choices, there is no reason why they cannot be effective for Hindus. This is one place where the exercitant might benefit from the addition of stories from the Hindu tradition, but she might also benefit from the exposure to new stories and images from a different tradition that prompt her to see things in a different light, so as always, directors must follow the spirit's lead on what is needed. One text from the Hindu tradition that may prove helpful during the first week is the story of Arjuna on the battlefield in the *Bhagavad-Gītā*, so paralyzed by fear and sadness— and utterly bound up in his ego attachments and his sense of separation from others—that he cannot bring himself to fulfill his duty as a warrior:

Arjuna saw them standing there: fathers, grandfathers, teachers, uncles, brothers, sons, grandsons, and friends. He surveyed his elders and companions in both armies, all his kinsmen assembled together. Dejected, filled with strange pity, he said this: "Krishna, I see my kinsmen gathered here, wanting war. My limbs sink, my mouth is parched, my body trembles, the hair bristles on my flesh. The magic bow slips from my hand, my skin burns, I cannot stand still, my mind reels. I see omens of chaos, Krishna; I see no good in killing my kinsmen in battle. . . ." Saying this in the time of war, Arjuna slumped into his chariot and laid down his bow and arrows, his mind tormented by grief. Arjuna sat

---

15. Richard Gula, *Reason Informed by Faith: Foundations of Catholic Morality* (New York: Paulist Press, 1989), 92.

dejected, filled with pity, his sad eyes blurred by tears. Krishna gave him counsel. (*Bhāgavad-Gītā*, 24–29)

At multiple points in the Exercises, the exercitant is asked to use her imagination to place herself before Jesus suspended on the cross. Ignatius's text includes several instructions bound in thick theology here; exercitants are to ask themselves, "How is it that he, although he is the Creator, has come to make himself a human being? How is it that he passed from eternal life to death here in time, and to die in this way for my sins?" (SE 53). Hindu exercitants might instead simply follow the concluding part of Ignatius's instructions: "As I look upon Jesus as he hangs upon the cross, I ponder whatever God may bring to my attention."[16] Although it will be important for Hindu exercitants to have an opportunity to make a colloquy with Jesus on the cross, it may be helpful for them to first make colloquies with more familiar figures from their own tradition. For instance, they might be invited to consider what sort of colloquy they would have with Krishna if they were in Arjuna's position on the battlefield. Looking back on the times that they have found themselves bound up in their own ego attachments, what would they say to Krishna? What would he say to them? This will help to set the stage not only for a colloquy with Jesus, but for the second exercise of the first week, which involves a meditation on one's own personal history of sin. The exercitant may then wish to have another colloquy with Jesus, revisiting this exercise after engaging sources and images from her own tradition.[17]

The next exercise of the first week is a meditation on one's own personal history of sin, followed by a colloquy of mercy, and finally, a triple colloquy addressed to Mary, Jesus, and God the Father. For Hindus, it will be helpful to focus on what O'Brien calls "the beauty of the triple colloquy: even in our very real and visceral struggle with sin, Ignatius reminds us that we are surrounded by divine company and help. We

16. David Fleming, SJ, *Draw Me into Your Friendship: A Literal Translation and a Contemporary Reading of The Spiritual Exercises* (St. Louis, Mo.: Institute of Jesuit Sources, 1996), 49.

17. Another figure from the Hindu tradition that may be a helpful point of reflection for Hindus at this stage of the Exercises is the demon-king Ravana in the *Rāmāyana*, the antagonist of the epic poem and opponent of Rama (an incarnation of Vishnu). He is particularly interesting to consider in relation to the sin of the angels and the sin of Adam and Eve.

are not alone."[18] This view is just as fundamental to Hinduism as it is to Christianity. While exercitants should be exposed to—and ideally, try— the traditional form of the triple colloquy, here is another place where an adaptation may be appropriate for some Hindu exercitants, depending upon whether they find it to be a stumbling block. Some may find it difficult to pray to deities that are unfamiliar; others may feel comfortable addressing them. A Hindu might simply pray a colloquy to deities she normally addresses in prayer, but this would represent a heavier form of adaptation, and it is important not to dismiss the opportunity for Hindus to acquaint themselves with Mary, Jesus, and God the Father. Of course, other parts of the Exercises will afford this opportunity, as well, but the triple colloquy reminds us of their relationship and allows us to experience it firsthand. A more moderate adaptation would be a quadruple colloquy that includes a Hindu deity but without the removal of Mary, Jesus, and God the Father. One of the key questions here will be whether and where the Hindu exercitant encounters a stumbling block: Is there difficulty with all three parts of the triple colloquy, or only part of it? Regardless of who the prayer is addressed to, its content should remain intact: most important is to pray for an interior knowledge of one's sinful tendencies, choices, and actions, to truly abhor them, to understand how they have caused disorder in one's life and in the lives of others, to recognize the things that get in the way of loving and serving God, and to pray for a desire to turn away from worldly and vain things. Also essential to the effectiveness of the triple colloquy is the repetition of these prayers multiple times (addressed to different persons), as is the sense of humility and reverence that is generated by beginning with Mary and then praying to Jesus, and finally to God the Father. These are important elements to remember and to try to keep intact even if the triple colloquy includes Hindu deities.[19]

18. O'Brien, *The Ignatian Adventure*, 101.

19. Whenever I suggest the possible adaptation of addressing prayers to deities from one's own religious tradition, it is intended only for exercitants who are encountering a stumbling block, and it is designed to serve as a stepping stone or intermediary step that will help her to become more comfortable with Ignatian ways of praying. The aim is to make it possible for her to encounter Jesus and God the Father in prayer over the course of the Exercises, but for some, this may require a gradual process of introduction. Spiritual directors who are uncomfortable having exercitants include other deities might instead consider removing the colloquy entirely, or they may decide to shift to an eighteenth-annotation retreat.

The final exercise of the first week is a meditation on hell, which in the original text of the *Exercises* presents a medieval Christian picture of hell. The Hindu tradition, throughout its history, conceives of hell in a variety of ways, but hell is typically understood as a temporary place of punishment that is governed by Yama, the god of death; after punishment, one is reborn according to one's karmic merit. The number and names of hell vary, but many Hindu scriptures describe twenty-eight hells, and they are depicted vividly in literature and art. Such descriptions and images may be helpful for some Hindu exercitants at this stage of the Exercises, but the fact that the hells are usually regarded as *temporary* places of punishment in Hinduism helps to illustrate why a "replacement" approach to adaptation is problematic. There is not a simple analogue to Ignatius's view of hell in the Hindu tradition. In this case, the fact that hells are not permanent or eternal places might make it more difficult for Hindus to appreciate the significance of the meditation on hell in the Exercises, much of which is tied to the fact that it is a permanent state of hopelessness and purposelessness. In order to better accommodate this aspect of the Exercises, another possible adaptation would follow Fleming, who moves beyond a literal picture of hell to capture the larger significance of this meditation. He suggests that we "try to experience the breadth and length and depth of hell—the despair of facing a cross with no one on it, the turning out upon a world which has no God, the total emptiness of living without purpose, an environment pervasive with hatred and self-seeking, a living death."[20] This part of Fleming's contemporary translation, like Ignatius's medieval images of hell, includes some thick theology that will differ in important ways from Hindu religious views. However, what *would* be accessible to Hindus making the Exercises is the idea of a world with no God and no purpose. Exercitants might focus on what this means within the context of traditional Hindu views of *moksha*: a world without hope would mean a world in which there is no possibility of liberation from the cycle of rebirth, no possibility of ever breaking free of the illusion that we are separate from others, no possibility of awakening to our true identity with God and others. Hindu exercitants can also focus on doing what Fleming suggests next: "I let all the horror of

20. Fleming, *Draw Me into Your Friendship*, 59.

sin which has been the fruit of my previous prayer periods wash over me in an enveloping flood."[21] O'Brien offers further suggestions that would be accessible here: "We have seen hell on earth in photographs and video images in the news—from Dachau to Darfur, from distant battlefields to our own city streets. We hear the screams of those crushed by systemic poverty and victimized by greed and the lustful pursuit of power."[22] A reflection on contemporary images of hell and a consideration of the horror of sin, drawn from previous prayer periods, together with the idea of a world without any God and without any purpose can achieve the ends of the meditation on hell even for someone who does not accept or is unfamiliar with Christian views of hell—for it "confirms God's mercy and inspires our gratitude. The meditation further reminds us of the ultimate freedom God gives us to embrace or refuse God's love."[23]

An Adaptation of the Ignatian Spiritual Exercises for Hindus: The Second Week

In the Exercises, God's boundless mercy is the ultimate source of our liberation from sin. It is not surprising, then, that much of the Exercises focus on Jesus Christ. For some, this is precisely where we encounter difficulties in adapting the Exercises for non-Christians, but it is important to recall that those who have a desire to make the Ignatian Spiritual Exercises are not—and should not be—clueless as to their Christian content. To the contrary, it is reasonable to assume that this is a part of why they are drawn to the Exercises in the first place. As a result, the adaptations that I suggest in this book for the second week, which turns on the task of accompanying Jesus Christ on mission, will be oriented toward helping Hindu exercitants have a deeper experience of Jesus Christ. Once again, the exercitant should focus on the gift she is seeking, the graces of the second week of the Exercises: to know Jesus more intimately, to love him more dearly, and to follow him more closely. Some of the central questions for exercitants to consider in the second week stem from looking long and hard at the person of Jesus Christ: What attracts me to this

21. Ibid.
22. O'Brien, *The Ignatian Adventure*, 105–6.
23. Ibid., 104.

way of being? What attracts me to goodness? How do I grow in my desire to follow that path? The colloquy before the cross has exercitants prayerfully consider what they have done for Christ, what they are doing, and what they ought to do.

Having experienced God's faithful love in the first week, the second week of the Exercises offers a way for exercitants to respond generously to God's love: through knowing, loving, and following Jesus Christ. The transition from the first to the second week, then, is seen in the orientation of the second week toward the life and person of Jesus. The second week traditionally opens with the Contemplation on the Kingdom of Jesus Christ. However, John Veltri, SJ, moved it so that it follows the Contemplations on the Incarnation, the Nativity, and the Hidden Life, a change also adopted by O'Brien. Throughout this book I will follow this adaptation because it gives members of other faith traditions the opportunity to get better acquainted with who Jesus is through the Contemplations on the Incarnation, the Nativity, and the Hidden Life before considering the Call of Christ, our King. As Veltri points out, "The call of Jesus in the Kingdom Exercise is an overview of how Jesus calls us to follow him as we are contemplating his public life," and one of the graces sought is "to be open to his call to me in the unique and concrete circumstances of my own life; and to know him with that deep-felt knowledge, that I might love him more and follow him more closely."[24] It will simply be easier for exercitants from other faiths to seek this grace if they have more time to get acquainted with Jesus first.

With this amendment, then, the second week opens with the Contemplation on the Incarnation, the Contemplation on the Nativity, and the Contemplation on the Hidden Life. In a way, the adaptation of the second week for members of other faiths seems more straightforward than that of the first, because it is fundamentally about getting acquainted with Jesus; as O'Brien puts it, "God lifts our gaze and turns our attention to Jesus as he walked and talked, healed and preached, among us. The grace of the second week is fundamental: to grow in a heartfelt knowledge of Jesus Christ so that we can love him more deeply and follow him more closely. But to grow in this intimate love, we need to get

---

24. John A. Veltri, SJ, *Orientations*, vol. 2, *A Manual to Aid Beginning Directors of the Spiritual Exercises according to Annotation 19* (Guelph, Ontario, Canada: Loyola House, 1981), A16.

close."[25] The challenge of adapting the second week for members of other faiths, however, is that it is not readily apparent to members of other faiths that they should love and follow Jesus—and *why* they should do this. However, it is important to remember that a part of the power and beauty of the Exercises for Christians is the way in which it allows them to experience all of this in a new way. One of the aims of the Exercises is to allow us to experience the attractive power of Jesus firsthand: "In this part of the adventure, the Gospels come alive for us. We are there with Jesus, immersed in the Gospels with the help of our senses and imagination. We do not simply obtain more insight or information. With our attentiveness fine-tuned and our imaginations sparked, we see the living God in daily life as we pray through the Exercises."[26] This aspect of the second week will not be all that different for Hindus. We will, though, need to work through some of the theological views that are interlaced with the second week, and also work to help Hindu exercitants to experience how Jesus might stand in relation to central themes, images, stories, and values from the Hindu tradition. All of this will be done with an eye toward the graces that are sought.

When the second week opens with the Contemplation on the Incarnation, the graces that are traditionally sought are to know Jesus intimately, to love him more intensely, and so to follow him more closely. For those who are not Christians, seeking the gift of knowing Jesus intimately will be primary, though they should also look for what is appealing in this way: What about Jesus makes them want to follow him, and what inspires in them feelings of admiration and love? Gazing on the world with the Trinity—with God the Father, Son, and Holy Spirit—will be in some respects challenging and in others quite natural. While the doctrine of the Trinity is obviously Christian, actually imagining the three Divine Persons does not necessarily come naturally or easily to Christians, so once again, this is not a part of the Exercises that should automatically be assumed to be more difficult for non-Christians. This doctrine is not typically embodied for us in a real way; while imagining the person of Jesus is not a problem, imagining the Holy Spirit and God the Father gazing on the earth beside Jesus is much more of a chal-

---

25. O'Brien, *The Ignatian Adventure*, 124–25.
26. Ibid., 125.

lenge for Christians.[27] Interestingly, it may be easier for Hindus to imagine multiple Divine Persons gazing on the earth because most Hindus believe in multiple divine beings who are depicted in art and iconography. They believe, too, in divine beings who become human to offer assistance. It makes sense for Hindus to draw upon these images as they imagine the three Divine Persons in the Contemplation on the Incarnation. But it is equally important not to become overly concerned with theology here, or simply with the details of what the Divine Persons look like; this contemplation centers on what the Divine Persons see "on the whole surface or circuit of the world, full of people" (SE 102), which leads them to decide that the Second Person should become human. Fleming's suggestion that we "try to enter into the vision of God" will be just as easy for a Hindu to follow as a Christian: "looking upon our world: men and women being born and being laid to rest, some getting married and others getting divorced, the old and the young, the rich and the poor, the happy and the sad, so many people aimless, despairing, hateful, and killing, so many undernourished, sick, and dying, so many struggling with life and blind to any meaning. With God, I can hear people laughing and crying, some shouting and screaming, some praying, others cursing."[28] There are a rich variety of images from Hindu texts that may serve as an aid here, as well. One, in the first teaching of the *Gītā*, is Arjuna's description of the world, which prompts his despair.

Arjuna saw them standing there: fathers, grandfathers, teachers, uncles, brothers, sons, grandsons, friends. He surveyed his elders and companions in both armies, all his kinsmen assembled together.... "The greed that distorts their reason blinds them to the sin they commit in ruining the family, blinds them to the crime of betraying friends. How can we ignore the wisdom of turning from this evil when we see the sin of family destruction, Krishna? When the family is ruined, the timeless laws of family duty perish; and when duty is lost, chaos overwhelms the family. In overwhelming chaos, Krishna, women of the family are corrupted; and when women are corrupted, disorder is born in society. This discord drags the violators and the family itself to hell; for ancestors fall when rites of offering rice and water lapse. The sins of men who violate the family

---

27. Religious art and icons, such as Rublev's icon of the trinity, can serve as a helpful resource here.

28. Fleming, *Draw Me into Your Friendship*, 91.

create disorder in society that undermines the constant laws of caste and family
duty. (*Bhāgavad-Gītā*, 24–26)

One reason why this passage would be helpful is that it helps to highlight the need for assistance, and thus helps the exercitant to consider
how she feels and how the three Divine Persons feel as they as they gaze
upon the world. The exercitant must understand the context that leads
the three Divine Persons to say, "Let us work the redemption of the human race" (SE 107), the context that leads God to become one of us.

Next, the Exercises shift more precisely to the Christian story, to the
Annunciation, followed by the Contemplation on the Nativity. Fleming's
suggestion that the exercitant "try to stay with the eyes of God, and look
upon the young girl Mary as she is greeted by God's messenger, Gabriel,"[29] is helpful, for it reminds us that the goal is not to convey Christian
doctrines but to provide the opportunity to experience the story of Jesus, to encounter Jesus and those around him directly. We do not follow
a movement, idea, or principle, but a person. So, most important is to
"notice how our triune God works—so simply and quietly, so patiently.
A world goes on, apparently oblivious to the new creation which has begun. I take in Mary's complete way of being available and responding
to her Lord and God."[30] I would add here that the fact that it is a "triune God" is not particularly critical; the point for exercitants from other faiths will be to acquaint themselves with how God works—and who
God is—in this story. These contemplations both end with a colloquy,
and Ignatius specifies that this may be addressed "to the Three Divine
Persons, or to the eternal Word made flesh, or to our Mother and Lady"
(SE 109). Further adaptation is encouraged by commentators, as well,
here. Fleming notes, "Perhaps there is little to say because this style of
contemplation is often more a 'being with' experience than a word-
response."[31] O'Brien suggests concluding with a colloquy with Mary, Joseph, or God the Father, or by speaking to the baby Jesus while holding him, or remaining in silence.[32] Unlike the triple colloquy of the first
week, there is more latitude here, which will be helpful for members of

29. Ibid., 93.
30. Ibid.
31. Ibid., 99.
32. O'Brien, *The Ignatian Adventure*, 139.

other faiths, particularly as the three Divine Persons can be imagined in a wide variety of ways.

As Hindu exercitants contemplate Jesus' birth and his life, they will need to grant the possibility that certain events—some of them quite miraculous—occurred. The idea that God has intervened in history by appearing in human form to offer loving assistance is not foreign to Hinduism, and that idea prepares the ground for Hindus making the Exercises. Nevertheless, the events that are a part of Jesus life, from the appearance of the angel Gabriel to Mary to the events of Jesus' public ministry, are not a part of Hindu teachings. Hindus who make the Exercises will need to imagine these things happening, and entertain the possibility that they occurred. This can be done in different ways. One is simply to ask, "What if it's true?" and to allow one's imagination to freely engage this possibility, thus allowing God to work through one's imagination. Resolving the question of whether this is the only instance of God's appearing in human form should not be the focus for any exercitant, and it is important to recognize that Christians who make the Exercises often have theological questions that are just as pressing and just as difficult to resolve. The aim, as always, during the prayer periods, is to set aside these questions and remain focused on experiencing and witnessing firsthand Jesus' life.

The Contemplation on the Kingdom of Jesus Christ differs in the challenges it poses for Hindus making the Exercises, because it uses a central symbol in the biblical tradition: the kingdom of God. O'Brien points out that most basically, the kingdom expresses God's dream for the world: "Imagine what the world would look like if everyone acknowledged God as Creator and Lord and if everyone followed God's law of love and life! Jesus spoke of the kingdom of God and revealed most completely God's dream of the world in how he lived, taught, healed, and served others. . . . Christ calls us out of great love and concern for us and our world; ideally, we respond also in love and not in fear or obligation."[33] Consider Paul's definition here: a kingdom of justice, peace, and love. Again, it will be important to continually work to identify the graces that Hindu exercitants may be seeking in the second week; many Christians will seek to become more eager to do what Christ wants, while Hindus will be seek-

33. Ibid., 153.

ing a broader range of graces. At this juncture, given that the Exercises have highlighted the need for redemption in the world, Hindus making the Exercises may be working through questions relating to how they can better use their gifts to serve others, how they can live out their faith in a more meaningful way, or what role this encounter with Christianity ought to play in their lives. The Contemplation on the Kingdom of Jesus Christ offers the opportunity to recognize explicitly that the Exercises include an opportunity to follow Christ. One of the key questions for this adaptation is what following Christ would mean for a Hindu. Let us first review the details of the Contemplation on the Kingdom, and then proceed to considering what adaptations might help to make it more accessible to Hindus making the Exercises.

The Contemplation on the Kingdom first asks us to contemplate an admirable worldly leader, or as Ignatius puts it, "a human king, chosen by God our Lord himself, whom all Christian princes and all Christian persons reverence and obey" (SE 92). O'Brien writes that if the medieval imagery that is a part of Ignatius's subsequent description is distracting or unhelpful, we might consider a person of our time who "personifies virtue and integrity, fights against injustice, or labors for the oppressed and marginalized. This person may be a civic leader, a modern-day saint or prophet, or a personal friend. Or you may rely on some mythical figure in literature or film. Reflect on anyone who inspires you and summons your zeal to make the world a more just and gentle place."[34] This part of the contemplation is something that should not be a stumbling block for members of other faiths, and it is worth noting that there are a number of values that are shared by Hindus and Christians that are highlighted here; the leader described here would be regarded as an admirable individual in both traditions. The second part of the Contemplation of the Kingdom of Jesus Christ will be a bit more challenging for Hindus, as it asks us to consider the call of Jesus Christ, as well as his *lordship*, which grounds or lends authority to the call: "If we give consideration to such a call from the temporal king to his subjects, how much more worthy of our consideration it is to gaze upon Christ our Lord, the eternal King, and all the world assembled before him. He calls to them

---

34. Ibid., 155.

all, and to each person in particular he says: 'My will is to conquer the whole world and all my enemies, and thus to enter into the glory of my Father. Therefore, whoever wishes to come with me must labor with me, so that through following me in the pain he or she may follow me also in the glory'" (SE 95). Ignatius then suggests two responses: "all those who have judgment and reason will offer themselves wholeheartedly for this labor" (SE 96), but those "who desire to show greater devotion and to distinguish themselves in total service to their eternal king and universal Lord," will not only dedicate themselves to laboring for the kingdom, but to being *with* Christ and imitating his way of living. It is important not to underestimate what Ignatius has in mind here, seen in the prayer of those who make the second response: "Eternal Lord of all things, I make my offering, with your favor and help. I make it in the presence of your infinite Goodness, and of your glorious Mother, and of all the holy men and women in your heavenly court. I wish and desire, and it is my deliberate decision, provided only that it is for your greater service and praise, to imitate you in bearing all injuries and affronts, and any poverty, actual as well as spiritual, if your Most Holy Majesty desires to choose and receive me into such a life and state" (SE 98). Now, as Ivens notes, "the exercitant does not at this point actually make the concluding offering ... its function is preparatory."[35] However, even though its role is preparatory, the very consideration of this offering may create a number of challenges for some Hindu exercitants.

There are two contrasts set up for us in this Contemplation. The first is between a good worldly king and Christ the king, and as we have seen, the image of a good leader is one that Hindus can easily share. But as Fleming points out, "The parable of the temporal king is meant only to help contemplate the life of Christ our eternal king."[36] We should all want to follow a good leader in this world, and as a result, "how much more worthy of our consideration it is to gaze upon Christ our Lord, the eternal King" (SE 95). For Hindus making the Exercises, the most obvious challenge here is in the very quick move from an admirable worldly leader to Christ, which stems from the claim that Christ is *the* eternal

35. Michael Ivens, SJ, *Understanding the Spiritual Exercises* (Leominster, U.K.: Gracewing, 1998), 77.
36. Fleming, *Draw Me into Your Friendship*, 83.

King. There are other deities in Hinduism that would come to mind as eternal kings; why should Christ be the point of contemplation here? This issue could be handled in multiple ways in an adaptation for Hindus, and as always, much depends upon the particular individual making the Exercises. One of the aims of adapting the Exercises for members of other faiths is to help remove stumbling blocks that emerge as they make the Exercises, and specifically stumbling blocks that are tied to the differences between their beliefs and practices and those of Christianity. Some Hindus may not feel a tension at this point; they may, for instance, be struck by the distinctiveness of Christ's call or they might simply feel the movement of the spirit in their own life, calling them to consider this call. For these individuals, little adaptation will be needed at this juncture; they should simply attend to the stirrings of Christ in their hearts. Others, though, will be very much aware that Christ for them is not *the* eternal King, and this could prove to be a significant stumbling block.

I think Ivens's remark that the Call is preparatory is particularly helpful in determining how to adapt this exercise for Hindus. The Call comes at a pivotal time in the Exercises for members of other faiths: it is prior to the consideration of Jesus' public ministry and the three meditations of the second week (the Meditation on Two Standards, the Meditation on the Three Classes of Persons, and the Meditation on Three Kinds of Humility), and also prior to the consideration of Jesus' death and resurrection in the third and fourth weeks. As a result, the Call represents an important opportunity for Hindu exercitants to become more open to, and more comfortable with, engaging the person of Jesus Christ. Of course, it may also serve as an opportunity for exercitants to recognize that they are not ready to continue the Exercises at this time. After all, it will not be possible for exercitants to continue the Exercises without the story of Jesus being central, and without entertaining the possibility that Jesus has a special and unique role in relation to humanity. As I argue in the first two chapters of this work, there are several reasons why we should not try to remove Jesus from the Exercises and replace him with figures from other traditions, one of which is that such an endeavor simply is not an adaptation; rather it is to create new and different exercises. While there is nothing wrong with the creation of new exercises inspired by or based on the Ignatian Spiritual Exercises, it is important to recognize the difference between that task and the task of adapting the Exercises, which is our concern in this chapter.

With the right adaptations, the Call might help exercitants to develop the ability to see Jesus in a special role, and can thus serve as preparation for the rest of the Exercises. What would the right adaptations be? Well, much rests on what the purposes of the adaptations are. As Ivens writes, the Kingdom exercise "prepares the exercitant to meet Christ in a new way, not only as personal saviour but as Lord of the universe, who calls his friends to share his work in building the Kingdom of God in the world."[37] This is true for Christians and Hindus alike, though much more literally so for most Hindus. If we see the Call as preparatory in this way, then it should serve as a bridge to more fruitful, comfortable engagement with Jesus in the remaining movements of the Exercises. This will require us to use resources from Hinduism to move the exercitant toward a deeper engagement with Jesus, and I propose adding an additional step in the Kindgdom exercise, in between the call of a worldly leader and the call of Christ. After considering the call of a worldly leader, Hindu exercitants who find it difficult to consider Christ as the eternal King might consider, perhaps with additional readings from the Hindu tradition, the question of who, for them, *is* an eternal king, and how he (or she) calls them. The Kingdom exercise might thus serve as an opportunity to consider how they are being called by God within the context of their own faith tradition. While the choice should ultimately be left up to each individual exercitant, most Hindus would not have difficulty envisioning Vishnu or a particular avatar (incarnation) of Vishnu, such as Krishna, in this role. Indeed, some of Krishna's teachings in the *Bhāgavad-Gītā* may prove helpful to consider alongside the call of Christ, the king:

Look to your own duty; do not tremble before it; nothing is better for a warrior than a battle of sacred duty. The doors of heaven open for warriors who rejoice to have a battle like this thrust on them by chance. If you fail to wage this war of sacred duty, you will abandon your own duty and fame only to gain evil. . . . Be intent on action, not on the fruits of action; avoid attraction to the fruits and attachment to inaction! Perform actions, firm in discipline, relinquishing attachment; be impartial to failure and success—this equanimity is called discipline. (*Bhāgavad-Gītā*, 34–36)

37. Ivens, *Understanding the Spiritual Exercises*, 78.

After considering the call of an eternal king within the Hindu tradition, exercitants should move on to the call of Christ the king and focus closely on the content of his call. Ivens points out that the exercitant is invited to "contemplate"—"to 'see' and to 'hear'—the now risen Christ calling all people to his service. This is not a moment for analysis, simply for hearing."[38] This point is particularly relevant, for it will be important for Hindu exercitants to immerse themselves in Christ's call, hearing it for themselves, and not to immediately begin comparing it with the previous calls. Fleming's contemporary translation might be helpful here, as its language is a bit broader: "Jesus's call goes out to all peoples, yet he specially calls each person in a particular and unique way. He makes this kind of appeal: 'It is my will to win over the whole world, to overcome evil with good, to turn hatred aside with love, to conquer all the forces of death—whatever obstacles there are that block the sharing of life between God and humankind. Whoever wishes to join me in this mission must be willing to labor with me, and so by following me in struggle and suffering may share with me in glory.'"[39]

Ivens points out that while we want the exercitant to simply hear the call, "to hear this direct and simple appeal is to begin to absorb the basic theological principles which undergird Ignatius' concept of union with Christ in the work of the Kingdom."[40] Indeed, upon hearing the call, the Hindu exercitant will be confronted with the opportunity to consider the similarities and differences between the call of Christ and the call of the king she has contemplated from the Hindu tradition—and to consider also the theology that undergirds Ignatius's view. We should not shy away from an honest recognition of these questions. What is unique about Christ's call, and what is there to learn from it? Where does it come from, and how does it differ from the call of the eternal king the exercitant has considered from her own faith tradition? Where are the resonances between these calls? At this point in the Exercises, there are a number of important topics for Hindu exercitants to note, topics that do not involve any sort of theological tension. For instance, the Kingdom exercise highlights the ways in which faith involves real sacrifices—a kind

38. Ibid., 83.
39. Fleming, *Draw Me into Your Friendship*, 85.
40. Ivens, *Understanding the Spiritual Exercises*, 83.

of surrender, a commitment to always looking for how we can give more. It also calls us to notice that living a life of faith involves very practical moral commitments as well as religious commitments. While many of the things that the worldly king and Christ the king labor for are shared, Christ calls us to work not just to fight against disease, poverty, and oppression, but "whatever obstacles there are that block the sharing of life between God and humankind"—as Fleming translates it. In other words, we are to work for all to experience the fullness of a life of faith. This is something that members of different faith traditions, including Hindus and Christians, share. On the other hand, there are also tensions between these traditions that are apparent in certain aspects of the Call. For instance, the idea of conquering all the forces of death may be problematic for Hindus who firmly believe in reincarnation. For them, death lacks the finality that it does for those who do not believe in reincarnation, and as a result, this may not be an aspect of the Call that they would accept.

Ivens also highlights the emphasis on a deep unity with Christ that is a part of the call of Christ the king, adding that "Christ carries out this work through his disciples, and in sharing Christ's work the disciple shares in the suffering inseparable from it.... '[W]ith me' (conmigo) is a key phrase. The disciple labours and suffers not just 'for' Christ but 'with' him."[41] As we have seen, unity is a theme that is at the very heart of Hinduism, and this distinction—laboring *with* Christ as opposed to *for* him ought to resonate deeply with Hindu senses of oneness. At the same time, though, there is a distinctly ethical variety of oneness here, as opposed to the metaphysical variety that is most characteristic of Hinduism, and it will be important to encourage Hindus to think about the form of solidarity that embodies the Christian sense of oneness in the Exercises, compared with other senses of oneness. Indeed, Ignatian insights might be brought to bear upon Hindu texts and practices on this point: What does it mean to labor *with* God or in solidarity with God, in contrast to being one with God in a monistic sense that eliminates all distinctions? The model of sharing Christ's work extends to and is embodied in the Jesuit commitment to extend this sense of oneness to others, including being not only friends and companions of the Lord and each other, but friends and companions of our partners in mission.

41. Ibid., 83.

The call of Christ, our King, also makes clear that all of us are called to "poverty of spirit," and this idea, too, can serve as an interesting point of resonance with Hinduism. As O'Brien points out, when we assume the stance of utter dependence before God that spiritual poverty describes, "While we are grateful for our talents, abilities, wealth, and achievements, we are free enough to offer them to the service of God and others and to let go of them when they get in the way of that self-giving. In short, poverty of spirit is an emptying of self so that God can fill us with life and love."[42] This theme is touched on beautifully in the text of the *Bhāgavad-Gītā*, as we find Arjuna struggling to surrender himself to God. Spiritual poverty also resonates in interesting ways with the Hindu tradition in its emphasis on recognizing how our attachment to particular roles or positions separates us from God—something we see clearly in the text of the *Bhāgavad-Gītā*. Hindu exercitants might find it fruitful to explore the value of spiritual poverty as it is presented in that text, while also considering how the Ignatian concept of spiritual poverty can be enriching. The Ignatian view entails letting go of excessive attachments to oneself, which finds many deep points of resonance with themes in the Hindu tradition, but one of the distinctive features of the Ignatian view is its ethical focus on loving and serving other human beings, and actively laboring to meet their needs—a focus that is underdeveloped in the Hindu tradition.[43] Also, we let go of excessive attachments so that we can be more fully who we are; we empty so as to be filled beyond our imagining.

Next in the second week is Jesus' public ministry, which will be especially important for members of other traditions, as it affords them the opportunity to get acquainted with Jesus in a more intimate way. This should not require any special adaptations, but the use of imagination is key: exercitants must place themselves in each scene, experiencing and encountering firsthand the people and places that are a part of Jesus' story. Interspersed throughout a consideration of Jesus' life we have a sequence of three meditations, beginning with the Meditation on Two Standards, in which Ignatius has us consider the opposing values and tac-

---

42. O'Brien, *The Ignatian Adventure*, 159.

43. This is seen, for instance, in the fact that the Hindu religion has not been a great promoter of social justice, historically. The role of the caste system has presented (and continues to present) a variety of challenges here.

tics of Christ and Lucifer. A standard here refers to a banner or flag under which the followers of different leaders stand, and this meditation asks us to consider the two alternatives and choose where we will stand. For members of other faiths, it will be important to remember that, although Lucifer is a particular figure from the Christian tradition, he is referred to in the Exercises in a number of ways: the enemy of our human nature, the father of lies, the evil one, the deceiver.[44] These references ought to allow members of other faiths to envision a broader alternative to Christ—an alternative that is fully comprehensive to anyone, regardless of their tradition and regardless of whether or not they believe in or have an understanding of Lucifer. This alternative is one that opposes all that is good in us as human beings and that employs substantial levels of deception. And the precise kinds of deception are clearly spelled out in the Meditation itself. The reason the choice is not an easy one for us is that it does not appear to be a simple choice between good and evil; rather, as O'Brien writes, "The enemy begins by seducing us with riches. Such riches can win for us honors and the esteem of others, which we can begin to excessively desire. Fixation on riches and honors devolves into a self-serving pride, leaving little room for God or anyone else."[45] As Joseph Tetlow, SJ, points out, it boils down to the following exclamations: "Look at all this stuff I have!" Leads to "Look at me with all this stuff" and finally "Look at me!"[46] It is important to highlight the way in which these are *deceptions*. The enemy seduces us with riches and honors because we are especially drawn to these things and they seduce us in a very effective way. Material goods are not bad in themselves, but they are temptations away from what is good for us. It is difficult for us as humans to desire these things in a properly ordered way. Like an addict, we are drawn to the idea that these things will make us happy—and of course they often do bring satisfaction and pleasure—though never the deep, lasting kind of fulfillment and joy that truly leads us to flourish in the ways that God's love and the service of others can. In this way, we can see clearly how the Meditation

44. O'Brien, *The Ignatian Adventure*, 168.

45. Ibid.

46. Joseph A. Tetlow, SJ, *Making Choices in Christ: The Foundations of Ignatian Spirituality* (Chicago: Loyola Press, 2008), 108. See also Dean Brackley's discussion of solidarity with the poor in relation to these movements in the *Exercises* in his *The Call to Discernment in Troubled Times: New Perspectives on the Transformative Wisdom of Ignatius of Loyola* (New York: Crossroad, 2004), 100–101.

on Two Standards is very much about something that is the enemy of our human nature: the pursuit of riches and honors draws us in quickly and easily, eroding away our generosity and our sense of being loved and created uniquely for the service of God and others (and note here the very things that are at the heart of the Principle and Foundation), instead fostering selfishness, envy, and doubt. In calling these things the enemy of our human nature, Ignatius highlights the fact that we are created for a good purpose and, with God's help and through a relationship with God, capable of becoming people who are loving, compassionate, generous, and humble. The seductive appeal of riches and honors opposes those things, robbing us of the opportunity to become the people we are truly meant to be. But there is another element of our human nature that this meditation highlights, and that is the darker part of our nature that is inherently drawn to riches and honors, and easily seduced by them.

I focus intentionally on this dimension of the Two Standards because it resonates deeply with one of the most fundamental teachings in Hinduism: *desires*—including desires for wealth and honor—although they are a natural part of us, are a serious problem for human beings, because they lead us to be trapped in an illusory world in which we believe that we, as individuals, are essentially disconnected from others. In short, they lead us to believe that it's all about us (and here we should be reminded of Tetlow's phrase, "Look at *me*!"). Now, there are a number of key differences between Hindu views on these matters and the views Ignatius held, most notably the different metaphysical foundations that are in play (i.e., the view that we are all fundamentally one, versus the view that we have individual souls and are separate from God and each other) and the issue of whether all of our desires (or only some of them) are a problem. With respect to the latter, as I mentioned earlier in this chapter, it is worth noting that, in practice, most Hindus seek to develop a liberating sense of selfless love of and devotion to God, which shows that certain types of desires are acceptable and even deemed holy. For the purposes of this meditation, Hindu exercitants also should be aware of the deep resonances with their tradition, most notably the fact that Hinduism, like Christianity, teaches that we ought to work against our disordered desires for riches and honors, and work instead to serve others in a spirit of self-giving and humility. Both traditions call us to stand beneath the banner that is opposed to disordered desires. Ignatius calls this the banner of Christ, and the Exercises offer Hindus an opportunity to experience why they would ultimately choose, with Ignatius, to stand beneath this banner. This should continue the process of helping Hindu exercitants to hear and respond to the call of Christ, the king.

It may be helpful here to ask Hindu exercitants to look to the texts of their own tradition for a text that offers a description of one who stands beneath the banner of Christ, albeit a banner that is not so named. For instance, the *Bhāgavad-Gītā* contains a passage describing the perfect sage, which Gandhi called "the essential wisdom of the *Gītā*." In these lines we find a description of someone who is free of a desire for wealth and honor, and who embraces the countercultural values Ignatius encourages: poverty, self-giving, and humility:

"He does not waver, like a lamp sheltered from the wind" is the simile recalled for a man of discipline, restrained in thought.... Since he knows that discipline means unbinding the bonds of suffering, he should practice discipline resolutely, without despair dulling his reason. He should entirely relinquish desires aroused by willful intent; he should entirely control his senses with his mind. He should gradually become tranquil, firmly controlling his understanding; focusing his mind on the self, he should think nothing. Wherever his faltering mind unsteadily wanders, he should restrain it and bring it under self-control. When his mind is tranquil, perfect joy comes to the man of discipline; his passion is calmed, he is without sin, being one with the infinite spirit. Constantly disciplining himself, free from sin, the man of discipline easily achieves perfect joy in harmony with the infinite spirit. Arming himself with discipline, seeing everything with an equal eye, he sees the self in all creatures and all creatures in the self. He who sees me everywhere and sees everything in me will not be lost to me, and I will not be lost to him. I exist in all creatures, so the disciplined man devoted to me grasps the oneness of life; wherever he is, he is in me. (*Bhāgavad-Gītā*, 65–67)

It may be helpful for Hindu exercitants to apply an Ignatian method to their consideration of texts such as this, placing themselves in the presence of this sage and seeing what they might observe about how he handles himself, or what he might say to them. Exercitants should relate passages they consider from the Hindu tradition to the two standards and see what light might be shed on this meditation as a result. For instance, this passage from the *Gītā*, by virtue of its description of the sage as having achieved the utmost states of calm and peacefulness, serves to point up some additional features of the two standards. Most notably, whereas the enemy is repulsive and harsh and seeks to deceive, Christ is inviting and gentle and seeks only to move people to love God and serve others.

The Meditation on the Three Classes of Persons (SE 149–57) follows the Meditation on Two Standards in the second week of the Exercises. While the Meditation on Two Standards encourages us to consider the ways in which we might be seduced by a desire for material wealth and worldly honor—which ought to cause all of us to reevaluate our choices, the Meditation on the Three Classes of Persons takes us into the deep waters of Ignatian discernment. One of the distinctive features of the Exercises, especially relative to other contemplative practices across different faith traditions, is that they include rules for discernment. Ignatius intended the Exercises to help individuals to develop the ability to make choices grounded in their faith. This is an aspect of the Exercises that can serve members of different faiths in rich and meaningful ways. Ignatius's aim is to have individuals strive for indifference, asking for the grace of interior freedom: to be free of disordered loves and fears so that they can respond with generosity to God's call, whatever it might be. In the Meditation on the Three Classes of Persons, Ignatius paints a vivid picture of what that spiritual quality looks like and what it entails. This meditation, unlike some others, will not require as many special adaptations for Hindus, especially because most Hindus are already comfortable with the idea of a God who might call them in various ways. This meditation asks us to imagine three good people who are trying to serve God and who acquire something that is very attractive to them. Ignatius suggests a large sum of money, but as O'Brien suggests, "you can imagine something especially attractive to you, such as a certain material possession, a place to live, a high-profile job, or a particular honor. None of these things is intrinsically evil; each one can be used for good. But each of the three typical persons is excessively attached to the possession in some way. This preoccupation risks getting in the way of a greater good or more generous response to God's call."[47] The first person has good intentions and would

47. O'Brien, *The Ignatian Adventure*, 177.

like to let go of the attachment—and thinks and talks about doing so regularly—but is always too busy to do so. The second person, like the first, worries about being too attached and desires to be free of this possession while at the same time wanting to keep it. So she compromises and does a lot of good works, in a way trying to buy God off in order to avoid facing up to the truth. Like the first person, the second person on some level knows she is unfree as a result of her attachment to this possession, but fails to do the one thing she must do to address it. The third person wishes to be free of any attachment that gets in the way of God's invitation to her and recognizes that this possession is one of those attachments. As Ignatius puts it, "The person typical of the third class desires to get rid of the attachment, but in such a way that there remains no inclination either to keep the acquired money or to dispose of it. Instead such a one desires to keep it or reject it solely according to what God our Lord will move one's will to choose, and according to what the person himself or herself will judge to be better for the service and praise of the Divine Majesty" (SE 155). O'Brien notes where the third person begins: "she is not sure whether or not God is asking her to give up the possession; she simply desires to be free to do what God wants her to do. So she begins by asking God what she should do. She is open to how God directs her through her prayer, her experience, her reasoning through different options, her discernment of consolations and desolations, and the wise counsel of others."[48] As a result, as Fleming points out, "the graced desire to be better able to serve God becomes clearly the motivating factor for accepting or letting go of anything."[49]

One of the keys to understanding Ignatian discernment is to appreciate that attending to one's desires is central. Whenever we make a choice, we ought to choose from a desire to better serve God and others. In order to choose from such a stance, we must attend to what Ignatius calls "motions of the soul," or interior movements—including thoughts, emotions, inclinations, desires, repulsions, and attractions. Ignatius believed that some of our interior movements come from God while others do not, and the task of spiritual discernment is to reflect on our interior movements in order to determine where they come from and where they are

48. Ibid., 179.
49. Fleming, *Draw Me into Your Friendship*, 119.

leading us. He distinguishes between spiritual consolation, which includes "every increase in hope, faith, and charity, and every interior joy which calls and attracts one toward heavenly things and to the salvation of one's soul, by bringing it tranquility and peace in its Creator and Lord" (SE 316), and spiritual desolation, which is quite the opposite, including experiences of the soul in heavy darkness or turmoil which "move one toward lack of faith and leave one without hope and without love. One is completely listless, tepid, and unhappy, and feels separated from our Creator and Lord" (SE 317). Our goal, which Ignatius describes with the third person, is to be indifferent: to desire only what God wants for us. This is what it means to have interior freedom, and it is called freedom because we are not bound by disordered loves and self-preoccupations.

When one looks to the classic texts of Hinduism, one finds a deep resonance with the ideal of interior freedom, seen in the tranquility of the ideal sage, and at the same time a deep contrast between the sage's thoroughgoing detachment from his desires and the Ignatian view that some desires are good, such as the desire for whatever God wants, as well as those desires through which God speaks to us. But it is important in an adaptation to remain focused on the specifics of each exercise. In the Meditation on Three Classes of Persons, much depends upon the exercitant's ability to distinguish between the person who procrastinates, the one who compromises, and the one who is truly free or indifferent—and to appreciate why the third person represents the ideal. Hindu exercitants may find it helpful here to focus on the way in which the interior freedom of the truly indifferent person resonates with Hindu views of oneness. As *Katha Upanishad* puts it, "What is here is also there, and what is there is also here. Who sees the many and not the ONE, wanders on from death to death. Even by the mind this truth is to be learned: there are not many but only ONE. Who sees variety and not the unity wanders on from death to death" (62–63). If one truly understands that all things are one, in the Hindu sense, one will not have an inclination to keep or dispose of the kind of possession that we are asked to consider in this meditation. Again, the *Upanishads* are a helpful resource here: "Behold the universe in the glory of God: and all that lives and moves on earth. Leaving the transient, find joy in the Eternal: set not your heart on another's possession. Working thus, a man may wish for a life of a hundred years. Only actions done in God bind not the soul of a man. . . . Who sees all beings in his own Self, and his own Self in all beings, loses all fear. When a sage sees this great Unity and his Self has become all beings, what delusion and what sorrow can ever be near him?" (*Isa Upanishad*, 49). So a Hindu exercitant might have different reasons for agreeing that the third person represents the ideal she wishes to follow, but she can still agree that this person represents the ideal, and that indifference is the appropriate goal.

The concluding meditation of the second week is the Meditation on Three Kinds of Humility (also sometimes called the Three Ways of Loving). This meditation is highly theistic, for all three kinds require obedience to God's law, but it is also Christocentric, for as Fleming notes, "Humility lies in the acceptance of Jesus Christ as the fullness of what it means to be human. To be humble is to live as close to the truth as possible: that I am created in the likeness of Jesus, that I am meant to live according to the pattern of his paschal mystery, and that my whole life fulfillment is found in being as near to Jesus as he draws me to himself."[50] The first kind of humility involves humbling oneself so that one might obey God's law, and that is all. The second, "more perfect" kind of humility, in addition to living according to God's law, involves indifference: "It is what I have when I find myself in this disposition: If my options are equally effective for the service of God our Lord and the salvation of my soul, I do not desire or feel myself strongly attached to having wealth rather than poverty, or honor rather than dishonor, or a long life rather than a short one" (SE 166). The third and "most perfect" kind of humility encompasses the second and third but adds, "in order to imitate Christ our Lord better and to be more like him here and now, I desire and choose poverty with Christ poor rather than wealth; contempt with Christ laden with it rather than honors. Even further, I desire to be regarded as a useless fool for Christ, who even before me was regarded as such, rather than as a wise or prudent person in this world" (SE 167). As Fleming puts it, "By grace, I find myself so moved to follow Jesus Christ in the most intimate union possible, that his experiences are reflected in my own. In that, I find my delight."[51]

Given that this meditation is deeply Christian in its orientation, the

50. Ibid., 129.
51. Ibid., 131.

key question for us is how it might be adapted for Hindus who do not share the view that Christ should be at the center of our lives. This adaptation aims to give exercitants from other faiths a real encounter with Jesus Christ, but it also aims to remove stumbling blocks, caused by differences between our traditions, that might prevent exercitants from growing in their faith. It should be expected that different individuals will be at different places on their journey at this point, which is of course true for Christians who make the Exercises, as well. There may be more dramatic differences between members of other faiths, since some, at this stage, may have experienced or may be experiencing different types of conversion. This could take the shape of a traditional conversion to Christianity, but it might also take the shape of "multiple religious belonging," where one acknowledges Christ as Lord, or begins to do so, without renouncing Hinduism. Others might still struggle at this point with the strong focus on Christ as the central individual to be imitated, and for those exercitants it will be helpful to focus on the gift that is sought at this point in the Exercises: we pray to know Jesus more intimately, love him more intensely, and follow him more closely, but we also pray for humility. As O'Brien points out, "Christian humility is not about demeaning yourself; hating the self is a failure to honor the goodness of God's creation in us. Authentic humility is a way of loving God and ourselves. A humble person recognizes his or her need and dependence on God, and thus is another expression of spiritual poverty. A humble person embraces the liberating truth of our humanity: we are not the center of the universe—God is! Authentic humility helps us rejoice in who we are and Whose we are, with all of our gifts and limitations. The three kinds of humility are really just three ways or degrees of loving God."[52] One thing to note about O'Brien's language here is that it is theocentric, as opposed to Christocentric, which will make these remarks especially helpful for Hindus who are struggling with the Christocentric character of this meditation. O'Brien's remarks highlight features of this meditation that are shared by Hindus, and which serve as a basis for rewriting this meditation in a way that would be more accessible for Hindus: "in order to imitate Jesus better and to be more like him here and now, I desire and choose poverty rather than wealth; contempt

52. O'Brien, *The Ignatian Adventure*, 183–84.

rather than honors. Even further, I desire to be regarded as a useless fool with Christ, who before me was regarded as such, rather than as a wise or prudent person in this world." It is not that we want to remove Christ from the Meditation on Three Kinds of Humility; it is that we want to highlight the reasons why Christ is someone worthy of imitating, not just for Christians but for others, as well. This may involve—for those who stumble over the Christocentric language and that language which takes Christ as the center, to the exclusion of other religious figures—removing language that emphasizes Christ's central place in the Christian tradition. For Hindus, the reasons *why* this kind of humility is worth embracing might include the fact that that we are not the center of the universe—from a Hindu standpoint, I cannot be the center of the universe if I am continuous with all of creation. But I am in desperate need of help to realize that and live that out in a tangible way. One of the points of the Exercises, for Hindus, is to allow them to experience and encounter Christ as an exemplar who lives out this shared value in a powerful way. Jesus points beyond himself, to the Father, to the Kingdom.

An Adaptation of the Ignatian Spiritual Exercises for Hindus: The Third and Fourth Weeks

In the third and fourth weeks, exercitants contemplate the passion and the resurrection. As Ivens notes, these final contemplations belong to the structure of the Exercises and are connected with the sequence as a whole "first in the sense that they presuppose, while at the same time enhancing, the graces characteristic of the previous weeks." At the same time, the transition from the second week marks "a certain change of spiritual climate. This is pinpointed in the requested graces which in the final weeks shift from the more external graces of knowledge, love and committed discipleship to graces of a more immediately participatory sort—suffering *with* Christ, joy *with* Christ."[53] These remarks remind us that exercitants from other faiths will need to have established a considerable comfort level with Jesus by this point in the Exercises. But it is important not to mistake this comfort for an embrace of Christian the-

---

53. Ivens, *Understanding the Spiritual Exercises*, 146.

ology. The focus of the third week is *being with Jesus*, accompanying him
through his suffering. This is something that anyone—not only someone
who accepts a particular doctrine of the atonement—can do. The grace
we seek is compassion—literally, "suffering with." As O'Brien puts it, "We
reflect not merely on the physical pain he endured but also on the emotional, interior suffering of a person who is misunderstood, isolated, rejected, and alone."[54] The fact that the colloquy is a key part of the third
week underscores the fact that being with Christ in his suffering is not
about accepting a particular theological view concerning Jesus and his
death. Rather, we are to be with Jesus as we would be with a friend, and
speak to him as we would speak to a friend. This makes the third week
very accessible to members of other faiths, who probably for the first
time will experience and immerse themselves in the days leading up to
Jesus' death on the cross.

However, it will be helpful for many if not most Hindu exercitants if
certain elements recede to the background. One such element is a focus
on the idea that Jesus endures suffering *for me*, or that he dies for my
sins. In place of this Christian focus, Hindu exercitants might focus instead on how Jesus' opponents are concerned with self-seeking, while
Jesus genuinely seems to recognize his unity with others, and the contrast between Jesus and his self-seeking opponents ought to lead us to
embrace the model of the former rather than the latter. Without embracing a Christian theological view on the atonement, one can still affirm
the image of the three divine persons saying, "Let us work the redemption of the human race," and sending Jesus into the world with this purpose.[55] While it is not a Hindu theological conception of oneness, there is
nevertheless a sense of unity in Jesus' teachings, and this can serve as an
important point of focus for Hindu exercitants, since it meets up in interesting ways with the centrality of oneness in their own tradition. This
sense of unity is seen most clearly perhaps in the final judgment scene
of Matthew's Gospel, where people are judged by their compassion, that
gift of the third week: "Come, you that are blessed by my Father, inherit

---

54. O'Brien, *The Ignatian Adventure*, 216.

55. For a discussion of the excessive reliance on atonement theology, see Elizabeth Johnson,
Abounding in Kindness (Maryknoll, N.Y.: Orbis, 2015). Johnson emphasizes the passion as a sign of
God's faithfulness, loving to the end, a natural consequence of remaining faithful to the kingdom,
which might serve as a helpful resource for adaptations of the Exercises.

the kingdom prepared for you from the foundation of the world; for I was hungry and you gave me food, I was thirsty and you gave me something to drink, I was a stranger and you welcomed me, I was naked and you gave me clothing, I was sick and you took care of me, I was in prison and you visited me" (Mt 25:34–36). This passage highlights something important about Jesus' story as it unfolds in the third week: as we walk beside Jesus in his suffering, it ought to deepen our compassion, not just for him but for others also, and our solidarity with all those who suffer. Jesus regards himself as one with the most marginalized, as he says in Matthew's Gospel: "Truly I tell you, just as you did it to one of the least of these who are members of my family, you did it to me" (Mt 25:40). As Gerald Fagin points out, "The Third Week calls us to a deep personal union with Jesus. . . . Our love for the suffering Jesus shapes our own hearts into the compassionate heart of Jesus. This confirms our commitment to live our lives in service to those in need. The root of our compassion is our compassion for Jesus and for our suffering brothers and sisters who are Christ's body today."[56]

More challenging than the third week is the fourth week, for the latter focuses on the miraculous event of Jesus' resurrection, making it less easy to simply follow along with the story while bracketing theological questions. One way of approaching the challenges raised by considering Jesus' resurrection is to ask Hindu exercitants who struggle with this to use their imagination to entertain the possibility that it happened. Exercitants should ask the question, "What if it's true? What did it look like? What did it mean to those who were present? What does it mean to me, as a friend who walked with Jesus through his suffering in the days leading up to his death?" In this way, the fourth week represents an opportunity for exercitants to use the skills they have developed thus far in the retreat to *see with the eyes of their imagination*. Indeed, for anyone who finds it difficult to believe that the resurrection actually occurred, the fourth week comes at the ideal time—after much practice in using the imagination over the course of the first three weeks of the Exercises. At this point, we stand with Mary and the beloved disciple or Thomas as they experience the risen Lord. This serves to remind us that making the

---

56. Fagin, *Putting On the Heart of Christ*, 168.

Exercises is not only about encountering God and deepening one's faith; it is also about learning to pray in a variety of different ways. This is why the Exercises have often been called a school of prayer.

As Hindu exercitants pray through the fourth week, it will be helpful once again to focus on the gift that is sought during this final movement of the Exercises: joy. This is more than just happiness; the type of joy we seek here is deeply felt consolation. While considering Jesus' resurrection, Hindu exercitants should be encouraged to look to the texts of their own tradition for stories and passages that deepen their sense of the gifts of life, hope, and joy, and how these gifts frequently arise out of the darkness. Even for those who believe in reincarnation, death is still a reality; the loss of loved ones is felt deeply even if one believes their soul continues on another journey. Jesus' resurrection, then, is just as radical, just as astonishing, and just as hopeful. As O'Brien points out, "The Resurrection reveals how God is always bringing life from death, hope from despair, love from hate, and light from darkness. So we celebrate 'risings' as well, such as reconciled or new friendships, unexpected opportunities, renewed vigor, and meaningful learning experiences that come from losses."[57] If the cross reveals Jesus' faithfulness, the resurrection reveals the Father's; for the resurrection is also a creative act that demonstrates God's faithfulness. One important thing to notice about the fourth week is that Ignatius himself departs from scripture in his contemplation of Jesus' resurrection when he asks us to imagine the risen Christ appearing first to his mother.

Without departing from Ignatius's own approach, then, a variety of other stories and images from the Hindu tradition might be added to the journey of the fourth week to deepen and enrich exercitants' experience of Jesus' resurrection. It is worth noting something here for those who worry that the Exercises here might stray too much toward "resurrection," broadly construed, and away from the resurrection of Jesus Christ. All of the suggestions I offer here are intended as *additions* or accompaniments to the more traditional core of the Exercises. Hindu exercitants are not considering additional stories and texts in place of the Gospels. Rather, these supplemental adaptations are designed to help those who find

57. O'Brien, *The Ignatian Adventure*, 244.

it more difficult to access the story of the risen Christ. By picking up on common themes, the aim is to help all exercitants to go deeper in their engagement with the risen Christ, in order to facilitate an experience of God and a growth in their faith through the Exercises.

The final contemplation of the Exercises, the Contemplation of the Love of God (SE 230–37), invites us to consider how the experience of God's love in the Exercises has changed us, and how it ought to inform our lives as we move ahead. This contemplation hinges on themes that will be familiar to Hindu exercitants from their own tradition. We look back on the course of our lives and the many gifts we have received, thanking God for these gifts; we look at creation, other people, and ourselves, finding God in all things; we consider how God labors in all that we see: "For example, he is working in the heavens, elements, plants, fruits, cattle, and all the rest—giving them their existence, conserving them, concurring with their vegetative and sensitive activities" (SE 236). And we praise God, who labors for us in all of these ways. Finally, we "consider how all good things and gifts descend from above; for example, my limited power from the Supreme and Infinite Power above; and so of justice, goodness, piety, mercy, and so forth—just as rays come down from the sun, or the rains from their source," and we praise God who is the source of all goodness (SE 237). Exercitants look to creation and to their lives, and are asked: Does it move you to wonder and awe? The response of feeling gifted then prompts the desire to want to give back, and this is what makes the Take, Lord, Receive prayer (SE 234), which follows each of the four points of this contemplation, so appropriate. This prayer ought to be accessible to Hindus.

The second and third points of this contemplation might be enhanced by a variety of companion readings from the Hindu tradition. For instance, the vision of Krishna's totality—his unity with all things—from the *Bhāgavad-Gītā* offers a variety of rich images: "Arjuna, see my forms in hundreds and thousands; diverse divine, of many colors and shapes.... See all the universe, animate and inanimate, and whatever else you wish to see; all stands here as one in my body" (98). The narrator remarks of the vision, "Everywhere was boundless divinity containing all astonishing things, wearing divine garlands and garments, anointed with divine perfume. If the light of a thousand suns were to rise in the sky at once, it would be like the light of that great spirit. Arjuna saw all the universe in its many ways and parts, standing as one in the body of the god of gods" (98–99). What follows is a vivid description of all things, including a variety of Hindu gods, and of course there are brilliant contrasts with Ignatius's view here, not only the contrast to Ignatius's concept of God, but also the fascinating contrast between finding God at work in all things, and believing that God is one with all things—seen here in the vision of Krishna's totality. The latter view is one of identity—God is one with all things—whereas Ignatius believes we can see how God labors in the world in all things, working in and through them, without believing that God *is* those things. These are important differences to acknowledge, and doing so can deepen a Hindu's sense of connection to her own tradition and its distinctive value. At the same time, there is enough resonance to make the Contemplation of the Love of God accessible for Hindus—resonance seen most clearly in the shared belief that God is present to us at each moment, in very real ways, and is inviting us into a relationship, loving us and abiding with us in joy and sorrow, eliciting our gratitude and praise, and inviting us to consider how we might return that love in tangible ways by serving others.

Suggested Further Readings

Francis Clooney SJ. *Beyond Compare: St. Francis de Sales and Sri Vedanta Desika on Loving Surrender to God.* Washington, D.C.: Georgetown University Press, 2008.

———. *Divine Mother, Blessed Mother: Hindu Goddesses and the Virgin Mary.* New York: Oxford University Press, 2010.

———. *Hindu God, Christian God: How Reason Helps Break Down the Barriers between Religions.* New York: Oxford University Press, 2010.

———. *His Hiding Place Is Darkness: A Hindu-Catholic Theopoetics of Divine Absence.* Stanford, Calif.: Stanford University Press, 2013.

4

Buddhist Adaptations of the Spiritual Exercises

ONE OF THE TRULY remarkable features of Buddhism is the diversity of belief and practice one finds in this tradition—not just historically, but speaking descriptively of Buddhists today. This feature of Buddhism makes it especially challenging to describe a single adaptation of the Exercises that would be helpful for Buddhists. As a result, this chapter makes two different sets of recommendations—one set that concerns adaptations for more philosophical forms of Buddhism, which are non-theistic and very prevalent in the West, such as Zen; and another set of adaptations for forms of Buddhism, popular in East Asia, that are theistic in practice and which represent the beliefs and practices of a majority of Buddhists in the world today. As we shall see, these two groups differ dramatically in thought and practice, though they do share certain beliefs and doctrines in common, and their common beliefs will be the focus of the broader adaptation I outline here.

I wish to begin by noting the specific nature of this chapter: my aim is not to offer a study in comparative theology—such studies can be found in other works, which have sought to compare elements of Ignatian spirituality with Zen Buddhism—but to outline in detailed form an adaptation of the full and complete Ignatian Spiritual Exercises (all four weeks) for Buddhists who are good candidates for making the Exercises, based on the standards outlined in the opening chapters of this book. Additionally, my work here seeks to address not only Zen Buddhism but other forms of

Buddhism as well, including those that are practiced by most Buddhists worldwide. Finally, the content of what I will have to say about Buddhism in this chapter is a notable contrast to studies of Zen Buddhism and Ignatian spirituality. Unlike Ruben Habito's *Zen and the Spiritual Exercises*, which is the most detailed comparative study of these two traditions, this work does not contend that the Zen and Ignatian traditions are fundamentally in agreement, in some ultimate sense. Habito, for instance, contends that the three fruits of Zen practice "roughly correspond" to different stages of the Exercises, at times making the stronger claim that these fruits *are* the stages of the Ignatian Exercises.[1] It is hard to know how to assess these claims, but in any case, the purpose of this work is not to offer a critique of Habito's view. I will, however, provide evidence throughout this chapter of the deep and important differences between these traditions, thereby offering an alternative view. I argue that these differences are what make specific adaptations of the Exercises for Buddhists necessary. If one believes that these two traditions offer the same basic view of human beings, their spiritual needs and proper end, then there is little if any reason to make an adaptation of the sort that I outline here.

On that note, it is essential to remember to which Buddhists this adaptation applies, namely those who wish to deepen their faith through the Ignatian Spiritual Exercises and who are open to encountering God and Jesus Christ. As I argue in the first two chapters of this work, a careful consideration of the aims and purposes of the Exercises point toward this subset of individuals as the best candidates from other traditions to make the Exercises—and also those who are most likely to express an interest in doing so. Once we understand this, it is easy to see why the adaptation for Buddhists that I outline in this chapter keeps most of the content of the Exercises intact and *adds* Buddhist texts and practices to the Exercises, as opposed to *replacing* large portions or elements of the Exercises with them. In addition to the fact that it would be neither possible nor advisable to replace key elements of the Exercises with texts and figures from Buddhism, such replacement also would not be necessary for the Buddhist exercitants in question. The goals of the Buddhist

1. See, for example, Ruben Habito, *Zen and the Spiritual Exercises* (Maryknoll, N.Y.: Orbis, 2013), xxii–xxiii: "The third fruit flows naturally from the second and is called 'the embodiment of the peerless way,' or the actualization of Zen enlightenment in our daily lives. This fruit is the Ignatian stage of Union, which takes an entire lifetime to fulfill."

adaptations described in this chapter are the same as adaptations for Christians who make the Exercises: to remove stumbling blocks that prevent individuals from benefiting from the Exercises and to do so with the least amount of change or adaptation necessary, with the aim of preserving the distinctive character of the Exercises and those features that make them effective. What is unique about this adaptation is its engagement with Buddhist texts, practices, and ideas, and its more specific aim of helping Buddhists who make the Exercises to carefully work through the tensions and resonances between their tradition and that of Ignatius. The primary goal of this exercise is not to teach Buddhists about Christianity—although this certainly may occur as an added benefit—but to open up the Exercises as a tool for deepening their faith through a different sort of religious experience or encounter. For some, this in turn may lead to important shifts in their religious beliefs, including the degree to which they identify with the Buddhist tradition. This reality will be more striking in the case of Buddhism compared with Hinduism because—as we shall see—some forms of Buddhism differ from Christianity even more dramatically than Hinduism. However, in keeping with the spirit and practice of the Exercises, I will not attempt to specify what the outcome of the Exercises might be for different exercitants; it is Ignatius's contention that this is ultimately up to God and the exercitant.

Since Buddhism contains a vast and remarkable set of contemplative practices that are dedicated to helping Buddhists to grow and reach various states of religious fulfillment, I especially want to emphasize that the adaptation I outline in this chapter is not a competing or alternative path to achieve Buddhist metaphysical ends, such as particular states of consciousness—though it certainly may be helpful with respect to some Buddhist ethical ends. The central goals of Ignatian spirituality, as I have argued and as we shall see throughout this chapter, differ in a variety of important ways from the goals of Buddhist contemplative practices. Accordingly, this adaptation is for those Buddhists who have a particular interest in engaging with Christian spirituality, who wish to explore a different set of ends (most notably encountering God and having a personal relationship with Jesus Christ) but who are not (or not yet) prepared to leave the Buddhist tradition behind and who believe that their faith might be enriched by Christian spiritual practices.

How, then, can Ignatian spirituality serve as a helpful resource for these Buddhists? In what areas, specifically, might it offer assistance? My adaptation focuses on two areas in particular. First, I show how the Exercises offer an opportunity to have a different sort of religious experience, namely to encounter and cultivate a relationship with God and Jesus Christ[2]—an aim that differs significantly from the aims of Buddhist contemplative practices, most of which aim to help individuals extinguish desires and move closer to enlightenment (which will be discussed in the first section of this chapter). Second, I show how the Exercises can help Buddhists to cultivate some of the same traits and abilities that certain Buddhist practices aim to cultivate, most notably virtues such as humility and generosity, mindfulness of oneself, others, and the world, and the ability to make decisions that are grounded in one's faith. Whereas Ignatian spirituality serves as a unique resource for Buddhists with respect to the first goal, it simply provides another way of cultivating the second set of goals—albeit one that some Buddhists might find constructive since it makes use of different approaches and practices.

A Brief Overview of Buddhism

Buddhism is a remarkably diverse tradition—arguably more diverse in thought and practice than any other religious tradition, including Christianity. Indeed, while it has become popular for scholars of religion to refer to religious traditions in the plural—"Christianities," "Hinduisms," and so on—as a way of emphasizing their diversity, sometimes at the expense of their similarities, referring to "Buddhisms" makes a good deal of sense. Nevertheless, the Buddhist tradition contains a number of foundational teachings that are shared by virtually all Buddhists, and I will begin by introducing these ideas before moving on to discuss the diversity of other beliefs and practices one finds among Buddhists today. It should always be remembered, however, that the foundational teachings I discuss are

---

2. In specifying "God and Jesus Christ," I aim to emphasize that many Buddhists are not theists, and as a result, encountering God in any form (and not just God as revealed in Jesus Christ) will be new to them. This marks an important difference from Hinduism. Of course, the Triune God is central to the Exercises, and my aim here is to underscore the fact that non-theistic Buddhists not only do not share the Christian belief in three Divine Persons; they do not believe in any deity at all. Accordingly, encountering God in any form—as well as Jesus—will be new.

in any given case accompanied by different practices and accompanying doctrines in different schools of Buddhism, which makes them a bit like matching frames surrounding very different paintings. While different schools of Buddhism are as different as the works of Monet and Pollock, there are also reasons why people with such diverse beliefs and practices call themselves Buddhists—a number of which are seen in these shared foundational teachings.

The Buddhist tradition takes its name from a particular individual who came to be known as the Buddha ("awakened one"). Since many later individuals became awakened as a result of following the Buddha's teachings, and since there subsequently developed in the tradition a belief in many previous buddhas, the Buddha is widely referred to as "the historical Buddha" (or simply "*the* Buddha"). Gautama Siddhartha (563– 483 BCE), who came to be called Shakyamuni Buddha ("awakened sage of the Shakya clan") was born a wealthy prince in north India. The first complete biography of his life was not written until the first century, but most accounts agree on some fundamentals: his father was the king of one of the many large clans that dominated north India, and at the time of his "awakening" to the reality of suffering in the world, he was already a young man, married with a son. He grew up sheltered by wealth and privilege, but when he witnessed the sights of old age, disease, and death for the first time as a young man, he was struck by the illusion that had been created for him inside the palace walls. He awakened to the reality of pain and suffering in the world as if from a dream, and vowed to find a way to free all beings from suffering. He departed the palace, leaving his family behind, and became a Hindu ascetic or renunciate (*sadhu*), living without the comforts of food, clothing, and shelter. But after experiencing the most meager existence, and in comparison with the lavish existence he had known previously, he had an epiphany: if a string is too slack it won't play; if it is too tight, it will break; the correct path is one in between self-indulgence and self-denial—a teaching that came to be known as the Buddhist "middle way."[3]

In addition to rejecting the extreme practices of Hindu asceticism,

---

3. There is an interesting resonance with an element of Ignatius's autobiography here: in his conversion, Ignatius adopted a variety of ascetical practices at Manresa but discerned with the help of a spiritual director that they were not of God. He details this experience in the *Autobiography*.

the Buddha also rejected the most fundamental teaching of Hinduism: the reality of atman—the essential self or soul. As we saw in the previous chapter, the Hindu tradition contends that the key to our salvation is to recognize our true identity: *ātman* is *brahman*—we are one with all things. One of the foundational teachings of Buddhism is an explicit rejection of the doctrine of *Brahman-Ātman*. In its place, the Buddhist tradition defends the doctrine of *anātman*, or no self. This doctrine is precisely what it sounds like: a rejection of the view that there is any essential self or soul. There is no self or soul that thinks, animates us, is immortal, is constant and enduring, or that continues to exist after death. The illusion, on the Buddhist view, is not that each of us is a separate and distinct self, as the Hindu tradition maintains; the illusion is that there is any self at all. There is no permanently abiding entity such as the soul or self. This teaching is grounded in the doctrine of impermanence—the view that nothing, not even the self or soul, is permanent, enduring, or immortal. Rather, all that exists are what Buddhists call the five aggregates: sensations, perceptions, emotions, memories, and volitions. These five are what "we" are, but they are always changing; no part of us is constant. There is not even a self that "has" the five aggregates; in each of our cases, only the five aggregates exist in an ever-changing state. While most Buddhists, like Hindus, believe in reincarnation, they do not believe that the atman, or soul, is reincarnated. Rather, five fluctuating aggregates are reborn, like an ever-changing flame that is passed from one candle to the next.

The historical Buddha is sometimes referred to as "the great physician," because traditional Buddhists maintain that humanity is plagued by an illness and the Buddha offers a cure through his teachings. We see the diagnosis and cure outlined in another set of foundational teachings known as the four noble truths, which aim to answer the fundamental question of why we—human beings and other sentient beings as well—experience pain and suffering. Few questions are bigger and more fundamental than this one. The first noble truth, "All is suffering" (*sarvam duhkha*) affirms the reality and pervasiveness of suffering. It is a part of every aspect of life: even pleasure is bound up with frustration and fragility, and even the greatest joys in life contain seeds of pain. Suffering here includes not only the standard sense of the term but various other forms of suffering as well, including incompleteness and dissatisfaction. And our suffering, from a Buddhist standpoint, is largely rooted in a fear of loss, which is why all of life involves suffering, even our greatest experiences of joy. The more you love someone, the more you fear losing them; the more you enjoy something, the more difficult it is when it is taken away. To draw a brief point of comparison, Christianity and Buddhism both teach that the worldly goods we experience in this life are finite, fleeting, and ultimately unsatisfactory; but whereas Christianity points us to transcendent spiritual goods (indeed, to an infinite, divine Good that is the source of all goodness), Buddhism teaches instead that genuine flourishing or well-being can be attained—and suffering overcome—only by giving up the belief that there are permanent, eternal goods or sources of good.

The second noble truth posits the origin or source of suffering: desire, or more literally, "thirst" (*trishna*). We suffer because we desire, crave, and thirst for things. Ultimately, all desires are a problem for us: both selfish and unselfish desires, material and immaterial desires are at the root of our suffering, on the Buddhist view. Just as desiring our own success leads to suffering, so too does desiring the happiness of others; likewise, desiring to acquire a lot of possessions leads to suffering, but so too does desiring peace and happiness. It is a hallmark of the Buddhist tradition that *all* desires are problematic, not just selfish desires, for all of our desires are ultimately rooted in the same illusion about the self: the view that I am a real self who can and does possess or have things. But it is a mistake, on the Buddhist view, to think that anyone can ever really possess anything, for not only is everything that we might possess impermanent; we, too, are impermanent.

While the first and second noble truths outline the illness that plagues humanity, the third and fourth noble truths outline the cure. The third noble truth specifies the way to stop suffering: we must extinguish all of our desires, just like a candle flame is snuffed out. Since the source of suffering is desire, release from suffering can come only from eliminating desires. The traditional Buddhist term for "extinguish," *nirvāna*, ultimately points toward an ineffable state: complete freedom from all desires and complete cessation of suffering can only be experienced, not described. It is an experience of absolute reality and absolute truth, for it represents the full and complete embodiment of the reality that nothing is permanent—not even you or me.

The fourth noble truth aims to answer the question of *how* to extinguish desires: we must follow *the middle way* (*madhyamarga*) between self-indulgence and self-denial (both of which reaffirm the very idea of a self), just as the historical Buddha did when he found the way between his lavish upbringing and an ascetic lifestyle. This is a middle way between a hedonistic lifestyle, in which one's passions and desires are continuously indulged, and a lifestyle that involves depriving oneself of all sensual pleasure. While some traditional forms of Hinduism maintained that such deprivation, practiced by Hindu ascetics, was the best way to detach from one's desires, on a traditional Buddhist view such practices betray an attachment to one's desires and oneself, as one's sole concern is to deprive oneself of fulfilling those desires. From a Buddhist standpoint, rather than focusing on either fulfilling or denying the fulfillment of one's desires, one ought to seek to detach oneself from all desires, aiming to extinguish them completely.

The noble eightfold path outlines the specific ways of living that traditional Buddhists believed could help one to walk this middle way between self-indulgence and self-denial. The first two paths, right understanding and right thought, concern one's wisdom or knowledge. Right understanding involves seeing things as impermanent, while right thought concerns turning from craving to compassion, nonviolence, and unconditional love. The third, fourth, and fifth paths concern ethics: right speech, right conduct, and right livelihood specify the importance of eliminating untrue and hurtful speech; contain the prohibition of intoxication, stealing, cheating, immoral sexual activity; and outline the importance of earning a living morally, which would prohibit earning money through the sale of drugs, weapons, poisons, prostitution, and the killing of animals. The sixth, seventh, and eighth paths concern meditation: right effort filters out non-edifying thoughts and stops the mind's indulgences and obsessions; right mindfulness concerns attentiveness to and awareness of one's thoughts at each present moment; right concentration involves the highest levels of mental calm. When one reaches the final stages of right concentration, one approaches nirvana.

The noble eightfold path contains rules not just for behavior but for the mind, as well. This concern is seen in a variety of Buddhist texts. The Parable of the Piece of Cloth says, "Just as soiled and dirty cloth, plunged in clear water, becomes pure and clean; or just as gold, passed through the furnace, becomes pure and clean ... one who has reached this state in virtue, in mental discipline and in wisdom, may partake of the choicest rice with all manner of sauces and curries." The rules for the mind that are outlined in the noble eightfold path aim to purify the mind, cleansing it of desires and attachments, which, as this parable indicates, will allow one to proceed in the world and encounter the objects of worldly desires without becoming attached to or desiring those things. Here we see clearly the ideal of extinguishing desires completely, for on a traditional Buddhist view, desire is the root of all suffering.

How are these foundational teachings lived out in practice by Buddhists today? I want to focus on two particular forms of Buddhism that are prominent in the contemporary world. One is a more philosophical form of Buddhism that is embraced by a majority of Western Buddhist converts; this form of Buddhism is strongly influenced by and associated with Zen—a Japanese school of Buddhism that has its origins in fifth century Chinese Buddhism and that focuses strongly on meditation as a way of achieving Buddhist goals. The second form of Buddhism I want to discuss is the theistic Buddhism that is embraced by the overwhelming majority of Buddhists worldwide and seen especially in East Asia. This form of Buddhism focuses primarily on worshipping and offering prayers of supplication to a variety of Buddhist deities. I want to emphasize that in discussing these two forms of Buddhism in fact I am referring to two different *families* of Buddhism; there is diversity within each of these, including multiple sects or schools in each group. For the purposes of this book, it makes sense to group them for practical purposes: similar kinds of adaptations of the Ignatian Spiritual Exercises would be helpful for members of the various sects that comprise the first form of Buddhism (which I will call philosophical Buddhism) on the one hand, while other kinds of adaptations would be helpful for most members of the sects that comprise the second form of Buddhism (which I will call theistic Buddhism) on the other.[4] As we shall see, the most press-

---

4. I use the terms "philosophical Buddhism" and "theistic Buddhism" because they describe the strong emphasis that the former places on Buddhist philosophy (including the four noble

ing reason that this is the case is that philosophical Buddhism takes a non-theistic view in which there is no analogue to God, whereas theistic Buddhism is polytheistic. God is central to the Exercises, and thus much rests on our ability to address different individuals differently, according to their theistic or non-theistic beliefs and practices. I am not denying that there might be other forms of Buddhism outside of these two basic groups, though I think most would fall more or less into one category or the other; I focus here on these two forms of Buddhism because I believe they describe the two main types of Buddhists today who would be most likely to express an interest in making the Exercises.

The form of Buddhism that I am calling philosophical Buddhism is heavily influenced by, and includes, Zen Buddhism. Self-discipline and self-reliance are hallmarks of Zen tradition, and so too is the practice that requires these qualities, namely *zazen*: silent, seated meditation in which the goal is to cleanse the mind of all thoughts and desires. There are many kinds of meditative exercises that are designed to cultivate this state, but the Zen Buddhist tradition as a whole contends that when one's mind is completely and utterly still, empty, and devoid of content, it becomes possible to achieve *samādhi*: a state of consciousness in which the thinking mind is at rest. *Samādhi* provides an ideal condition for the spontaneous emergence of enlightenment, or nirvana, though according to the Zen tradition it does not cause nirvana. Now, one of the points of Zen practice is to help individuals not just to know but to experience firsthand the truth of certain Buddhist teachings—that there really is no self, soul, or conscious essence of the human person, that everything is impermanent, and that we can be freed from suffering only when we extinguish all desires, because they are the root of our suffering. Buddhist meditation also is designed to help individuals to extinguish their desires—a process that is facilitated by the experience of no self and impermanence, and by training the mind to operate in ways that reflect that experience. Accordingly, a rich variety of Buddhist meditative practices are geared toward the realization that when one gazes inward, one beholds nothing but pure emptiness (Sanskrit: *sunyata*). There is no God or

---

truths and the doctrines of anatman and impermanence) in relation to contemplative practice, and the latter's focus on the veneration of Buddhist deities. There is an important contrast here, especially because most theistic Buddhists do not focus on Buddhist philosophy and many are not even aware of these teachings.

Spirit, and no soul in any shape or form that one perceives here, and this marks the most striking difference from both Christianity and Hinduism.

Despite the overwhelming popularity of Zen Buddhism and Buddhist meditation in the West, most Buddhists in the world today do not meditate.[5] The overwhelming majority of Buddhists engage in devotional practices that involve offering petitionary prayers to a variety of deities. The form of Buddhism that is practiced by most Buddhists thus looks very different from the form of Buddhism that is practiced by most Western Buddhist converts, or by monks in Buddhist monasteries throughout Asia—many of whom include meditative practices to varying degrees in their daily collective monastic practices. But even in most monasteries in Asia, Buddhist monks do not typically take meditative practice as their primary work; it is included alongside the work of running a temple that typically houses a variety of representations of Buddhist deities that are venerated.

Who are those deities? They include buddhas—awakened ones who have extinguished their desires and ended their suffering, and, for Mahayana Buddhists (the form of Buddhism that dominates Central and East Asia), bodhisattvas—enlightened beings who, out of unlimited compassion, postpone their final freedom from samsara and their entry into buddhahood until all sentient beings can also be freed and achieve awakening. There are many of each and a rich variety of stories and texts about these individuals, but it is important to remember that they are all limited in power, and those who frequent Buddhist temples typically pray to them for specific needs. As Meir Shahar and Robert Weller point out, when we refer to deities or gods in relation to Chinese religions (including Confucianism, Daoism, Buddhism, and popular religion), "Such use should be taken to imply not the omniscience and omnipotence of the Abrahamic god, but something more akin to Catholic saints: spirits of dead worthies who can respond to requests from the living."[6] Some contemporary interpreters object to the use of the term "gods" on the basis that it brings to

5. As a leading study of the history of Buddhist insight meditation points out, devotional forms of practice have been more dominant: "While over the course of Buddhist history relatively few people have meditated, many have worshipped the Buddha's relics," and "mass meditation, by both monks and laypeople, was born in Burma only in the early years of the twentieth century and at a scale never seen before in Buddhist history." See Erik Braun, *The Birth of Insight: Meditation, Modern Buddhism, and the Burmese Monk Ledi Sayadaw* (Chicago: University of Chicago Press, 2013), 3.

6. Meir Shahar and Robert Weller, eds., *Unruly Gods: Divinity and Society in China* (Honolulu: University of Hawaii Press, 1996), 2.

mind God (with a capital *G*). Yet if we deny that spirits, deities, or spiritual agents other than a single, omni-predicate God should be referred to as "gods," we (perhaps inadvertently) privilege certain theistic views over other views by denying that any other deities should be referred to as "gods." This also minimizes—either intentionally or unintentionally—the continuity between different kinds of religious views that involve belief in and interaction with powerful and benevolent spiritual beings. A majority of Buddhists in the world today are clearly theists of a certain kind—polytheists, to be precise—but it is important to remember that this does not mean they believe in any deity that resembles the God that is central to the Ignatian Spiritual Exercises. Indeed that is what makes an adaptation for theistic Buddhists at once challenging and necessary. It is also worth noting that, especially in China but in other parts of East Asia as well, it is not uncommon for those who frequent Buddhist temples to visit other kinds of temples as well, including Daoist temples, where they venerate a variety of other deities. Many if not most theistic Buddhists in East Asia are not exclusively theistic Buddhists; their theism is highly syncretic, for it includes deities from Buddhism, Daoism, and perhaps other traditions as well.

Most often, the contemporary practice of Buddhism in East Asia involves petitioning Buddhist deities in temples or in small shrines kept in the home. One normally bows and kneels, burns incense, and offers silent prayers before the icons. Such practices are not always directly related to fundamental Buddhist teachings about the self or the four noble truths, but some Buddhists believe that divine assistance is needed to follow Buddhist teachings and to achieve Buddhist ends. For well-educated theistic Buddhists, there is a wedding of theism—the belief that those who achieve enlightenment and become buddhas or bodhisattvas are present spiritually to hear our prayers and offer assistance—with the belief that desires are the root of our suffering. For a majority of people who frequent Buddhist temples in East Asia, there is little to no awareness of foundational Buddhist teachings: Buddhism, for them, involves belief in the existence of Buddhist deities who can help them with their problems. Witness the fact that people in East Asia often pray for wealth when they visit Buddhist temples: such a prayer is clearly out of line with Buddhist teachings concerning the central importance of extinguishing desires. But at a practical level, this is how Buddhism functions for most of the people who visit Buddhist temples in East Asia.

Compared with the literature examining Christianity in relation to Hinduism, Daoism, and Confucianism, there is an especially large body of literature that has been dedicated to engagement between Buddhism and Christianity. Much of this literature focuses on comparing the theological views of these two traditions, but some studies have sought to compare the spiritual practices of Buddhism and Christianity. This literature has overwhelmingly focused on Zen Buddhism, which is not unproblematic, since most Buddhists worldwide are not Zen Buddhists and do not meditate, which means that, as far as interreligious engagement goes, it addresses the practices and beliefs of only a small subset of Buddhists. Some of this literature is comparative in nature—comparing and contrasting practices and the theological views associated with them in order to better understand them and to see what each religion might learn from the other—while some of it is syncretic—mixing together elements of Christianity and Zen Buddhism to try to form a different coherent whole.[7] Much of this literature is identity-driven, with some more prominent works written by Jesuits or former Jesuits who have found meaning and purpose in Zen meditation but are not (or not yet) prepared to leave the Jesuit order or the Christian tradition—at least not entirely. As a result, many of these studies tend to read Christianity through a Zen lens, giving it a Buddhist shape. For instance, Habito—a Zen teacher and former Jesuit—suggests "that we set aside as much as possible any conceptual content that people tend to associate with the term 'God'," and make the Exercises while "emptying out the conceptual content of what we understand by 'Jesus'."[8] This, of course, makes sense for a Zen Buddhist, since one of the fundamental goals is to completely empty one's mind and recognize that nothing exists, not even the self; but such a goal

---

7. See William Johnston, SJ, *Christian Zen: A Way of Meditation* (New York: Fordham University Press, 1987), *The Still Point: Reflections on Zen and Christian Mysticism* (New York: Fordham University Press, 1989), and *The Mirror-Mind: Zen-Christian Dialogue* (New York: Fordham University Press, 1990); Robert Kennedy, SJ, *Zen Gifts to Christians* (New York: Bloomsbury Academic, 2004), and *Zen Spirit, Christian Spirit: The Place of Zen in Christian Life* (New York: Bloomsbury Academic, 1995); Ruben Habito, *Living Zen, Loving God* (Somerville, Mass.: Wisdom, 1995), *Healing Breath: Zen for Christians and Buddhists in a Wounded World* (Somerville, Mass: Wisdom, 2006), and *Zen and the Spiritual Exercises* (Maryknoll, N.Y.: Orbis, 2013).

8. Habito, *Zen and the Spiritual Exercises*, 8, 15.

stands in direct tension with the aims and the movements of the Exercises. Habito seems to understand the Exercises in a Buddhist light and as a
result molds them into something new—something with a very Buddhist
shape, as well as Buddhist goals. There is also a strong tendency in this
literature to minimize or gloss over the differences between Buddhism
and Christianity. For instance, Daniel O'Hanlon—writing as a Jesuit for
forty years, with five years of experience practicing Zen—maintained that
Ignatius's visions are "remarkably similar" to descriptions of Zen enlightenment experiences, and that Zen's detachment and goal-lessness and
Ignatius's ideal of spiritual freedom are "another way of expressing the
same thing."[9] His work does not, however, deal with the tensions that
undermine these claims, most notably that Ignatian freedom involves
attending to one's desires, since God speaks through them, while Buddhist detachment involves extinguishing one's desires completely, since
they are all ultimately a source of suffering. When O'Hanlon stresses that
Zen and the Exercises both offer methods of direct religious experience,
he does not address the fact that the experience is *of* different things—
which would seem to make the resemblance a very thin one.

Here we can see some of the dangers involved in not considering
carefully and intentionally the differences between different traditions:
one ultimately ends up with versions of the two traditions that make
them look very much alike. This is problematic to an adaptation of the
Exercises for Buddhists for multiple reasons, including the fact that it is
hard to see why a Buddhist ought to make the Exercises if they are ultimately the same as Buddhist practices. As we have already seen in the
preceding chapters, one of the likely reasons that a member of another
faith would be interested in making the Exercises is that they differ in
significant ways from her own practices and thus might be enriching in
new and different ways. But if we change the content of the Exercises so
much that they have Buddhist goals rather than Ignatian ones, then we
are not in fact adapting the Exercises anymore; we are inventing new,
Ignatian-inspired Buddhist practices. The primary purpose of this chapter is to deal honestly and openly with the tensions and resonances that
would be felt by a Buddhist making the Ignatian Spiritual Exercises, and

9. Daniel J. O'Hanlon, "Zen and the Spiritual Exercises: A Dialogue between Faiths," *Theological Studies* 39 (1978): 743–44.

to find ways of helping her to work through and benefit from those tensions and resonances so that the aims of the Exercises might be realized. The goal of this adaptation, then, is not to blend Buddhist and Ignatian practices into some new set of spiritual practices—which seems to be the goal of many if not most of the works focused on Buddhist and Christian spirituality.

In the rest of this chapter, I will focus especially on the obstacles that Buddhists might face when making the Exercises, and suggest ways of working through those obstacles. O'Hanlon formulates some of the more acute differences that distinguish Zen practice from the Exercises, including the content of the religious practices in these two traditions: "In the means which Zen uses, we find ourselves in a different world. Instead of laying out a detailed description of a series of spiritual exercises, using thoughts, reasonings, memories, visualizations, images, feelings, stories, personal colloquies, optional bodily positions, and the like, the Zen student is asked to simply sit still with an erect back and let go of all thoughts and images."[10] As O'Hanlon describes it, the process "is always one of trying to get unhooked from thoughts in order to activate a level of awareness deeper than that of the merely rational and discursive."[11] Here I want to note the implicit normative judgment in O'Hanlon's language, namely that Zen practice allows us to achieve a deeper (and hence superior) form of religious awareness than the Ignatian Spiritual Exercises offer, since the Exercises rely upon different forms of discursive prayer. He correctly notes that in Zen "the ordinary discursive processes of the mind are put aside and considered hindrances to the experience of enlightenment."[12] It is not just the methods—mental reasoning, including discursive prayer such as reading over Scripture or weighing certain thoughts (which Ignatius terms "meditation") and the use of the imagination (which Ignatius terms "contemplation") as opposed to letting go of all thoughts and images—that differ; the goals differ as well. God speaks to us through our desires, according to Ignatius, and so we must learn to attend carefully to them; desires are the root of the problem, according to the Buddhist tradition, and so we must learn to extinguish them completely. While Ignatius seeks to help us to grow closer

10. Ibid., 746.
11. Ibid., 747.
12. Ibid., 754.

to God and follow God's will, the Buddhist tradition seeks to help us to recognize that there is no self (or any being such as the God of Christian faith) and that all is impermanent, and, ultimately, to help us to achieve freedom from samsara and enlightenment. Even O'Hanlon—who saw a great deal of continuity between these two traditions—acknowledged that these differences make it hard to see how one might incorporate Zen practice extensively into the Ignatian Spiritual Exercises: "The question, whether the Zen mode of meditation should not simply be used as a preliminary mind-settler but given a more central position in the Exercises, is a more difficult one. The question is not whether it is an authentic or good practice, not even whether it can be sound Christian practice. It is rather a question of the degree to which it can be a practice at the heart of the Exercises without interfering with their particular dynamism."[13]

With these differences and challenges in mind, I turn to the details of an adaptation of the full and complete Exercises for philosophical Buddhists, on the one hand, and theistic Buddhists, on the other, with the aim of opening each of them up to a different kind of religious experience and a different approach to cultivating Buddhist virtues and making decisions grounded in their faith.

An Adaptation of the Ignatian Spiritual Exercises for Buddhists: The First Week

As we saw in the chapter on Hinduism, one way of understanding the dynamics of the Exercises is by attending to the graces or gifts that are sought. As exercitants from different religious traditions gain a sense of the traditional movements of the Exercises through conversation with a spiritual director and through readings in an accessible guide to the Exercises, they can begin to identify the graces they are seeking at different stages of the Exercises and discern the ways in which they are being invited to grow. This provides a helpful starting place, since the exercitant is anchored to the dynamics of the Exercises; she can then be invited to look to the texts and practices of her own tradition as a source of further reflection on the gift she is seeking. In some places in this chapter I will suggest different adaptations from the Buddhist tradition that aim

13. Ibid., 748.

to deepen the experience of the Exercises for philosophical Buddhists on the one hand and theistic Buddhists on the other. Given the tremendous diversity of texts in the Buddhist tradition (and disagreement between different branches of Buddhism over which texts are canonical), whenever possible I will draw upon Buddhist stories and texts that are shared or recognized widely, such as stories about the life of the historical Buddha and his sermons, since these would be accessible to a wide range of Buddhist exercitants. However, the diversity of texts will make it especially important for Buddhist exercitants to be invited to bring texts and stories that speak to them and with which they are familiar. In addition to suggesting additional readings and adaptations for particular exercises, I will highlight those parts of the Exercises that might contain stumbling blocks and suggest possible ways around them. However, in keeping with Ignatius's own approach, it should always be remembered that these are only general suggestions and guidelines; the appropriate adaptation for each person can be found only in the relationship and conversation between the exercitant and the director. Each exercitant should be encouraged to see what Buddhist texts she is drawn to and which Buddhist stories capture her imagination, especially in relation to the gift she is seeking.

Additionally, as we saw in the previous chapter, in the early stages of the Exercises it will be especially important to help a member of another religious tradition continue to discern whether the Exercises, grounded as they are in the Christian tradition, will be helpful; she must ask whether a Buddhist retreat would be more helpful, and whether she is searching for an opportunity to contemplate, and even encounter, God and the life of Jesus deeply, for a considerable period of time. I stress here the importance of not just being *comfortable* with God and Jesus, but of *searching for an opportunity* to get acquainted with and even encounter God and Jesus; such a distinction is especially critical here, because there are no analogues to God in either philosophical or theistic forms of Buddhism. Philosophical Buddhists will also need to consider whether they feel comfortable with a very active, imaginative, discursive type of prayer—which stands in contrast to forms of Buddhist meditation that are focused on silence and emptiness of thoughts and desires. An added challenge—to be discussed in detail as this chapter progresses—will be attending to their desires in prayer rather than working to eliminate them. Theistic Buddhists, on the other hand, will need to consider how they feel about addressing and encountering a single deity through forms of prayer that are not petitionary in nature. Prayer in the Ignatian tradition, in contrast with prayer and worship in theistic Buddhism, does not center on asking for assistance with particular problems or needs, but on creating a relationship. Now, these two are not mutually exclusive; Ignatius endorsed petitionary prayer, and it is a part of the Exercises (e.g., we ask for what we desire, and offer colloquies). One can offer petitionary prayers while also desiring and working to create a relationship with a deity. Additionally, many Christians who make the Exercises must make a shift from simply or primarily making requests or reciting prayers to Ignatian ways of praying. But I think the challenges will be even greater in the case of theistic Buddhism. It is not uncommon for people in East Asia to visit Buddhist temples primarily in order to offer petitionary prayers asking Buddhist deities to grant certain blessings. Theistic Buddhists who make the Exercises will be able to benefit more if they are made aware of these important differences from the outset, and offered the opportunity to reflect on whether they are not just open to but interested in departing from their own tradition in these ways.

It is important to remember that this book seeks to outline *adaptations* of the Exercises for members of other religious traditions, which means that the core of the Exercises will remain intact. Such an adaptation is easily distinguishable from a new, syncretic set of spiritual exercises that are inspired by the Ignatian Spiritual Exercises but are partly Christian and partly Buddhist. Making the Exercises—even in a form that is adapted for Buddhists in particular—demands more of the exercitant than making a syncretic set of spiritual exercises, because they require her as a Buddhist to engage in much greater depth with Christianity. As noted in the previous chapter, the preparatory days that precede the first week are important, and the Principle and Foundation and the Examen are helpful introductions to the reality of what the purposes of the Exercises are, the extent to which they are grounded in Christian beliefs, and the kind of prayer that will be involved in making the Exercises. The Examen requires a very active way of praying, which will give Buddhists an opportunity to experience firsthand how Ignatian prayer differs from forms of Buddhist meditation such as insight meditation, and how it differs from prayers of supplication directed toward particular Buddhist deities. A Buddhist praying the Examen may also begin to experience some of the specific ways in which the Exercises might deepen her faith and also challenge her beliefs. One of the purposes of our modern practice of the Examen—which is an adaptation and a departure from the examination of conscience in the Exercises, which is primarily concerned with naming sins—is to help us find God in all things and discern how God is calling us in both large and small ways; we do this by reflecting back on a period of time and attending carefully to what was happening in and around us, and then looking ahead to see how we might act in a way that is worthy of our vocation. While there are many different ways of praying the Examen, it will be important in Buddhist adaptations of the Exercises not to remove the monotheistic content from the Examen, because it provides a helpful—and quite gentle—introduction to some of the fundamental dynamics of the Exercises. In a way, only by praying in a different way (for theistic Buddhists) or engaging in a different type of contemplative practice (for philosophical Buddhists) can exercitants—or potential exercitants—really gauge whether or not the Exercises will be a good fit for them. For instance, if philosophical Buddhists find themselves unable or unwilling to try praying to God in the Examen, or unable to entertain not only the idea that God might exist but also the possibility that God might be calling them to live in a certain way or to embrace a certain vocation, it is difficult to see how the full and complete Exercises will be feasible, let alone fruitful, for them. Such individuals should be encouraged to reflect on what drew them to the Exercises initially; exercitants might find it very challenging to pray the Examen but sense that there is something there worth pursuing, something that beckons, and in such cases exercitants will need further support in praying the Examen—something I discuss further below. Directors must be sensitive to the situation, listening closely to the needs and desires of each potential exercitant, allowing God to lead in each instance. We should not turn people away too quickly, but neither should we be so eager to give the Exercises to members of other faiths that we push too hard. It is also important to remember that some individuals might benefit in other ways from Ignatian spirituality—and suggestions to that end will be offered in the chapter on Confucianism (many of which would be accessible to theistic Buddhists, too, since the suggestions are oriented toward those of East Asian cultural backgrounds, broadly speaking). As I argued earlier, however, that is quite different from making the full and complete Exercises.

I mention above that some exercitants may need further support in praying the Examen, and one of the primary aims of this chapter is to suggest specific ways of supporting Buddhists who make the Exercises. A philosophical Buddhist who finds it challenging to pray the Examen because she is not sure if she believes in God may find it helpful to precede the Examen with a more familiar contemplative practice. James Skeehan, SJ, suggests incorporating an adapted form of Buddhist insight meditation (which he calls "Christian Insight Meditation") into the Exercises, and, while his adaptation was not intended for Buddhists making the Exercises, his model for doing this may be helpful, since his approach shows how Buddhist meditation can be a helpful companion to (though not a replacement for) various parts of the Exercises.[14] Skeehan especially suggests using meditation in a preparatory way, in order to "reduce the amount of thinking that you do and pray more with the heart," and he recommends beginning the Examen with silent meditation.[15] For Buddhists, this approach might be helpful, because it could help to ease the transition from Buddhist meditation to Ignatian prayer and show how they can be complementary, at least in some cases. Skeehan does not present a form of the Examen that removes God, but the steps he outlines might be more accessible for those who are still growing accustomed to praying to God, especially since one moves through the first two steps of the Examen (silent meditation and a prayer of gratitude) before one begins talking directly to God.[16] Such a gradual, slow process will be helpful to many who are new to theistic prayer; this is a reminder that adaptation is not just about *what* one does in the Exercises, but *how* one does it (e.g., how quickly one moves through the parts of an exercise).

14. James Skeehan, SJ, *Place Me with Your Son: Ignatian Spirituality in Everyday Life* (Washington, D.C.: Georgetown University Press, 1991), 10–12.

15. Ibid., 10.

16. Ibid., 12.

A Buddhist who struggles with the Examen, especially since it is addressed to God (in the sense that we ask for God's inspiration and perspective as we review our day or sift through our interior landscape) may also find it helpful to reconsider the gifts that she is seeking from the Exercises. What is it about the Exercises that draws her to them? It will be especially important for such individuals to have an opportunity to articulate their uncertainties, including the beliefs they are questioning, as opposed to slipping into the more comfortable waters of blurring the lines between different traditions. Making the full and complete Exercises is much more challenging—and *should be* much more challenging—than reading one of the many books one can find on Buddhist and Christian spirituality. It may be comforting and attractive to think that one can simultaneously embrace both of these traditions fully, and such an idea allows one to avoid what really may be happening—a change or shift in her beliefs, and a change in what her needs are, spiritually. The Exercises will prompt her to plumb the depths of what is provoking that shift; even if a philosophical Buddhist is not certain that she believes in God, the Exercises will present the opportunity to explore whether God is calling her to a different life, or a different kind of commitment. It is important to see how allowing exercitants to evade the hard questions here can be a way for them to avoid hearing and responding to God's voice. At the same time, directors must be sensitive to the temptation to push too hard in any direction. At this early stage, though, it is important to determine whether the person is ready to make the full and complete Exercises, and for a philosophical Buddhist much of this rests on her degree of openness to the possibility that God is real and speaks to us. For theistic Buddhists, the Examen is likely to pose less of a challenge, though it may be helpful for them to note and discuss the fact that this way of praying does not involve—and is actually opposed to—petitionary prayers (e.g., for wealth, children, etc.) of the sort that are often offered to Buddhist deities. Like Hindus, theistic Buddhists should not have difficulty addressing God in prayer or considering how God is calling them, although they may have difficulty with the idea of one God and feel a need to consider which God they are praying to. Indeed, this may be felt more keenly by theistic Buddhists than by Hindus, since Hindu philosophy affirms the view that all, ultimately, is one. In contrast, there is a multiplicity of deities in popular Buddhism. If we consider the matter from the standpoint of religious inclusivism, it may be helpful during the early stages of the Exercises to encourage a theistic Buddhist to focus more on the content of the Examen in prayer than the deity to whom it is addressed; if she struggles with the latter, she might try addressing it to a familiar deity, with the understanding that God may be reaching out to her even if she understands God in very different terms. Indeed, part of what a Buddhist adaptation of the Exercises should do is open up the opportunity to understand God in a new and different way. In the early stages of this process, however, theistic Buddhists may need an adaptation that allows them to address their prayer to a familiar deity in order to help them feel comfortable offering the prayers that are a part of the Exercises, such as the Examen.

The Principle and Foundation offers another opportunity to deepen the sense of what the Exercises are about. The grace of indifference or spiritual freedom that we seek with the Principle and Foundation, which urges us to hold all created things reverently and gratefully, treating them as gifts from God, while also holding them loosely, frees us to love and serve however God calls. Now, for some Buddhists the idea of freeing oneself from attachments is not foreign at all; a central tenet of Buddhism is that all things are impermanent, and we should be mindful of this truth in everyday life. This is a point that Buddhist exercitants should reflect upon: Buddhist teachings are oriented toward helping us to become freer—free of attachments, and thus free to make better decisions. This aim is central to the Exercises, but what differs is the idea that we should hold things loosely because they are gifts from God and we wish to use them only in keeping with God's greater desire for us and our world—not because all things are impermanent and our attachments ultimately cause us to suffer, thereby moving us further away from enlightenment. Here we can see some of the contrasting beliefs and aims of these two traditions. The ultimate goal of the Exercises (and, more broadly, of Christianity) is a certain kind of relationship with God, which in turn facilitates a host of other ends, including the ability to respond to God's call and to take one's place in the kingdom of God. Our aim is to be free not of all desire but only of disordered desires. In fact, spiritual freedom is all about tapping into deep, holy desires, which are God-given; our deepest desires are God's own, for God, as creator, is the source of them. The ultimate goal in the Buddhist tradition is to completely free ourselves from desires, and to reach (and help others reach) the state of nirvana, enlightenment, complete freedom from suffering and liberation from samsara.

Additionally, however, the centrality of God will not be lost on any Buddhist who reads the Principle and Foundation. In his seminal study of the Exercises, *Spiritual Freedom*, John J. English, SJ, describes spiritual freedom as "acceptance of oneself as historically coming from God, going to God, and being with God."[17] The sort of interior freedom that is central to the Exercises is one that places God at the center of our lives and thus makes us more aware of God's call and how we can respond to it generously. Nowhere is this more boldly stated than in the opening lines of the Principle and Foundation: "Human beings are created to praise, reverence, and serve God our Lord, and by means of doing this to save their souls." Unlike Ignatian indifference, Buddhist detachment does not involve belief in God or individual souls.

Since the centrality of God to the Exercises will, I think, be the most significant challenge for many Buddhists throughout the four weeks of the Exercises, I would like to pause to address potential strategies for dealing with this issue now, before beginning to work our way through the details of the four weeks. Although no one has yet outlined a detailed adaptation of the full and complete Exercises for Buddhists, there are Jesuits and former Jesuits who have offered suggestions on how to approach this type of challenge. In the work of Habito and Haight, for instance, we find two basic approaches. One is to take the view that God is essentially a mystery pointing to the unknown, and therefore not necessarily a stumbling block for a non-theist. This type of view is seen in Habito's claim that the Principle and Foundation is an invitation to "be opened to an experience of encounter with Mystery right in the midst of our lives, seen in the light of that someone so intimate and yet so beyond reach on the horizon of our mind."[18] Haight, on the other hand, acknowledges that for those who are "agnostic toward religious beliefs in

17. John J. English, *Spiritual Freedom: From an Experience of the Ignatian Exercises to the Art of Spiritual Guidance*, 2nd ed. (Chicago: Loyola Press, 1995), 18.

18. Habito, *Zen and the Spiritual Exercises*, 42, cf. 31–32. This particular reconstruction of the concept of God was developed by the liberal Protestant theologian Gordon Kaufman. According to Kaufman (following Tillich), God should not be thought of as a divine being or person.

God, a personal colloquy with God represents fairly precisely where he or she cannot go. . . . How can seekers who have had no encounter with a personal God entertain such a colloquy?"[19] He recommends offering "a prayer to an unknown God," standing "before the unknown in silence," but does not specify what this colloquy might entail, other than silence, and it is unclear how such an individual would proceed with the rest of the Exercises.[20] Habito's suggestions for how a Zen Buddhist might make the Exercises offer more detail, but they strip away the theistic content of the Exercises, seen his "Recommended Exercises" for each of the four weeks, which do not describe adapted forms of the Ignatian Spiritual Exercises, but new Exercises altogether, such as the following Exercise, which he suggests for the first week: "Take the daily newspaper and examine the sections on international, national, and regional news, noting the items that depict violence in different forms. After noting a particular incident and finding out the details as described, set the newspaper aside, and imagine yourself as a family member (mother, father, son, daughter, brother, sister) of one of the victims of violence. Sit and breathe in this place for half an hour."[21] Such Exercises are certainly potentially fruitful, and one can see how they might have been inspired by the Exercises, but they are not recognizable adaptations of Ignatian Exercises. Notably absent from them, much like Haight's suggestion that individuals "stand before the unknown in silence," is any engagement with God or even the possibility of God.

The biggest challenge is that within the context of the Exercises, God is *not* simply regarded as a mystery or "the great unknown." This is a difficult truth for those who wish to adapt the Exercises for members of other faiths, because it means that we cannot just gloss over or ignore the question of how to give the Exercises to those who are not theists. Ignatius is grounded in the Christian tradition, the Exercises are shaped by his own experiences with God (which he understands through a Christian lens, particularly a triune God: Father, Son, and Holy Spirit), and while we typically bracket theological questions when making them, the

19. Roger Haight, *Christian Spirituality for Seekers: Reflections on the Spiritual Exercises of Ignatius Loyola* (Maryknoll, N.Y.: Orbis, 2012), 95.

20. Ibid., 96.

21. Habito, *Zen and the Spiritual Exercises*, 65.

Exercises still rest upon a number of basic Christian theological commitments. For instance, the idea that God is a personal being who creates us and loves us unconditionally lies at the very heart of the Exercises. This view may seem to Christians to involve only minimal theological commitments, but the commitments may be significant to members of other faith traditions who hold different views. As I argued in the opening chapters of this book, it is essential to remain focused on the aim of offering the Exercises to non-Christians. Habito contends that the intended outcome of the Exercises is "awakening and personal transformation." However, on my view, this is problematic because it not only re-describes the aims of the Exercises in Buddhist terms but also contends that the aims of the Exercises are Buddhist (i.e., awakening), which represents a departure from the aims that Ignatius outlines. While most would agree that a certain kind of personal transformation is a part of the overarching aims of the Exercises, as I argued earlier in this book, these aims are much more specific, and to claim that the Exercises are simply a path to personal transformation is to remove most of what is distinctive, and, perhaps, effective, about the Exercises, relative to other contemplative practices and self-help strategies.

Buddhists who make the Exercises must wish to pursue some different ends than they pursue through meditation; as I argued earlier in this work, it is hard to imagine why they would want to make the Exercises otherwise. And as I also argued, while some might wish to simply experience what the Exercises are like in order to better understand another tradition, that is not a good reason to make the full and complete Exercises; such an aim could easily be achieved through a weekend retreat or by reading about the Exercises. As we saw earlier in this work, given the extraordinary investment of time on the part of spiritual directors, as well as the purposes of the Exercises, and considering the fact that when exercitants begin and do not complete the Exercises, they may have a sense of failure, and others who might more successfully make the Exercises will have missed the opportunity to do so, it is important to try as hard as we can to ensure that exercitants have the right motivations up front. Much, then, hinges on the aims of individuals who are not sure they believe in God. Philosophical Buddhists who would be good candidates to make the Exercises are individuals who believe there is something of value for them in Christianity, and who thus are not completely satisfied with their spiritual lives and who hope to discover more. One of the differences between pursuing contemplative practices in the Ignatian tradition and other forms of Buddhism or Hinduism is, to be sure, the centrality of God and Jesus. To me, one of the aims of the Exercises for those who are uncertain that they believe in God is to offer them an opportunity to encounter God, and to explore the possibility that God might exist—and not just God but God in Jesus Christ.

Here it may be helpful to consider the contemporary value of Pascal's wager in relation to the case of non-theists such as philosophical Buddhists who are interested in making the Exercises.[22] Pascal famously argued that since we cannot be rationally certain of God's existence, all of us must "wager" and live either as though God exists or doesn't exist. Pascal contends that we ought to wager "yes," since we have everything to gain, and doing so involves living in the way we would live if God existed. On his view, religious faith can develop only when we reach out and make ourselves available to God through our actions; those who do not pray or attend Mass, for instance, never really give faith a chance.[23] Many of these individuals—philosophical Buddhists and religiously unaffiliated individuals alike—already (to use Pascalian terms) live as though there is no God. They are familiar through their daily living with what unbelief looks like. Yet many if not most of these individuals have not had an extended opportunity to live as though God does exist, and the Exercises offer one of the most powerful ways of doing so—much more powerful, I would argue, than many other forms of religious practice, since the Exercises engage our hearts and minds deeply and (in the case of the full and complete Exercises) over an extended period of time. Ignatius consistently asks us to engage our imaginations; indeed, the use of the imagination in prayer is one of the most distinctive features of the Exercises, compared with other contemplative practices. Based on the centrality of the imagination to Ignatian methodology, a sound approach to adapting the Exercises for many non-theists—including philosophical Buddhists—is to ask them to imagine that God exists, and that Jesus

22. Pascal's wager is apt here, even though Pascal himself was an influential critic of the Jesuits.

23. Blaise Pascal, *Pensées and Other Writings*, trans. Honor Levi (New York: Oxford University Press, 1995), 152–58.

Christ is the revelation of God in humanity. Within the context of this approach, there is much room to adapt the Exercises on an individual basis, but without stripping away the theistic content of the Exercises. Moreover, there is the added benefit of allowing Buddhist exercitants to consider openly and honestly the differences between Buddhism and Christianity, instead of suggesting to them that our fundamental beliefs are all really the same. Such a claim not only misrepresents both traditions, robbing both of the distinctive insights they might contribute to our understanding of ourselves and the world; it also robs exercitants of the opportunity for spiritual growth to be found in a potential relationship with God, which may indeed be what drew them to the Exercises initially.

In this adaptation, both philosophical and theistic Buddhists would be invited to consider the Principle and Foundation in light of the possibility that God exists (which will likely be more challenging for philosophical Buddhists to entertain, since they are not already theists) and in light of the possibility that God creates us uniquely and out of great love and invites us to praise, reverence, and serve in response to this gift. The latter is a particularly striking contrast to the view that we, like all sentient beings, come into being as a result of the law of karma, and that our lives and bodies are shaped and determined by our previous actions. There is a reverence for life in the Buddhist tradition, a reverence that stems not from the idea that we are all created uniquely by God but from the idea that all sentient beings (animals and humans) are linked according to Buddhist beliefs about reincarnation: at the most basic level, perhaps I am a human in this life because I lived a good life as an animal in my previous life, and thus am experiencing the results of good karma through my human form. Buddhist views about the nature of the self also play an important role here. If there is no such thing as an essential, substantial self, then there is no essential, substantial difference between "my" suffering and that of others. If I fully grasp this truth, I should be led to seek not only my own liberation from suffering, but also that of all other sentient beings, who do not essentially differ from me. But, of course this sort of view differs markedly from a Christian view of, and care for, life, even if these views arrive at some similar conclusions.

At this juncture, Buddhists making the Exercises should be invited to reflect on the rich variety of resonances and contrasts between Ignatian spirituality and Buddhism, and they will likely need additional time with the Principle and Foundation in order to do this. Two aspects of the Principle and Foundation that ought to resonate with Buddhist sensibilities are, first, the invitation to experience the ways in which we are intimately related to all of creation—including not only other humans but other creatures and the natural world—and, second, the grace of indifference, which means that we hold all of God's gifts reverently, gratefully, and also loosely, embracing them or letting them go depending on how they help us to fulfill our vocation. The first resonates with the Buddhist tradition's emphasis on the value of all sentient life, while the latter resonates with Buddhist teachings concerning the suffering that results from becoming attached to impermanent things. However, there are deep and important differences between the Ignatian and Buddhist traditions on these matters; most notably, for Ignatius, as the Principle and Foundation makes clear, we are related to but not equal to or one with the rest of creation ("The other things on the face of the earth are created for the human beings, to help them in pursuit of the end for which they are created," SE 23). Buddhists do not view the world—or persons—as the creation of a loving God, and it is hard to overemphasize the significance of this difference. According to Buddhist teachings, we are not creatures whose existence depends on our Creator (a fact that also links us to one another). Rather, we are all the dependently arisen products of a vast, impersonal causal nexus that has no beginning. Such a view is much more similar to Western materialist views than it is to Christian theism. As a result of this deep contrast, Buddhists may need to spend more time simply considering the meaning of the phrase, "I am created" in their consideration of the Principle and Foundation. Additionally, it will be helpful to consider carefully what it means to regard the things of this world as *gifts*. While both traditions highlight the value of gratitude, for Ignatius this means being grateful for the gifts we are given in this world while also not clinging to them; Buddhists cannot really view these things as gifts proper, because a gift is something that is intentionally given by one person to another. Even to view our lives this way assumes a theistic view, and this feature of the Exercises will be much harder for many Buddhists to accept than Hindus. Yet both Ignatius and the Buddhist tradition emphasize the importance of not becoming overly attached to the things of this world, and this is an important point of resonance: Ignatius urges us to keep our entire life oriented toward the service of God and to remember that everything (even things that are painful and difficult) has the potential to call forth in us a more loving response to our life with God,[24] while Buddhism teaches that our attaching ourselves to things as though they are permanent ultimately leads only to suffering.

I want to stress that Buddhists need not reject traditional Buddhist teachings about attachment in order to appreciate and benefit from Ignatian insights about indifference. Indeed, the idea that we ought to hold all things loosely in order to make ourselves more available to serve God and others is not incompatible with the idea that attaching ourselves to impermanent things leads to suffering. Buddhists might see the Ignatian conception of indifference—and especially its emphasis on embracing different gifts lightly and letting them go depending upon how they help us to fulfill our vocation—as providing added strength and urgency to the claim that we should guard against unhealthy attachments to things, people, and ourselves. Indifference leads us to a certain passion or devotion or giving of self. The Ignatian emphasis on vocation offers an added dimension for Buddhists to consider, especially as it stems from the idea that each person is created uniquely and created to serve. While the latter stands in tension with certain aspects of Buddhism, as noted above, many Buddhists nevertheless have a strong sense of vocation, rooted in a commitment to working to liberate all beings from suffering. The Ignatian tradition, through the Exercises, offers an opportunity for Buddhists to consider further their vocations in light of another tradition.

One text that may be a helpful companion as Buddhist exercitants consider Ignatius's Principle and Foundation is the Buddha's sermon, "Getting Rid of All Cares and Troubles" (*Sabbasava-sutta*). The following selection presents a traditional Buddhist understanding of what it would mean to embrace different things lightly, guarding ourselves against attachment even to basic sources of physical sustenance:

Bhikkus [monks], what are the cares and troubles to be got rid of by use? Bhikkhus, a bhikku, considering wisely, makes use of his robes—only to keep off

---

24. Consider the encyclical letter *Laudato Si'*: Pope Francis discusses the sanctity of all natural life, but privileges human dignity (May 24, 2015, http://w2.vatican.va/content/francesco/en/encyclicals/documents/papa-francesco_20150524_enciclica-laudato-si.html).

cold, to keep off heat, to keep off gadflies, mosquitoes, winds and the sun, and creeping creatures, and to cover himself decently. Considering wisely, he makes use of food—neither for pleasures nor for excess (intoxication), neither for beauty nor for adornment, but only to support and sustain this body, to keep it from hurt (fatigue) and to foster the holy life, thinking: In this way I put out the feeling (of suffering, hunger) which is already there, and will not produce a new feeling, and my life will be maintained in blamelessness (harmlessness) and convenience.[25]

A crucial part of the first week centers on sin, and one of the graces or gifts sought is a sense of shame and confusion as we consider the destructive effects of sin in our own life and in the lives of others. Sin is a term that is strongly associated with Christianity, and this term may be a stumbling block, so it will be important to clarify for Buddhist exercitants the ways in which recognizing and confronting the reality of sin in the Exercises resonates with the emphasis on the reality of suffering in the Buddhist tradition, as well as Buddhist teachings about the Three Poisons, also known as the Three Root Evils, since they lie at the root of desire (and therefore suffering): attachment or greed (*rāga*), aversion or hate (*dvesa*), and delusion (*moha*). Sin need not be (and is not) understood exclusively in terms of a violation of God's laws or commands; as we saw in the previous chapter, for Hindus and also for Buddhists, as a result of our own sinful choices we are caught in the wheel of samsara, destined to be reborn again and again until we achieve enlightenment. According to the Buddhist tradition, only when we fully extinguish our desires do we become enlightened, and all desires lead to suffering and thereby represent sin. This is made clear in "The Fire Sermon," which may be a helpful Buddhist text to accompany the consideration of sin in the first week of the Exercises:

Bhikkus, all is burning. And what is the all that is burning? Bhikkus, the eye is burning, visual forms are burning, visual consciousness is burning, visual impression is burning, also whatever sensation, pleasant or painful or neither-painful-nor-pleasant, arises on account of the visual impression, that too is burning. Burning with what? Burning with the fire of lust, with the fire of

---

25. "Getting Rid of All Cares and Troubles (Sabbasava-sutta)" in *What the Buddha Taught*, trans. Walpola Rahula (New York: Grove Press, 1974), 103.

hate, with the fire of delusion; I say it is burning with birth, aging and death, with sorrows, with lamentations, with pains, with griefs, with despairs.[26]

The text continues, noting how every fiber of our being—ear, nose, tongue, body, mind—is burning with desire and attachment, finally noting what we must do to bring this suffering to an end:

Bhikkus, a learned and noble disciple, who sees (things) thus, becomes dispassionate with regard to the eye.... He becomes dispassionate with regard to the ear, with regard to sounds.... He becomes dispassionate with regard to the nose ... with regard to odours.... He becomes dispassionate with regard to the tongue ... with regard to flavours.... He becomes dispassionate with regard to the body ... with regard to tangible things.... He becomes dispassionate with regard to the mind.... Being dispassionate, he becomes detached; through detachment he is liberated.[27]

There are some important connections between Ignatius's understanding of sin and Buddhist views of suffering. Gerald Fagin, SJ, stresses that when we are sinful we "consume rather than cherish and misuse rather than share," which is why we ought to see sin as "rooted in possessiveness and a sense of self-sufficiency that leads to an inability and unwillingness to respond to the call of discipleship."[28] On a Buddhist view, these elements of sin point toward our tendency to attach ourselves to things as though they are permanent, and thus to desire them, which leads to our suffering and the suffering of others. As we proceed with considering the specific meditations that are a part of the first week of the Exercises, it is important to keep all of this in mind. As the adaptations outlined below suggest, Buddhist exercitants should be encouraged to explore understandings of sin and suffering in their own tradition alongside Ignatian views of sin, instead of simply focusing on Buddhist views of suffering as a *replacement* for the Ignatian meditations on sin that are a part of the first week. My adaptations will highlight the fact that Buddhist views of suffering cannot serve as a replacement for Ignatian views of sin because they differ in key

---

26. "The Fire Sermon (Adittapariyaya-sutta)," in Rahula, *What the Buddha Taught*, 95.
27. Ibid., 96.
28. Gerald Fagin, SJ, *Putting On the Heart of Christ: How the Spiritual Exercises Invite Us to a Virtuous Life* (Chicago: Loyola Press, 2010), 54, 56. See also the Meditation on Two Standards in the second week of the Spiritual Exercises (SE 136–48), where the temptations of riches, honors, and excessive pride are central.

ways. Additionally, we must remember that one of the aims of adapting the Exercises for Buddhists is to provide them with an experience that differs in important ways from Buddhist retreats and can thereby be enriching in new ways.

While at first glance it may seem that Buddhist accounts of suffering and the meditations on sin in the first week of the Exercises focus on the same aspects of human experience, in fact the content of these meditations can help us to see more clearly the differences between suffering in the Buddhist tradition and sin in the Christian tradition. Note that the graces or gifts we pray for at this point in the Exercises include a healthy sense of shame and confusion as we confront the reality of sin and consider the effects of sin in our lives and in the lives of others. This is most significant: the aim is not simply to appreciate the effects of sin, but to feel shame as a result of recognizing that we intentionally participate in sin by making choices that hurt God, others, and ourselves. Put simply, acknowledging our own sinful nature differs from acknowledging the reality of suffering, because sin takes into account our role in gravely wounding ourselves and the rest of creation. According to Christianity, *we* are to blame for this state we are in. As O'Brien points out, the goal is not "to become mired in guilt, self-hate, or despair," but to grapple with the reality of sin in our own lives, which is necessary for healing and growth: "Knowing how good God is to us, how and why do we still choose to sin, still choose to respond so meagerly to God's generosity?"[29] Now, certainly, the Exercises aim to help us to experience the depth and reality of the suffering that we (and others) cause through our sinful choices; this is where we can see the convergence with Buddhist affirmations of the reality of suffering and the fact that suffering characterizes every aspect of human life.

Another key way in which the concept of sin in the Exercises differs from Buddhist views of suffering is that, while sin can be described in many ways, all of them are inherently theistic: a breakdown of a relationship with God and others, a failure to love God, others, and self; a turning away from God; abuse of the freedom God gives us; choices that

---

29. Kevin O'Brien, SJ, *The Ignatian Adventure: Experiencing the Spiritual Exercises of Saint Ignatius in Daily Life* (Chicago: Loyola Press, 2011), 90.

hurt God, others, and ourselves.[30] This is the central reason why the first week is not simply an exercise in miring ourselves in guilt and despair: even as we experience the depth and reality of sin, "we recall that God loves us unconditionally and wants to free us from anything that blocks our growing into the people God calls us to be. We don't get very far just by counting our sins and trying to overcome them by sheer force of will. Instead, we need to keep our eyes fixed on God's ever-present mercy, which is the ultimate source of our lasting liberation from sin."[31] Here we can see very clearly the contrast between Ignatius's view of sin and Buddhist views, and not just in the different understandings of what constitutes liberation, but in the way it is achieved, as well. Fundamental to Buddhism is the recognition that as a result of our own sinful choices, we are caught in the wheel of samsara, destined to be reborn again and again until we extinguish our desires—and our suffering—completely. For philosophical Buddhists, meditative practice serves a key role in helping us to overcome suffering. While we do not do this entirely just by sheer force of will—most Zen Buddhists, for instance, would contend that it is only through the habit of disciplined practice over time, with the proper forms of guidance and support, that one makes progress—there is not an external force or entity that is the ultimate source of our liberation from sin. So this is one place where those Buddhists who align more with philosophical forms of Buddhism will need to engage their imaginations, and imagine that God exists, and see what that might mean for them. In contrast, theistic Buddhists, at this stage, may find it helpful to consider the ideal of the bodhisattva, who according to the Buddhist tradition extends mercy and compassion to those who are trying to work toward enlightenment. Pure Land Buddhists (the most widely practiced form of Buddhism in Japan) may also find it helpful to consider the boundless compassion and wisdom of Amida Buddha, the Buddha of Infinite Light. While the love, compassion, and wisdom of these figures differ in a number of ways from what Ignatius sees as God's ever-present mercy being the source of our liberation from sin, they will be helpful to theistic Buddhists as a stepping stone to help them understand and benefit from the Exercises.

30. See ibid.
31. Ibid., 91.

Three meditations make up the first exercise of the first week: a meditation on the sin of the angels, a meditation on the sin of Adam and Eve, and a meditation on the sin of one person, followed by a colloquy with Jesus on the cross. Since these meditations are designed to help us to understand that our sin is not an isolated act in human history, but a fundamental part of the human condition, it may be helpful for Buddhists to consider the stories of the sin of the angels and the sin of Adam and Eve alongside the early life of the historical Buddha. After being introduced to the sin of the angels and considering how they chose to use their gift of freedom by making the radical choice to reject God's love, Buddhist exercitants might consider the choice of the Buddha's father to shield his son from all pain and suffering by keeping him within the palace walls. Exercitants should use their imaginations to see what a radical choice this was, and the way in which it resulted in his son's isolation within the palace walls, and a life of hedonistic pleasure that was thoroughly devoid of generosity and concern for those less fortunate, a life not lived in service of others. Considering this scene and especially the dramatic choice of a parent to limit the possibilities of a child whose life has such potential to begin with, it may be helpful to revisit Ignatius's words from the meditation on the sin of the angels in the Spiritual Exercises: ". . . how they were created in grace and then, not wanting to better themselves by using their freedom to reverence and obey their Creator and Lord, they fell into pride, were changed from grace to malice, and were hurled from heaven into hell" (SE 50). Exercitants should avoid jumping further in the story of the historical Buddha, remaining with the scene of the Buddha's father's choices and the way in which they confined his son to a world of self-centeredness and prevented him from recognizing the deep suffering and needs of others. Exercitants then might consider those times when they have chosen to use their freedom in a rebellious, destructive way, choosing self-centeredness over concern for others.

Along similar lines, after considering the sin of Adam and Eve, it may be helpful to consider another vignette from the early life of the historical Buddha. One of the things that the sin of Adam and Eve highlights for us is the strong temptation to make ourselves something other than we are created to be. For Adam and Eve, this is the temptation to try to become like God or to make themselves valuable in God's eyes. Similarly, after realizing that his father created an illusory world for him inside the palace walls, the Buddha initially embraced the life of a Hindu ascetic, and in doing so went to the opposite extreme: instead of living a life of self-indulgence, he lived a life of self-denial, depriving himself of even the most basic forms of physical sustenance and comfort. Again, exercitants should imagine this scene in detail. It was very tempting for the Buddha to embrace the path that others had taken, and this was done partly out of rebellion against his early life, yet it did not lead him closer to the truth. In considering this story, Buddhist exercitants might consider not only how their own sinful choices have involved rebellion but also how such choices have involved attempts to make themselves into something they are not or to blindly follow along with others out of a desire for acceptance or recognition. This may be helpful in a preparatory way for the parts of the Exercises that will require consideration of one's own vocation.

The third meditation on sin—the sin of one person—lends itself to the consideration of stories from the Buddhist tradition even more than the first two, for Ignatius invites us to consider the particular sin of anyone who acts definitively against God. The language here is, of course, theistic, and Ignatius's view is very Catholic: he understands this to be a person who has gone to hell for a mortal sin. A Buddhist adaptation here will require us to help exercitants think about those who act in ways that are thoroughly self-centered and whose choices harm themselves and others. This is a good place for them to think about stories in their tradition of individuals who act sinfully, and who have isolated themselves from others through their sin. Traditional guides to the Exercises provide many suggestions that will be just as helpful for Buddhists as they are for Christians. O'Brien, for example, suggests that exercitants may wish to craft their own parables at this point in the Exercises, considering sin, violence, genocide, and injustice in the contemporary world, and ask themselves, "When have I failed to notice or respond to the needs of others? When have I felt isolated from God or others by my own sin?" It is worth noting that these questions are not exclusively theistic; in answering the second question, one might choose to focus on how sin has isolated one from others. But the adaptation must be balanced in this regard. In order to avoid bleaching out the content of the Exercises too much,

Buddhist exercitants should continue to examine biblical stories, such as the parable of the rich man and Lazarus (Lk 16:19–31), alongside stories and examples from their own tradition. This will continue to provide them with opportunities to learn more about Christian understandings of God, to entertain the possibility that God exists, and to consider who God is. It will be important to remember that the Exercises—for Christians and members of other faiths alike—represent an opportunity to open oneself up to a different kind of religious experience or encounter, and if the traditional content of the Exercises is thinned out too much, we may not be providing enough space for this to occur. Additionally, as non-theists (such as philosophical Buddhists) and those who have different conceptions of God or gods (such as theistic Buddhists) progress further in the Exercises, they will need to be able to engage, in increasing degrees of depth, with the very possibility and idea of God. The first week is preparatory for, and facilitates, the richness of that experience.

Following the first three meditations of the first week comes the first of multiple points in the Exercises where the exercitant is asked to use her imagination to place herself before Jesus suspended on the cross. As we saw in the previous chapter, Ignatius's text is fully grounded in Christian theology here, as exercitants are to ask themselves, "How is it that he, although he is the Creator, has come to make himself a human being? How is it that he passed from eternal life to death here in time, and to die in this way for my sins?" (SE 53). I suggested in the previous chapter that Hindu exercitants might instead simply follow the concluding part of Ignatius's instructions: "As I look upon Jesus as he hangs upon the cross, I ponder whatever God may bring to my attention,"[32] and this is what I would suggest for Buddhist exercitants as well. Additionally, like Hindu exercitants, Buddhists may find it helpful at this point to begin by making colloquies with more familiar figures from their own tradition. For instance, they might be invited to consider what sort of colloquy they would have with the Buddha when he was struggling to follow the way of a Hindu ascetic. Looking back on the times that they have found themselves tempted to try to be god-like or to be someone they are not, what would they say to him? What would he say to them? Buddhist exerci-

---

32. David Fleming, SJ, *Draw Me into Your Friendship: A Literal Translation and a Contemporary Reading of The Spiritual Exercises* (St. Louis, Mo.: Institute of Jesuit Sources, 1996), 49.

tants might also consider a colloquy with a particular bodhisattva such as Guanyin (Kannon in Japan), the Goddess of Mercy and the most popular Buddhist deity in East Asia (whom I discuss later in this chapter). Pure Land Buddhists may find a colloquy with Amida Buddha helpful here. By allowing exercitants to begin to experience colloquies within the familiar terrain of their own tradition, we can in some cases help to set the stage not only for a colloquy with Jesus, but for future colloquies.[33]

The next exercise of the first week is a meditation on one's own personal history of sin. Ignatius writes, "I will call to memory all the sins of my life, looking at them year by year or period by period. For this three things will be helpful: first, the locality or house where I lived; second, the associations which I had with others; third, the occupation I was pursuing" (SE 56). Traditional versions of the Exercises ask exercitants to invite God to lead them through their life history, revealing those moments where they failed to love God, others, or themselves. One always keeps in mind God's goodness and mercy. As O'Brien points out, one cannot help but be struck, as one reviews one's personal history of sin in this way, at the blessings, as well: "So many have loved me and helped me along life's journey. I am filled with wonder at God's generosity—and yet I am ashamed because I still choose to act selfishly or with excessive self-interest. I fail to notice or appreciate the gifts of God (including my talents and abilities). God offers me freedom, yet I choose to be bound by self-preoccupations and petty concerns."[34] For Buddhists, the obvious challenge is found in the idea of having *God* lead you through your life history, noting the ways in which you failed to love *God*, and noting God's generosity—including the idea that God is our creator, who gives us freedom and gifts like our talents and abilities. The Exercises are about offering a life-giving perspective that moves away from self to the divine perspective. How might we adapt the Exercises for Buddhists who find these ideas to be a stumbling block? Buddhists can certainly complete

33. As I indicated in the chapter on Hinduism, the possible adaptation of addressing prayers to deities from one's own religious tradition is designed to serve as a stepping stone or intermediary step that will help exercitants from other faiths to become more comfortable with Ignatian ways of praying. Spiritual directors who are uncomfortable having exercitants include other deities might instead consider removing colloquies or other prayers that are stumbling blocks for exercitants, or they may decide to shift to an eighteenth-annotation retreat.

34. O'Brien, *The Ignatian Adventure*, 99.

the meditation on our own sins without these specifically theistic elements, and the justification for such a practice may lie in returning to the text of the Exercises itself. If we look closely at SE 55–61, in which Ignatius details the five points of this exercise, we find that the first two points do not refer to God at all, while the third point contains a passing reference. The fourth and fifth points discuss God and the angels, but do not contain the heart of the exercise. If we simply look at the first three points, here is what Ignatius says:

The First Point is the court-record of my sins. I will call to memory all the sins of my life, looking at them year by year or period by period. For this three things will be helpful: first, the locality or house where I lived; second, the associations which I had with others; third, the occupation I was pursuing. *The Second Point* is to ponder these sins, looking at the foulness and evil which every mortal sin would contain in itself, even if it were not forbidden. *The Third Point*. I will reflect upon myself, by using examples which humble me: First, what am I when compared with all other human beings? Second, what are they when compared with all the angels and saints in paradise? Third, what is all of creation when compared with God? And then, I alone—what can I be? Fourth, I will look at all the corruption and foulness of my body. Fifth, I will look upon myself as a sore and abscess from which have issued such great sins and iniquities and such foul poison.[35]

I quote this passage in full because it is important to remember how dynamic the practice of giving the Exercises is and thus how much has been, and is, added to the Exercises when we give them to others. As we can see, Ignatius does not use theistic language in the bulk of his account of this meditation. He does not, for instance, say that one ought to review one's life history by imagining that God is leading one through it. In cases like this one, then, we are not in fact stripping away theistic content from the Exercises; Ignatius's own description of the first three points of this exercise do not contain stumbling blocks for those who do not share his view of God. The gift or grace that one prays for is, as Ignatius puts it, "growing and intense sorrow and tears for my sins," and this is certainly something that Buddhists can do without much adaptation.

---

35. George Ganss, SJ, trans., *The Spiritual Exercises of Saint Ignatius* (Chicago: Loyola Press, 1992), 43–44. It is worth noting how specific Ignatius is: the details of a human life are where our salvation history plays out; our choices matter, and this fact is a reflection of our freedom.

The meditation on one's own sins concludes with a colloquy of mercy, and finally, a triple colloquy addressed to Mary, Jesus, and God the Father. Theistic Buddhists, like Hindus, here might focus on what is really at the heart of the triple colloquy: "even in our very real and visceral struggle with sin, Ignatius reminds us that we are surrounded by divine company and help. We are not alone."[36] Theistic Buddhists, too, believe that humans are surrounded by divine company and help, and, as I argued in the chapter on Hinduism, there are varying levels or degrees of adaptation that one might use here for those who recognize multiple deities, and much depends on whether the exercitant finds praying to Mary, Jesus, and God the Father to be a stumbling block. It is important not to dismiss the opportunity for Buddhists to acquaint themselves with Mary, Jesus, and God the Father, but if exercitants struggle with the triple colloquy at this stage, they might first try a colloquy with more familiar deities, as an initial step that is preparatory for a more traditional triple colloquy. Again, it will be important to see this as a *process*, so what works for a colloquy early in the Exercises may help to facilitate something different later, and spiritual directors will have to help gauge what the exercitant wants and needs as she grows at each stage. Spiritual directors and exercitants must also continue to discern whether this retreat is an appropriate fit for exercitants who are encountering serious stumbling blocks. In the midst of adaptations, the content of the triple colloquy, however, should remain intact: most important is to pray for an interior knowledge of one's sinful tendencies, choices and actions, for the grace to truly abhor them, to understand how they have caused disorder in one's life and in the lives of others, to recognize the things that get in the way of loving and serving God, and for a desire to turn away from worldly and vain things. Also essential to the effectiveness of the triple colloquy is the repetition of these prayers multiple times (addressed to different persons), as is the sense of humility and reverence that is generated by beginning with Mary, and then praying to Jesus, and finally to God the Father. Here, the more that spiritual directors note and understand about the different elements of the Exercises and how they function, the better they will be able to help exercitants to find adaptations that are effective.

36. O'Brien, *The Ignatian Adventure*, 101.

For philosophical Buddhists, who are primarily non-theists, there are different approaches that might work better at this stage. As I suggested earlier, given Ignatius's emphasis on the imagination, it makes a great deal of sense to ask exercitants who are not certain that they believe in God to engage their imaginations and *imagine* that God is real in order to pray a colloquy. Given the nature of a colloquy—which for Ignatius involves speaking "as a friend speaks to a friend, as a person speaks to one whom he or she has offended, or as a child speaks to a parent or mentor, or as a lover speaks to his or her beloved"—this might be the easiest form of prayer for some exercitants to try, since it involves speaking very naturally, as one would speak to another person. Those who still find these colloquies to be a roadblock might focus more on the content of the prayer than to whom it is addressed. The exercitant might speak words of gratitude for her life, and propose amendment for the future. She might offer these words as a mantra or chant—words that in the Buddhist tradition are not necessarily directed toward a deity but are prayerful, in some ways analogous to the recitation of a creed. There are also a variety of traditional Buddhist chants that might be helpful additions here. For instance, Habito notes the resonances between the themes of the first week and the "Verse of Purification," a Buddhist scriptural text that is often chanted in unison by Zen practitioners: "All harmful karma ever committed by me since of old, On account of my beginningless greed, anger, and ignorance, Born of my body, mouth, and consciousness, Now I atone it all."[37] Such a verse could easily be incorporated into a colloquy offered by a Buddhist exercitant. But the content that Ignatius offers is unique and should not be left behind. Fleming captures this well in his contemporary reading of the Exercises, noting that in the triple colloquy we pray for "(1) a deep realization of what sin in my life is, and a feeling of abhorrence at my own sinful acts; (2) some understanding and a feeling for the disorder in my life due to sin and sinful tendencies, that I may begin to know how to amend my life and bring order into it; (3) an insight into the world that stands opposed to Christ, that I may put off from myself all that is worldly and vain."[38] It is worth noting that one need not hold Christian theological beliefs about who Jesus is to appreciate what it

37. Habito, *Zen and the Spiritual Exercises*, 53.

38. Fleming, *Draw Me into Your Friendship*, 55–57.

means to note the ways in which the world stands opposed to Christ, in its emphasis on worldly honors, prestige, and rampant materialism. For all of their differences, in their rejection of these values, the Buddhist and Christian traditions are in agreement.

A meditation on hell concludes the first week. Under the influence of the Hindu tradition, the Buddhist tradition, too, developed an account of multiple hells that are temporary places of punishment prior to rebirth. Also like the Hindu tradition, the Buddhist tradition depicts the hells vividly in literature and art. For theistic Buddhists, such images may be helpful at this point in the Exercises; most philosophical Buddhists do not accept such accounts of the hells. But like Hindus, even Buddhists who believe in the hells will likely find it challenging to fully grasp the meaning and significance of the meditation on hell in the Exercises simply with reference to their own tradition's hells, because the hells do not represent a permanent or eternal state. As a result, for both theistic and philosophical Buddhists, it will be helpful to follow Fleming's contemporary translation of this exercise, discussed in the previous chapter, but with some particular Buddhist adaptations. As a starting place, Buddhist exercitants may find it helpful to meditate on the first noble truth—all is suffering—and consider the possibility that the first noble truth is all there is. The basic aim of the meditation on hell is to appreciate what Fleming calls "the total emptiness of living without purpose, an environment pervasive with hatred and self-seeking, a living death."[39] Exercitants might focus on what this means within the context of traditional Buddhist views of enlightenment and suffering: a world without hope would mean a world in which there is no possibility of freeing any beings (let alone all beings) from suffering, no possibility of liberation from the cycle of rebirth, no possibility of ever breaking free of our desires and attachments. Theistic Buddhists might be invited to consider what a world without any divine assistance would look like: no bodhisattvas to offer compassion and mercy, and no god to offer a new and hopeful path away from the experience of sin that has been the focus of previous prayer periods. In order to better understand the emptiness and despair of a world without God, philosophical Buddhists might first

39. Ibid., 59.

need to engage their imaginations with respect to the possibility of God: the idea of one who comes to bring hope, meaning, and purpose to the lives of all, particularly in light of the depth of human sin and suffering. At the heart of the meditation on hell is the complete absence of hope in light of our suffering and brokenness. For both theistic and philosophical Buddhists, it will also be helpful to make use of O'Brien's suggestions concerning contemporary images of hell in the world today; along similar lines, Habito suggests that meditating on the current state of our world and then imagining a caring, harmonious world would be helpful to Zen Buddhists at this stage.[40]

An Adaptation of the Ignatian Spiritual Exercises for Buddhists: The Second Week

The conclusion of the first week and the beginning of the second week of the Exercises offers an opportunity to review the overarching aims of adapting the Exercises for Buddhists. The two primary things we identified as unique potential fruits of the Exercises for Buddhists are, first, the opportunity to have a different sort of religious experience—particularly in the possibility of an encounter and relationship with God and with the person of Jesus Christ; and second, the opportunity to cultivate virtues like humility, generosity, and mindfulness, and the ability to make decisions grounded in one's faith. While all of these aims relate to one's spiritual life, the latter are primarily focused on helping individuals to lead ethically better lives, while the former concerns religious experience and belief. Through a consideration of one's life in the first week (especially with reference to sin), the Exercises at this point have already offered considerable opportunities for ethical growth. But while the experience of the first week has helped to lay the groundwork for the opportunity to have a different sort of religious experience or encounter, the second week of the Exercises more squarely draws the exercitant into an encounter with Jesus. For many, this is precisely the problem or challenge of adapting the Exercises for non-Christians. However, readers must remember the argument presented in the first two chapters of this

---

40. See O'Brien, *The Ignatian Adventure*, 105–6; Habito, *Zen and the Spiritual Exercises*, 77.

book, especially in light of the fact that those who have a desire to make the Ignatian Spiritual Exercises are not—and should not be—clueless as to their Christian content—indeed, the content of the Exercises is an important part of why they are drawn to the Exercises. As a result, the adaptations that I outline in this chapter for the second week, which turns on the task of accompanying Jesus Christ on mission, are designed to help Buddhist exercitants to have a deeper experience of Jesus Christ. As with the first week, exercitants and spiritual directors will find it helpful to begin by focusing on the traditional graces of the second week of the Exercises, and then focusing on the gifts the exercitant is seeking. Some of the central questions for exercitants to consider in the second week stem from looking long and hard at the person of Jesus Christ: What attracts me to this way of being? What attracts me to goodness? How do I grow in my desire to follow that path? These questions help us to see that the twin aims or fruits of the Exercises for Buddhists—one of which concerns religious experience and the other of which is primarily ethical in nature—are in fact closely related.

In this chapter, I once again follow Veltri in moving the Contemplation on the Kingdom of Jesus Christ from its traditional place at the opening of the second week to later in the second week, so that it follows the Contemplations on the Incarnation, the Nativity, and the Hidden Life. This change allows members of other faith traditions to get better acquainted with Jesus through the Contemplations on the Incarnation, the Nativity, and the Hidden Life before considering the Call of Christ, our King—a change that is particularly important for an adaptation that addresses different kinds of Buddhism. Theistic Buddhists will need time to get acquainted with a different conception of God before considering how that God may or may not be calling them; philosophical Buddhists, on the other hand, are primarily non-theists and thus need more time to get acquainted with the very idea of a real, living God. In the Exercises, this occurs by becoming acquainted with the person of Jesus Christ, and it is helpful to recall the threefold sequence Ignatius offers: to know Jesus, to love Jesus, and follow Jesus. For those of other faith traditions, we begin with the first of these, simply offering the Exercises as what they are in their purest form: an opportunity to get to know Jesus "as he walked and talked, healed and preached, among us. The grace of the second week is fundamental: to grow in a heartfelt knowledge of Jesus Christ so that we can love him more deeply and follow him more closely. But to grow in this intimate love, we need to get close."[41] This closeness is pivotal in a Buddhist adaptation, where exercitants do not begin with an understanding of why one should love and follow Jesus, or what that might entail. While some Buddhists with an interest in making the Exercises may already be drawn to Christianity with the possibility of conversion in mind, others may be curious about Jesus or view Christianity as an alternative path toward enlightenment, with potentially enriching resources. In the latter case, individuals would likely be motivated to make the Exercises out of some sense of dissatisfaction with Buddhist practices, or some sense of wanting more. Such individuals will have different responses to the very idea of following Jesus and what it might mean for them. While it would be tempting to sort out these theological possibilities up front, this is not what the Exercises have us do. Spiritual directors, then, must simply allow the Gospels to come alive, and allow Buddhists, like Christians, to be there with Jesus, immersed in his story with the help of their imaginations. We must remember that this is not about gaining information; for those who wish to learn more about Christianity, there are many avenues. Rather, the Exercises allow us to see the living God in daily life. Nevertheless, a Buddhist adaptation will need to address some of the theological views that are woven into the second week, while also helping Buddhists to experience how Jesus might stand in relation to the central themes, images, stories, and values of the Buddhist tradition.

The second week opens with the Contemplation on the Incarnation, and the traditional graces sought are to know Jesus intimately, to love him more intensely, and so to follow him more closely. Buddhists will focus primarily on seeking the gift of knowing Jesus intimately, though they should also look for what is inspiring or appealing about his way. Philosophical Buddhists here can shift their energy away from imagining that God exists, to the task of contemplating the life of a real person. These two tasks are not unrelated, of course, but for now the focus should be on the real, lived details of Jesus' life. Theistic Buddhists are likely to have an easier time considering Jesus' divinity from the outset because

---

41. O'Brien, *The Ignatian Adventure*, 124–25.

there is a sort of analogue to this in the Buddhist tradition: humans who are also divine. Now, the opening contemplation of the second week, the Contemplation on the Incarnation, asks us to imagine the three Divine Persons gazing upon "the whole surface or circuit of the world, full of people" and, seeing their sin and suffering, deciding that the second person should become human in order to save the human race (SE 102). It is worth noting that Ignatius's text at this point in the Exercises is not concerned to explicate the three Divine Persons; he does not describe them, but instead, in all three points of this exercise his primary focus is on seeing what the persons on earth are doing and the response of the Divine Persons (SE 106–8). Once again, we see how remaining close to the text of the Exercises can help us avoid wading into deep theological waters in the process of adaptation. Buddhists should imagine the scene; spiritual directors can briefly introduce them to the idea of one God in three Persons, but there is no need for further explication here. For theistic Buddhists, the idea of multiple divine persons is not problematic or foreign. For philosophical Buddhists, it will be important to focus on the suffering of humanity that ultimately leads to Jesus' life and ministry. Additional theological detail is unnecessary; Ignatius's text invites us to operate with a thin theology, but it is important for any adaptation to take note of the words the Divine Persons speak: "Let us work the redemption of the human race" (SE 107). Jesus is not coincidentally born into the world; he is sent as a direct response to the needs of people. The idea that the world is filled with suffering is absolutely central to the Buddhist tradition, so the idea that this need existed should not be problematic for Buddhist exercitants, but what will be new is the consideration of the following questions: "How do the three Divine Persons respond to the joys and sufferings of the world? How does the God who is Love respond to us, God's children, who are lost, aimless, suffering, sinning, confused, and hurting?"[42] These can be presented as questions to consider as Buddhist exercitants witness the story for themselves. Here and in subsequent places that involve God's role and purpose, philosophical Buddhists will need to grant or imagine that God exists.

The Exercises next ask us to consider the Annunciation, followed by

42. Ibid., 130.

the Contemplation on the Nativity. In these contemplations, Buddhists should simply witness the story with their mind's eye, looking upon Mary as she is greeted by God's messenger and as she and Joseph struggle to make sense of the events unfolding in their lives. They should view this as precisely what it is: an opportunity to acquaint themselves with who God is and how God works, by observing those he has chosen and called. Throughout the Exercises, as Buddhists contemplate Jesus' life, they will need to grant the possibility that certain miraculous events occurred, and that God intervened in history. Most forms of Buddhism affirm the view that deities come out of pure and unlimited compassion to assist human beings, and for such Buddhists, miracles should not be particularly problematic in and of themselves. But the events of Jesus' life are not a part of Buddhist teachings. Accordingly, Buddhists will need to consider, as openly as possible, the idea that these events occurred, and ask themselves what that would mean for them. As I argued in the previous chapter on Hinduism, resolving theological questions relating to religious pluralism, such as whether or not God is one or many, should not be the focus for any exercitant, any more than they would be for Christians making the Exercises—whose theological questions are often just as complex. These questions must be set aside so that witnessing the events of Jesus' life can remain central during the prayer periods.

Mary is central to the contemplations that open the second week. Among the elements that exercitants should note about Mary in the Annunciation are what Fleming calls her "complete way of being available and responding to her Lord and God," despite the potentially disastrous consequences for her, and her initial fear followed by her tremendous faith.[43] The centrality of Mary as mother offers a unique opportunity to engage the Buddhist tradition. One of the most popular Buddhist deities today is the female bodhisattva Guanyin, the Goddess of Mercy, who is often depicted in iconography as having a thousand arms to reach out to those in need. While not a mother, Guanyin is also known as the "Giver of Sons;" many theistic Buddhists pray to her as a fertility goddess. Guanyin's name means "Perceiving the Cries of the World," which underscores her role as a responsive, merciful goddess who stands by to hear

43. Fleming, *Draw Me into Your Friendship*, 131.

the prayers of those in need. Theistic Buddhists who recognize Guanyin as an important figure might be invited to reflect on the differences between Mary, a human mother who responds with faith and a resounding "yes" to God—and whose response enables the birth of a savior into the world—and Guanyin, a deity with a posture of openness, generosity, and mercy. Guanyin's name describes her as one who hears the cries of the world; after contemplating the Incarnation, exercitants might recall those times when they have felt that Guanyin (or another bodhisattva) has heard them and responded. What feelings do these experiences evoke? How did Mary, in her situation, respond to the cries or needs of the world?

The Contemplation on the Kingdom of Christ offers the opportunity to recognize explicitly that the Exercises include an opportunity to follow Christ, and helps guide the exercitant through a process of understanding what this means over and against other possibilities. We begin by contemplating an admirable worldly leader—someone who inspires us to follow him in order to make the world a more just and loving place. One example of such a leader that might resonate with many Buddhists is the ancient Indian Buddhist emperor Ashoka (304–232 BCE), and reviewing his story may be helpful for this contemplation. Next we are asked to contemplate following Christ, as he calls to each of us, asking us to be with him and labor with him. Ignatius suggests that there are two responses: the response of those who dedicate themselves to laboring for the kingdom, and the response of those who not only do that, but devote themselves also to being with Christ and imitating his way of living. While individuals are not expected to make this offering at this point of the Exercises, the consideration of it will be challenging for Buddhists. One of the primary questions raised in the first part of the contemplation for members of other faiths is why Christ should be regarded as the eternal King. As I noted in the chapter on Hinduism, the Call comes at a pivotal time in the Exercises; it will not be possible for exercitants to continue on with the Exercises (to the consideration of Jesus' public ministry, the three meditations of the second week, and the consideration of Jesus' death and resurrection in the third and fourth weeks) without at least seriously entertaining the possibility that Jesus has a special role in relation to humanity. Ivens notes that the Call is fundamentally *preparatory* in nature; it ought to prepare exercitants "to meet Christ in a new way."[44] The right sort of adaptation for Buddhists, then, ought to facilitate a more comfortable, deeper relationship with Jesus.

Fleming writes that there are two unequal parts in this exercise, "the first one naturally leading to the more important second part. The parable of the temporal king is meant only to help contemplate the life of Christ our eternal king."[45] This insight is particularly helpful in considering how to adapt the Exercises, because it directs our attention to the *purpose* of the exercise and can thereby help us to think of ways to achieve that purpose for those who might struggle with this exercise in its traditional form. In the previous chapter the adaptation I recommended for Hindus involves adding an additional step in between consideration of a worldly leader and Christ, during which Hindus would consider the call of an eternal king from their own tradition. The added step is designed to help make the contemplation of the Call of Christ the King more accessible for those who find it difficult, by first contemplating a deity or other figure from their own tradition. I want to recommend an added step for Buddhists, as well, but instead of contemplating a deity from the Buddhist tradition, I suggest the use of a widely known and beloved parable from the Buddhist tradition. John Veltri, SJ, notes how helpful engagement with myths or parables can be at this point in the Exercises; he suggests adapting the Call by having exercitants write out their own personal myths, "a story that captures imaginatively all the desires of one's heart and then brings that story to prayer. Since the Kingdom exercise is built around Ignatius' own personal story or myth (that is, how he longed to serve an earthly king and conquer the moors and create a Christian world!) the directee can create her own parable too."[46] Veltri highlights the way in which such an adaptation is faithful to Ignatius's own vision of the Exercises. Picking up on the key role of personal story or myth, I suggest the use of a Buddhist story to help translate the Exercises for Buddhists. This particular story has the potential to resonate with many different kinds of Buddhists, and serves as a powerful exam-

44. Michael Ivens, SJ, *Understanding the Spiritual Exercises* (Leominster, U.K.: Gracewing, 1998), 78.

45. Fleming, *Draw Me into Your Friendship*, 83.

46. John Veltri, SJ, *Orientations*, vol. 2, *A Manual to Aid Beginning Directors of the Spiritual Exercises according to Annotation 19* (Guelph, Ontario, Canada: Loyola House, 1981), 89.

ple of what the call of a leader in the Buddhist tradition sounds like. It will, as we shall see, also offer an interesting and productive comparison with Christ's call—one that shines a light on important differences and similarities between Buddhism and Christianity.

The Platform Sutra, one of the most influential and widely known texts in the Buddhist tradition, opens with the story of Huineng (638–713 CE), the man destined to become the leader (the sixth patriarch) of the Southern school of the Chan Buddhist tradition. Patriarchs in the Chan tradition were believed to represent a direct line of disciples stretching back to the Buddha himself, and each time a new patriarch was named, the robe and bowl of the Buddha was passed on to him. Accordingly, Huineng's biography offers a window into how Buddhist leaders have been understood. The text tells us that Huineng's father died when he was a child, and his mother raised him alone. They were very poor and he did not go to school, instead helping his mother to earn a living by peddling firewood. One day in the marketplace he heard someone chanting the *Diamond Sutra*—one of the most famous Buddhist sutras in East Asia (and which also became a central object of study and devotion in Zen Buddhism)—and upon hearing it, Huineng said, "my mind became clear and I was awakened." Huineng realized that he was predestined to go and study with the Chan leader (the fifth patriarch) Hongren. Huineng's status as a commoner and his lack of education are central to the story; despite and perhaps even because of his lack of social status or formal education, he understood the highest truths of Buddhism.[47] After arriving at the Buddhist monastery, he was belittled by other monks for his illiteracy and lack of education, and assigned the most menial task in the monastery: that of a rice pounder. But soon after Huineng's arrival, Hongren held a competition to choose his successor: the monk who wrote the best poem to express the truths of Buddhism would win. The head

47. These features of the story express the view that spiritual wisdom is not a result of any form of privilege or learning, but rather "flows spontaneously out of an original and perfectly pure and innocent nature shared by all people—as well as all creatures and things. In Buddhist texts such as the Platform Sutra, this common endowment is Buddha-nature (*foxing*). The implications of this claim are many and profound but perhaps the greatest is that it entails an absolute spiritual and moral equality among human beings. All people are fundamentally Buddhas and would act as Buddhas do if only they could get in touch with and manifest their true natures; unfortunately, the Buddha-nature of most people is hidden or obscured by selfish desires" (Philip J. Ivanhoe, ed., *Readings from the Lu-Wang School of Neo-Confucianism* [Indianapolis: Hackett, 2009], 4–5).

monk, Shenxiu, got up at midnight to write his verse on a monastery wall so that he could remain anonymous—an expression of admirable humility: "The body is the tree of insight, the mind is like a clear mirror. Always clean and polish it, never allow dirt or dust!"[48] Huineng overheard others in the monastery reading the verse aloud. He composed his own poem, and the next night, since he could not read or write, he asked someone else to write it for him on the monastery wall: "Insight originally has no tree, the bright mirror has no stand. Buddha-nature is always pure and clean; how could there ever be dirt or dust?"[49] After reading it, everyone in the monastery was in awe. While Hongren had been impressed by Shenxiu's poem, he had not believed that it was the work of an enlightened man. Upon reading Huineng's poem, he immediately knew that it manifested enlightenment. However, he also knew that the more advanced monks would be outraged by a new, illiterate monk being given the authority of patriarch. So Hongren secretly passed on his authority to Huineng and asked him to depart and stay away until the monastery had a chance to process the news. He was right to do so; the news of Huineng's status created an uproar, and a group of monks took off after Huineng, eventually catching him and declaring him to be an imposter. When one of the monks demanded that he give up the robe and bowl of the Buddha, Huineng remained calm and placed the objects on a rock, but when the monk tried to lift the Buddha's robe, it would not budge. Astonished and trembling in fear, he said, "I thought I came here for the robe, but I see now that I came here for the Truth. Please; show me what it is that I seek." Huineng's response would become widely known in the Buddhist tradition: "If you wish to see the truth of your own nature, forget about these value judgments of who's right and who's wrong. Instead look deep inside yourself and tell me, what does your original face look like, before you were ever born?"[50] According to the story, the monk experienced enlightenment on the spot.

After contemplating the call of a worldly leader, Buddhist exercitants

---

48. Ivanhoe, trans., "The Dunhuang Version of the Platform Sutra (Selections)," in Ivanhoe, ed., *Readings from the Lu-Wang School of Neo Confucianism*, 15.

49. Ibid., 16.

50. For a readable version of this story and a helpful discussion of its larger significance, see Patrick Bresnan, *Awakening: An Introduction to the History of Eastern Thought* (Upper Saddle River, N.J.: Pearson Prentice Hall, 2007), 308–18.

should contemplate Huineng's story and imagine that he calls them to follow him. How does he speak to you and others? What does he say about his goals, and what he would like you to do when you accompany him? How should you and others respond to his invitation? Consider Huineng's call in light of the call of the worldly leader you have already considered. How much more worthy of our consideration is Huineng's call? Listen carefully and hear his call.

Next, exercitants will listen to the call of Christ. After doing so, it will be quite natural to consider both the resonances and differences between the call of Huineng and the call of Christ. What do the calls of Huineng and Christ share in common? What is unique about Christ's call, and what is there to learn from it? Where does it come from and how does it differ from Huineng's call? Both calls invite us to lead a different sort of life, a kind of surrender. In calling us to labor *with him* instead of just for him or for a larger cause, Christ's call also invites a personal relationship. By comparison, what is Huineng's call? There are many possible answers to this question, but all Buddhists should consider carefully who Huineng is, alongside who Jesus is. To assist with this, exercitants might consider Joseph Tetlow's adaptation of the loving disciple's offering, which concludes the kingdom of Christ meditation, especially the following lines:

I want it to be my desire, and my choice, provided that You want it this way, to walk this earth the way You walked it. I know that you lived in a little town, without luxury, without great education. I know that You suffered: Leaders rejected you. Friends abandoned you. You failed. I know. I hate to think about it. None of it looks romantic to me, or very useful. But it seems to me a toweringly wonderful thing that Your divine majesty might call me to follow after You.[51]

When considering this prayer, exercitants may find it helpful to compose an adaptation based on their consideration of Huineng's call.

The second week of the Exercises continues with consideration of Jesus' public ministry. Particular adaptations for Buddhists should not be needed at this stage, as the goal of this part of the Exercises is to allow exercitants to encounter Jesus and get acquainted with him. It is particularly important to allow this to happen for members of other traditions,

51. Joseph Tetlow, SJ, *Choosing Christ in the World* (St. Louis, Mo.: Institute of Jesuit Sources, 1998), 49.

many of whom will be hearing and experiencing the story of Jesus' life and ministry for the first time. While Buddhist exercitants might naturally notice some resonances and/or contrasts with the life of the Buddha, they should be encouraged to immerse themselves in the details of the story of Jesus as fully as possible, and to remember that there will be time to work through theological questions—including questions of similarity and difference between traditions—at a later time. Throughout the Exercises, as exercitants from other faiths notice similarities and contrasts between their tradition and Christianity, as much as possible it is also important to encourage a balanced approach to this natural process of comparison. If an exercitant only or mostly notes similarities, it will be helpful to ask them what differences they see; if she only or mostly notes differences, she should gently be encouraged to think about similarities. But again, the point of the Exercises is not to engage in theological study, comparative or otherwise, so we must remember and help exercitants to remain focused on opening themselves up fully to the experience of the Exercises.[52]

In the course of reflecting on Jesus' public ministry, the second week continues with three meditations. The Meditation on Two Standards invites us to consider the very different values and tactics of Christ and Lucifer—which represent two different banners under which their followers stand, as if on a battlefield—and to choose where we will stand. While Lucifer is a particular figure from the Christian tradition, Ignatius also refers to him as "the father of lies" and "the enemy of our human nature," signaling that what he represents is seen not just in a particular Biblical narrative but throughout the human experience. After an introduction to this meditation and Lucifer's invitation, an adaptation that may help Buddhists to better relate to the story is to consider the traditional Buddhist story in which Mara—a demon who personifies death, greed, and delusion, and who acts as a seducer and deceiver—tempts the historical Buddha in a variety of ways, including a vision of his daughters, in order to derail his quest for enlightenment.[53] After reviewing the story exerci-

52. Suggested readings are included at the end of each chapter of this work for exercitants who wish to further engage these questions after the Exercises, and for spiritual directors, as well.

53. Just as Christians have diverse understandings of Lucifer, not all Buddhists understand Mara literally; some interpret Mara as an aspect of the Buddha or the demons of his own internal struggle with doubt, weakness, and worldly desires. For this reason, the story of Mara could serve as a helpful resource for many different kinds of Buddhists making the Exercises.

tants might consider the invitation to stand beneath the banner of Mara. It is important to note that in the original story, the Buddha *was tempted* by the images and false promises of Mara, even though he did not give in to temptation. Exercitants might ask themselves: How would Mara entice me? What images and visions would be most tempting? After considering Mara's banner, Buddhist exercitants should be invited to consider what Lucifer does in the Exercise. He begins by tempting us "to covet riches (as he usually does, at least in most cases), so that they may more easily come to vain honor from the world, and finally to surging pride. In this way, the first step is riches, the second is honor, and the third is pride; and from these three steps the enemy entices them to all the other vices" (SE 142). Both Fleming and Tetlow note the vicious progression from a fixation on worldly possessions, to a growing fixation on worldly honors, to a fixation on the self: "riches (or 'this is mine') to honor (or 'look at me') to pride (or 'I AM . . .')."[54] There is also an implicit movement here from simple selfishness to a deep-seated form of self-centeredness. This progression is truly vicious because these things have an addictive quality for humans; their allure is incredibly difficult to resist, and yet they have a corrosive effect on all that is good about us, which is why Ignatius calls this "the enemy of our human nature." We are repeatedly drawn to the false promise that wealth, honor, and prestige will make us happy, and yet they do not, which is why Ignatius links them to "the father of lies." Our desire for riches and prestige, and the way in which these things lead to self-centeredness, resonate deeply with Buddhist teachings. Buddhist exercitants should consider how the picture Ignatius paints compares with the Buddhist claim that desires and a fixation on the self lie at the root of our suffering. Buddhists making the Exercises will need to recognize the reality of holy desires; grasping the difference between these desires, which ultimately come from God and bring us into properly ordered and fulfilling relationships with God and other persons, and our own selfish or self-centered desires for worldly or material goods, is a basic feature of Ignatian spirituality. While Ignatius does not regard all desires as problematic in the way that the Buddhist tradition does, there is nevertheless an important area of overlap here: a desire for material

54. Fleming, *Draw Me into Your Friendship*, 113; cf. Joseph Tetlow, SJ, *Making Choices in Christ: The Foundations of Ignatian Spirituality* (Chicago: Loyola Press, 2008), 108.

possessions and worldly honors is fundamentally destructive to us. Similarly, while Ignatius clearly believes in the soul, whereas Buddhists deny the existence of any soul or self, according to both views, a fixation on the self is destructive to us.

As we move to the second phase of the Meditation on Two Standards, Buddhists should be aware of how both Ignatius and the Buddhist tradition invite us to stand beneath a banner that is opposed to the pursuit of riches, prestige, and self-indulgence. At this point, Buddhists exercitants must be given the time and space to listen carefully to the invitation of Christ and to gaze upon him as he speaks to his disciples. Notice how his welcoming, gentle manner—as well as his desire to liberate people to love God and others—is an obvious contrast to Lucifer and Mara. When we allow ourselves to be fully immersed in the scene of that great plain near Jerusalem (SE 144), Christ's life is striking in its simplicity, and his humility and selflessness are striking, as well. Buddhists then might consider how and in what ways Buddhist teachings would lead one, when presented with this choice, to stand beneath the banner of Christ. For this task, I would suggest consideration of the noble eightfold path, which offers a path for the journey from ordinary human life (which is characterized by suffering) to a life of freedom and peace. The eight steps—right understanding, right thought, right speech, right action, right livelihood, right effort, right mindfulness, and right concentration—are not successive steps up a ladder, but are meant to be developed together in order to help one to embrace a life that is not rooted in the fulfillment of desires and attachments to things, people, and self. Exercitants should consider the questions: Which parts of the noble eightfold path offer a particularly strong contrast with the banners of Lucifer and Mara? Which parts resonate with Christ's banner, and which parts differ? Additionally, O'Brien suggests consideration of the following questions, which will be particularly helpful for exercitants from different faiths, since they highlight those aspects of the Two Standards that touch on fundamental aspects of human experience: "How do I experience the two standards playing out in my life or in the world around me? What role do riches and honors play in my life? What enslaves me? Where is the invitation to greater freedom in my life?"[55]

---

55. O'Brien, *The Ignatian Adventure*, 172.

The Meditation on Three Classes of Persons comes next in the Exercises, and this meditation represents an important opportunity for members of other faiths to become acquainted with Ignatian approaches to discernment, which can serve as a new and distinctive resource for making decisions grounded in one's faith. Discernment is not traditionally a core aim of Buddhist contemplative practice. Theistic Buddhist worship is primarily concerned with petitionary prayer, while meditative practices primarily hinge on the process of extinguishing desires, clearing the mind, and on attaining states such as *samādhi*. This meditation shows very clearly how Ignatian prayer is more active and discursive, aiming not to eliminate thoughts and feelings but to explore them. As we have already seen, Ignatius aims to have individuals strive for indifference: to be free of disordered loves and fears so that they can respond with generosity to God's call. In the Meditation on the Three Classes of Persons, Ignatius helps us to understand what indifference and a generous response to such a call involves. We pray for the grace of interior freedom. For some philosophical Buddhists, this meditation may pose a significant challenge, because it requires exercitants to entertain the possibility of a God who might call them to serve in various ways—a God who is also the Creator and Lord of the universe, which lends authority to this call. At this stage of the Exercises, philosophical Buddhists who have been following the adaptations suggested in this chapter will have had substantial practice imagining or wagering, in the Pascalian sense, that God exists, but this meditation invites them to go a step further, and to bring their experience thus far of Jesus' life, ministry, and call to bear upon the question at hand: What if God exists, and what if God calls me to serve in particular ways? Am I hearing that call? Where is it coming from and where is it leading me? A momentous decision is being called for here, one that requires the exercitant to move beyond the "as if" stage to genuine belief and commitment.

Now, there are aspects of the Meditation on Three Classes of Persons that can be re-described in thoroughly non-theistic terms. For instance, one might describe the three individuals as differing in the following way: the first person wants to let go of the attachment but ultimately avoids doing so by filling her life with other things; the second person, too, wants to let go of the attachment but is unable to do so and so instead makes a variety of other sacrifices; the third person differs because she doesn't just want to let go of the attachment, she wants to let go of any desire to keep it or get rid of it—she wants to become indifferent. The problem with adapting the meditation in this way is that in the end, one is left simply to choose from a place of indifference, but it is unclear how one would go about making a choice. Ignatius would have us become indifferent in order to be free to do what God wants us to do.

This meditation is important for Buddhists, because it at once resonates with Buddhist teachings about attachment—since the three classes of persons are all concerned to let go of an attachment, recognizing that it is unhealthy—while also highlighting a couple of fundamental differences between the Buddhist and Ignatian traditions: (1) Ignatius holds that the reason we want to be free of disordered loves and fears is so that we will be able to discern and respond fully to God's call, while in the Buddhist tradition freedom from attachment and desire is the only way to free ourselves and others from suffering, and (2) Ignatius holds that we ought to free ourselves from certain kinds of desires but not all desires, for God speaks to us through holy desires, while Buddhists view all desires as fundamentally destructive. What do these differences mean for an adaptation of this Meditation on Three Classes of Persons for Buddhists?

I think it will be helpful to focus closely on the graces or gifts that exercitants are traditionally seeking at this point in the Exercises. As Fleming puts it, "I ask that I may be free enough to choose to follow wherever God may be inviting me."[56] Buddhist exercitants might be invited to consider this meditation as having two components. The first component concerns spiritual freedom, and the difference between understanding that it is a good thing and wishing for it, and actively working to free oneself from disordered attachments. This is one of the things that distinguishes the third type of person from the first two. The Buddhist and Ignatian traditions can both agree that actively working to free oneself from disordered attachments is something we ought to do, and the contemplative practices of both traditions are dedicated to helping us to do this. For the purposes of this adaptation, I think it is reasonable for Buddhists to focus on identifying the attachments and disordered loves that are getting in the way of living well, and to consider, as well, how and when they have demonstrated interior freedom with respect to money,

---

56. Fleming, *Draw Me into Your Friendship*, 117.

possessions, priorities, work, or time. Thus, I do not think this meditation requires one to work through the particular theological differences concerning the nature of attachments and desires in the Buddhist and Christian traditions, and so I do not see those differences as an insurmountable stumbling block—although it may be helpful for those who are aware of the tension between the two traditions on this issue to acknowledge the important differences. Ultimately, though, this meditation, for Buddhists, can serve as a different opportunity to consider and respond to the destructive role of attachment in one's life.

Now, the second component of the meditation hinges on the fact that, in the Ignatian tradition, we must ask ourselves what attachments or disordered loves are getting in the way of our response to Christ's invitation. It is, I think, important not to bleach out or neglect this aspect of the Meditation on Two Standards out of a sense that this is problematic for Buddhists, because one of our goals in giving the Exercises to Buddhists is to offer the opportunity to have a different sort of religious experience. One of the distinctive features of the Ignatian tradition is the belief that God speaks to us not just from the outside, but from within, through our "motions of the soul" or interior movements—including thoughts, emotions, inclinations, desires, repulsions, and attractions. Ignatius believed that some of our interior movements come from God while others do not, and one of the purposes of the Exercises is to school us in how to discern where our various interior movements come from and where they are leading us. Particularly because the Buddhist tradition has an exceptionally wide range of practices dedicated to helping individuals extinguish desires and work through the destructive role of attachment in their lives, in adapting the Exercises it is important not to remove the elements of the Exercises that would make them different from Buddhist spiritual exercises and, therefore, the elements that would make them worthwhile for Buddhists. Additionally and even more importantly, if we remove theistic elements from this meditation, we remove the opportunity for Buddhist exercitants to open themselves up to a different type of experience or encounter, which, as I have argued in this work, is one of the reasons why they might be drawn to the Exercises in the first place. The image of God here is of a helping God, who helps us make good decisions; we are co-laborers with God.

I would argue, then, that the best adaptation at this stage is a much lighter one. Exercitants should simply be given the opportunity to see what happens if they try to begin where the third person in this meditation begins: "she is not sure whether or not God is asking her to give up the possession; she simply desires to be free to do what God wants her to do. So she begins by asking God what she should do. She is open to how God directs her through her prayer, her experience, her reasoning through different options, her discernment of consolations and desolations, and the wise counsel of others."[57] For philosophical Buddhists, this is a very active way of "wagering": one must *actually listen* for the God who might be there. But one is learning to listen not for an external voice, but for the movement of the Spirit within.

The final meditation of the second week is the Meditation on Three Kinds of Humility or three ways of loving God. The first kind of humility involves humbling oneself so that one might merely follow God's law, while the second, "more perfect" kind of humility brings about, in addition to obedience to God's law, spiritual freedom: "It is what I have when I find myself in this disposition: If my options are equally effective for the service of God our Lord and the salvation of my soul, I do not desire or feel myself strongly attached to having wealth rather than poverty, or honor rather than dishonor, or a long life rather than a short one" (SE 166). The third and "most perfect" kind of humility encompasses the second and third but in addition, "in order to imitate Christ our Lord better and to be more like him here and now, I desire and choose poverty with Christ poor rather than wealth; contempt with Christ laden with it rather than honors. Even further, I desire to be regarded as a useless fool for Christ, who even before me was regarded as such, rather than as a wise or prudent person in this world" (SE 167).

What is to be done with this meditation in order to make it more accessible to, and fruitful for, Buddhists? Once again, it will be helpful to focus on the gift that exercitants are seeking at this point. The gift that is at the center of this meditation is humility, and the meditation revolves around the view that humility is closely tied to a kind of selflessness: out of a recognition that one is not at the center of the universe (because

---

57. O'Brien, *The Ignatian Adventure*, 179.

God is) one is completely unconcerned with oneself and desires to give up everything (to God) as a result. For philosophical Buddhists, on the other hand, nothing (or no one) is at the center of the universe, and this is a stark difference. Without question, a different kind of selflessness is at the center of the Buddhist tradition, so one way of making this meditation more accessible to Buddhists would be to focus on humility and selflessness. Since the language of the Exercises is highly Christocentric, it may be helpful to begin by highlighting some broader differences between these three kinds of humility, before applying them specifically to one's consideration of God and Christ. The first kind of humility hinges on living a moral life, while the second kind of humility involves living ethically while also striving for interior freedom. The third involves wholeheartedly loving God by desiring and seeking to imitate Christ and to be with him in every possible way. Again, the meditation itself is very Christocentric, but notice how imitating Christ involves a kind of surrender of oneself. The third kind of humility involves a complete lack of attachment to oneself and one's life, and a thoroughgoing rejection of the desire for worldly possessions and honors: "I desire and choose poverty with Christ poor rather than wealth; contempt with Christ laden with it rather than honors. Even further, I desire to be regarded as a useless fool for Christ, who before me was regarded as such, rather than as a wise or prudent person in this world" (SE 167). Here we see more than a rejection of the world's goals and standards (such as wealth and honor); we see a call to become one with Christ. This involves leaving ourselves behind, in an important sense, and it provides an interesting opportunity for Buddhists to consider the various ways in which one might live out the doctrine of anatman, or no-self. One way of doing this is to follow the example of one who lived selflessly, and to follow his path rather than carving out our own path. Within the Buddhist tradition, and for Ignatius as well, this is deeply liberating.

In the concluding days of the second week, exercitants will continue to consider Jesus' public ministry. This provides an opportunity to practice, in contemplation, what it means to follow the self-less call of the Meditation on Three Kinds of Humility. As exercitants use their imaginations to become part of scenes from the gospels, speaking in a colloquy with Jesus or others, they are presented with ongoing opportunities to be close to Jesus and to learn to see, hear, speak, and feel as Jesus does, and to become like the one we gaze upon.

An Adaptation of the Ignatian Spiritual Exercises for Buddhists: The Third and Fourth Weeks

The third and fourth weeks of the Exercises invite exercitants to contemplate Jesus' death and resurrection. This marks a continuation of the experience of encountering Jesus throughout the Exercises, and one need not accept a particular theological view of the atonement in order to contemplate the events leading up to Jesus' death and his death on the cross. At the same time, Ignatius frames our consideration of these events in theological terms, and the adaptations that I describe here will be designed to address and reframe these movements of the Exercises in order to make them more accessible to, and fruitful for, Buddhists. My adaptations also take into account the fact that for many if not most Buddhists making the Exercises, this will be their first extensive engagement with the events surrounding the end of Jesus' life.

As I suggested in the adaptation for Hindus, one element of the third week of the Exercises that may need to be adapted is the prominence of the idea that Jesus endures suffering *for me*, or how he dies for *my* sins. This is seen, for instance, in Ignatius's description of the graces we seek at this stage of the Exercises: "to ask for sorrow, regret, and confusion, because the Lord is going to his Passion for my sins" (SE 193). Exercitants from other faiths may need to simply walk alongside Jesus through his final days, without too much theological baggage. It is worth noting that this is often true for Christians, as well; Jesus' death is one of the most difficult events to understand theologically, and the history of Christian theology testifies to that. For Buddhists, it will be important to focus on Jesus' suffering and the compassion it inspires in us—two hallmarks of Buddhism that resonate deeply with the third week of the Exercises. In accompanying Jesus we witness not only his physical suffering but his interior suffering, as he is misunderstood, mocked, isolated, and rejected. Here, some of the graces Ignatius suggests that we seek will be helpful, including "sorrow with Christ in sorrow; a broken spirit with Christ so broken" (SE 203). Similarly, one of Ignatius's instructions for the colloquy with Jesus on the cross during the first week of the Exercises will be helpful to members of other faiths in contemplating the third week, since it does not rest upon a particular theological view but encourages deep listening: "As I look upon Jesus as he hangs upon the cross, I ponder whatever God may bring to my attention" (SE 53).

The grace that Buddhists might seek throughout the third week is compassion, which has a special place in Buddhist ethics because it is the primary virtue associated with bodhisattvas, who extend pure and unlimited compassion to others by delaying their entry into nirvana until all beings can be freed from suffering. Such compassion is ultimately inspired by the historical Buddha's own compassion, and certain stories about the Buddha may serve as helpful companions for Buddhists during the third week. One such story tells of the Buddha's visit to a monastic community where a monk was suffering from an advanced skin disease, which had led his fellow monks to avoid contact with him. Upon learning of the man's plight, the Buddha took a basin of water and a towel and washed the monk himself. He then instructed the other monks, saying, "Monks, you do not have a mother or a father here who can tend to you. If you, monks, do not tend to one another, who is there to take care of you? Remember that whoever tends a sick person, as it were, tends me."[58] The story has obvious resonances not only with Jesus' response to the sick (including lepers) and his remarks about how we treat the "least of these," but also the way he washes the feet of his disciples.

As exercitants consider Jesus' final days, I propose an additional contemplation that will allow them to more easily connect these themes in the Exercises with their own tradition. This is a contemplation on the story of the Four Sights the Buddha experienced as a young man after being sheltered by his father from all images of pain and suffering. First, he encountered the sight of a crippled elderly man; second, a severely diseased man; third, a corpse; fourth, he saw a religious hermit practicing meditation. After witnessing human suffering in the first three sights, the Buddha felt moved to dedicate his life to putting an end to the suffering of others, and the sight of the meditator leads to his spiritual quest.

58. *Mahavagga*, VIII, 26, quoted in Donald W. Mitchell, *Buddhism: Introducing the Buddhist Experience* (New York: Oxford University Press, 2002), 27.

Using Ignatian contemplation, exercitants should place themselves in the scene as the Buddha encounters the three sights of old age, disease, and death. What do each of these scenes look like? Observe the Buddha's face as he witnesses the profound suffering in each of them. How does he respond? What does his compassion look like? Finally, consider these three sights in light of your journey alongside Jesus through his final days. Reconsider the following questions from the colloquy before the cross in the first week: "In the past, what response have I made to Christ? How do I respond to Christ now? What response should I make to Christ?" (SE 53)

At the conclusion of the third week, some exercitants from other traditions may feel a need to engage prayerfully with the overarching purpose of Jesus' life and the idea that through his life and death he redeemed humanity. A helpful starting place for thinking about God's purpose in sending Jesus into the world to redeem us, his children, might be Ruth Burrows's analogy of a happy couple who decides to have children of their own:

From then on their life undergoes a profound change. Now they are vulnerable; their happiness is wrapped up in the welfare of the children; things can never be the same again. If the children choose to alienate themselves and start on the path to ruin, the couple are stricken. They will plead, humble themselves, make huge sacrifices, go out of themselves to get their loved ones to understand that the home is still their home, that the love they have been given is unchanging. This perhaps, gives us some insight into redemption. In a mystery we cannot fathom, God "empties," "loses" Himself, in bringing back to Himself His estranged, lost children. And this is all the Father wants.[59]

The focus of the fourth week of the Exercises is Jesus' resurrection, which is likely to be more challenging for members of other faiths than the third week. In the previous chapter, I argued that one way of approaching the challenges involved in considering Jesus' resurrection is to ask exercitants from other faiths who struggle with this to use their imagination to entertain the possibility that it happened, asking, "What if it's true? What did it look like? What did it mean to those who were present? What does it mean to me, as a friend who walked with Jesus

---

59. Ruth Burrows, *Essence of Prayer* (Mahwah, N. J.: HiddenSpring, 2006), 74.

through his suffering in the days leading up to his death?" In this way, the fourth week represents an opportunity for exercitants to use the contemplative skills they have developed thus far in the retreat to *see with the eyes of their imagination*. As they consider the gift of joy that is sought during the final movement of the Exercises, Buddhist exercitants should be encouraged to look to the texts of their tradition for stories that deepen their sense of the gifts of life, hope, and joy, and how they can spring from places of suffering. For those who struggle with the particular story of Jesus' resurrection, it will be important to point toward the larger message and its significance for us: God brings hope out of despair, and this is central to God's very identity in the Christian tradition. More broadly, we are called to look for light in the darkness.

The final contemplation of the Exercises, the Contemplation of the Love of God (SE 230–37), invites exercitants to consider how the experience of God's love in the Exercises has changed them, and how it ought to inform their lives in the future. The contemplation contains four points: first, we call to mind the many gifts received over the course of our lives and offer thanks for these gifts; second, we are invited to find God in all things, noting how God dwells in all parts of creation, giving plants life and animals intelligence; third, we praise God who labors for us in all of creation, giving the elements, plants, fruits, cattle, and all things existence and conserving them; fourth, we consider how all good things come from above unceasingly: "God's love shines down on me like the rays from the sun, or God's love is poured forth lavishly like a fountain spilling forth its waters into an endless stream. Just as I see the sun in its rays and the fountain in its waters, so God pours forth a sharing in divine life in all the gifts showered upon me."[60] After each of these four points, we are to ask ourselves how we can respond, and then offer the Take, Lord, Receive prayer (SE 234).

For Buddhists, meditation on the things we are grateful for in each of the four points should not pose difficulties, but seeing these graces as *gifts* may be unsettling for philosophical Buddhists, since seeing them in this Ignatian way requires them to consider that God is the sources of these gifts. It is important not to avoid this dimension of the Exercises,

60. Fleming, *Draw Me into Your Friendship*, 181.

for it is one of the things that makes the Exercises distinctive and potentially fruitful for those who are engaged with other contemplative practices. For those who find the centrality of God and the Take, Lord, Receive prayer difficult, they may be better helped by simply allowing themselves to sit quietly in gratitude following the contemplation of each of the four points. As O'Brien points out, "Gratitude is freeing, for it opens us up to give what we have so abundantly received."[61] Indeed, most important is the response one makes to the gifts one has received. Exercitants look to creation and to their lives, and are asked: Does it move you to wonder and awe? The response of feeling gifted then prompts the desire to want to give back. From a Buddhist perspective, this means releasing and giving up one's gifts, and recognizing that they are not one's own (for nothing is)—a process that is fundamental to Buddhist teachings about attachment.

Buddhist exercitants might conclude by revisiting the two verses that are central to the *Platform Sutra*, discussed earlier in this chapter. Shenxiu's verse read, "The body is the tree of insight, the mind is like a clear mirror. Always clean and polish it, never allow dirt or dust!" Huineng's verse read: "Insight originally has no tree, the bright mirror has no stand. Buddha-nature is always pure and clean; how could there ever be dirt or dust?"[62] Huineng's poem corrects Shenxiu's in several places: there is no "tree of enlightenment" (i.e., the self), and instead of "polishing the mirror" (i.e., working to make oneself better), Huineng emphasizes that we simply need to realize that our fundamental nature is perfectly pure, and that all "specks of dust" are self-inflicted wounds that we generate by misunderstanding ourselves, others, and the world. While markedly different from Ignatius's view of the world, there is nevertheless an important point of resonance with the concluding insight of the Exercises, seen in the Contemplation of the Love of God: our own efforts to make ourselves better will never be sufficient to save us. From a Chan or Zen Buddhist perspective, this is because enlightenment does not involve gaining something new, but losing all that is false. From the standpoint of the Ignatian tradition in this final contemplation of the Exercises, the

---

61. O'Brien, *The Ignatian Adventure*, 253.
62. Ibid., 15–16.

full recognition that all we have, and ever will have, is a gift from God—and not an achievement of our own—lies at the heart of our salvation.

Suggested Further Readings

Patrick Bresnan. *Awakening: An Introduction to the History of Eastern Thought.* Upper Saddle River, N.J.: Pearson Prentice Hall, 2007.

David Clairmont. *Moral Struggle and Religious Ethics: On the Person as Classic in Comparative Theological Contexts.* Malden, Mass.: Wiley Blackwell, 2011.

Thich Nhat Hanh. *Living Buddha, Living Christ.* New York: Riverhead Trade, 1997.

Donald W. Mitchell. *Buddhism: Introducing the Buddhist Experience.* New York: Oxford University Press, 2002.

Walpola Rahula, trans. *What the Buddha Taught.* New York: Grove Press, 1974.

5

Confucianism, East Asian Cultures,
and the Spiritual Exercises

WHILE HINDUISM AND BUDDHISM are almost always included in lists of "the world's religions," Daoism and Confucianism—the indigenous religious and philosophical traditions of China—are often left out. This is largely because the two have not enjoyed the same popularity as Hinduism and Buddhism, because of the association of the latter two with the countercultural movement of the 1960s in America and the popularity of versions of transcendental and insight meditation, which are derived from those traditions. Yet both Daoism and Confucianism are rightly included in every major world religions textbook. And although most people are unaware of it, the versions of Buddhism that became most popular in the West—most notably Zen—were deeply influenced by Daoism. When Buddhism entered China in the first century CE, it was imprinted by Confucianism and Daoism, and by the time it reached Korea, Japan, and other parts of East and Southeast Asia, Buddhism had taken on a distinctive new set of flavors owing largely to the influence of the Confucian and Daoist traditions. The three came to be known as the "three teachings" of China—the three major traditions that most powerfully influenced Chinese religion, philosophy, and culture. The Confucian and Daoist traditions were changed by their encounter with Buddhism as well, something that is seen especially in the polytheistic character of Daoism today.

I do not devote a chapter of this book to an adaptation for Daoists because contemporary Daoism and contemporary theistic Buddhism are, in practice, very similar; most people who frequent Daoist temples today are polytheists and in both thought and practice strongly resemble theistic Buddhists. While many of the specific deities they petition differ (while others overlap), they share a similar and often overlapping set of beliefs and practices with theistic Buddhists. Indeed, many of these individuals also frequent Buddhist temples. As a result, the adaptation that I outline for theistic Buddhists in the previous chapter applies readily to those who associate with contemporary Daoism. It is important to note here how contemporary Chinese religious beliefs and the activities of Daoist priests and temples today differ from the beliefs and practices associated with early Daoism, as expressed in well-known and beloved texts such as the *Daodejing*. There are marked differences in the religious outlook that is presented in early Daoist texts and those of most worshippers in Daoist temples today, including most notably the fact that most people who frequent Daoist temples are not individuals who seek to follow an impersonal entity known as the *Dao*. Since my aim in this book is to address how to adapt the Exercises for members of other faith traditions today, and since there are very few people today who hold the beliefs associated with ancient Daoism, I have not included an adaptation relating to early Daoism.

The focus of this chapter, then, is Confucianism, but unlike previous chapters that offered adaptations of the full and complete Exercises for Hindus and Buddhists, this chapter does *not* offer an adaptation of the Exercises for Confucians. As we shall see in a moment, there are very few people who call themselves Confucians today, even though many people are influenced by Confucianism culturally. Instead, this chapter focuses, first, on how Confucianism can serve as a resource for making Ignatian spirituality (and Christianity more broadly) more accessible to members of East Asian cultures. I highlight resonances and tensions between Confucianism and Christianity with the aim of removing potential stumbling blocks for those from Confucian-influenced cultures who are interested in experiencing Ignatian spirituality. Second, this chapter argues that the Exercises can serve as a resource for reviving and strengthening elements of Confucianism by inspiring new contemplative practices. I outline practices that draw creatively upon the Ignatian tradition as a way of enlivening Confucianism today. This chapter, then, seeks not only to make Ignatian spirituality more accessible to members of other traditions and cultures, but to demonstrate some of the other ways in which elements of the Exercises might be "fruitfully appropriated" by non-Christians, as Father Nicolás has suggested.

A Brief Overview of Confucianism

Religion in China is anything but easy to sort out at first glance. Every so often the media will report that China is the least religious country in the world; a recent *Washington Post* article, for instance, reported that "90 percent of all Chinese consider themselves to be atheists or not to be religious."[1] But as sociologist of religion Anna Sun points out, most survey research done on religion in China is based on a Judeo-Christian framework and as a result fails to accurately capture Chinese religious life. For instance, in response to the 2001 World Values Survey question "Do you belong to a religious denomination?" 93.9 percent of Chinese respondents answered "No." But in another survey, which presented more nuanced questions regarding religious practices, 84.8 percent of respondents answered "Yes" to the question "Have you ever worshipped gods (*baishen*) or worshipped ancestors (*baizuxian*)?"[2] As Sun argues, research questions must be framed appropriately if we wish to gain any sense of the diversity and vitality of Chinese religious life. Questions about denominational or religious affiliation typically do not yield accurate results; Chinese people most typically do not describe themselves as "Buddhist" or "Daoist" even if they visit Buddhist and/or Daoist temples and offer prayers to Buddhist and Daoist deities regularly. Many see these terms as reserved only for monks and priests in Buddhism and Daoism, or for those who are exclusively committed to one of these traditions, whereas the norm in China has long been to visit multiple temples from multiple traditions, and to draw freely upon the expertise of Daoist and Buddhist priests, as well as

---

1. Rick Noack, "Map: These Are the World's Least Religious Countries," *Washington Post*, April 14, 2015, http://www.washingtonpost.com/blogs/worldviews/wp/2015/04/14/map-these-are -the-worlds-least-religious-countries/?tid=sm_tw. The survey was conducted by Gallup International and the WI Network of Market Research.

2. Anna Sun, *Confucianism as a World Religion* (Princeton, N. J.: Princeton University Press, 2013), 113–14.

spirit mediums. We see similarly misleading results when Chinese people are asked whether or not they are religious or whether they are a believer of any religion; in the World Values Survey, 55.3 percent of Chinese respondents claimed not to be religious, and the 2007 Horizon Survey reported that 78.1 percent of Chinese respondents claimed not to believe in anything.[3] Yet the same Horizon Survey also reported that about 70 percent of people interviewed said that they had visited their ancestors' graves in the past year, a practice that in China usually involves ancestral sacrifices (and, correspondingly, belief in the existence of ancestral spirits) with roots in the Confucian tradition. There are clearly distinctive understandings here of what it means to be "religious" and what constitutes "religious belief," and it is important to remember that plenty of Americans today would deny that they are "religious" in favor of being called "spiritual," partly because they do not consider themselves members of a particular faith or denomination. But there is an added layer of complexity in China. In addition to associating being "religious" with being ordained in or exclusively committed to a particular tradition, some Chinese people remain uncomfortable with describing themselves as "religious" in light of China's turbulent religious history and the officially Marxist views and policies of the Chinese government. In any case, the data shows that in order to get an accurate picture of religious life in China, we must ask the right questions.

The annual "tomb sweeping" festival known as Qingming is perhaps the best example of how pervasive traditional Confucian religious beliefs and practices are in China today. Officially reinstated in 2008 after being banned by the Chinese Communist Party in 1949, the ancient festival in which the living pay respect to their ancestors by tidying their graves, leaving offerings of food and drink, and burning paper offerings to ensure their comfort and happiness in the afterlife has had a resurgence in recent years. Paper offerings to be burned now sometimes include cardboard iPhones and iPads, which highlights the fact that those of different ages and economic circumstances are participating, and adapting traditional rituals to their way of life, instead of abandoning them.

Such practices help to show that traditional Confucian beliefs about

3. Ibid., 113, 116.

the spirits of dead relatives are alive and well, yet few people would describe themselves as "Confucians" today. This is not only because Chinese people tend not to describe themselves as members of a tradition in the way that many other religious people do. It is also because, unlike Hinduism, Buddhism, and Daoism, Confucianism is not a living tradition in any standard sense. Although remnants of traditional Confucian rituals survive in various East Asian cultural practices and in annual festivals like Qingming, most of them are not practiced in a traditional form anywhere today. While there are those who seek to revive Confucianism in a wide variety of ways—especially as a resource for political reform in China—these efforts are not centralized and there is no one today who is authorized to decide whose view, if any, would be accepted, nor is it clear what that would even mean. However, no single tradition has had such widespread cultural influence; Confucian values saturate the cultures of East and Southeast Asia, and Confucian religious beliefs and practices are tightly woven into the forms of Buddhism and Daoism, as well as of popular religion, that are practiced throughout East Asia today. People throughout East and Southeast Asia, regardless of whether they would describe themselves as Buddhist, Daoist, Christian, or atheist, are deeply influenced by the Confucian tradition in how they think about and lead their lives.

Confucianism is unique when compared with Buddhism, Daoism, and Hinduism not only because of the *breadth* of its influence—not only China, but the rest of East Asia and Southeast Asia, as well, bears its mark culturally—but also the *depth* of its influence. Not only those who have described themselves as Confucians historically but virtually all members of East Asian cultures have lived out Confucian values in their daily lives to varying degrees. While Buddhism, Daoism, and Hinduism—as well as Christianity, Islam, and Judaism—have certainly influenced a variety of cultures around the world, no other religion has had the same depth of cultural influence across such a large region, including so many different countries and cultures. More people have lived in China than anywhere else, and Confucianism quickly spread beyond China to Korea, Japan, Vietnam, Singapore, Thailand, and Malaysia. If you ask anyone to make a list of characteristic features of East Asian cultures, most of the likely items on the list—respect for elders, an emphasis on family, an appreciation for ritual, a commitment to learning and education—have their origins in Confucianism. This is why leading scholars of Confucianism have suggested that if we consider the *combined* influence of Jesus and Socrates on Western civilization, we might begin to get a sense of the influence of Confucius on East Asian cultures; no other single individual, tradition, or religion has had a comparable influence.[4]

Indeed, Confucius is the most influential thinker in history, if we measure influence by the number of people who have lived their lives according to a particular person's teachings (or teachings attributed to that person).[5] Obviously, traditions are much more than the thought and practices associated with their founding figures, but the historical figure of Confucius, known in East Asia as Kongzi, 孔子 (551–479 BCE), has nevertheless played a central role in shaping this tradition and its values.[6] Born in the state of Lu, located in what is now Shandong Province in the People's Republic of China, Kongzi lived and taught during a time of violence and warfare both between and within different states. Kongzi worked to recover and transmit the values and practices of earlier times, which he believed could help his society return to a time of peace and stability and help people to lead happier and ethically better lives. The tradition that we call Confucianism, then, began long before Kongzi, and he insisted that he was not an innovator of new ideas (*Analects* 7.1). But while he was building upon and working to pass down and revive the ideas and practices associated with his tradition, he was also putting it all together in a new way, and he—much more than any of the earlier sage-kings that he admired—became the rallying point for this tradition

4. Bryan W. Van Norden, introduction to *Confucius and the Analects: New Essays*, ed. Bryan W. Van Norden (New York: Oxford University Press, 2002), 3.

5. Roger T. Ames and Henry Rosemont Jr., trans., *The Analects of Confucius: A Philosophical Translation* (New York: Ballantine Books, 1998), 1.

6. Kongzi, 孔子, is known to many Westerners as Confucius, which is the Latinization of the name of a man whose surname was Kong, 孔. It was common practice in early China to refer to philosophers by appending the honorific suffix *zi*, 子 ("master") to their surnames, and so he became known as Kongzi ("Master Kong"). As a result of his exceptional influence, in time Kongzi was given the more elaborate honorific *fuzi*, 夫子, and from Kongfuzi, 孔夫子, we get the Latinized name Confucius. Although Confucius is his most recognizable name in English, from this point on I will refer to him as Kongzi, because that is how he is known throughout East Asia (the Japanese is Kosi and the Korean is Kongja). This seems appropriate, since the aim of this chapter is to discuss how the Exercises can be adapted for members of East Asian cultures and serve as a resource for reviving and reimagining Confucian practices.

throughout history. The text of the *Analects*, the earliest and most influential record of Kongzi's conversations with his followers and contemporaries, contains not only his teachings but descriptions of his conduct
and character. These descriptions distinguish him from philosophers like
Aristotle and make him look a lot more like the founding figures of other
religious traditions.

Confucians have always been concerned with what it means to follow
the Way (*Dao*, 道), a comprehensive way of life (likened to a well-trodden
path) that is defined by a particular set of virtues, certain kinds of roles
and relationships with others, and a traditional set of rites or rituals. This
path helps us to lead more meaningful, fulfilling, and happier lives. Making sacrifices to the spirits of deceased ancestors and cultivating the virtue
of filial piety are an important part of the Way, as are the rites—a broad set
of traditional moral and religious practices that include a variety of rituals, social customs, and rules of etiquette. The rites govern interactions
between members of families, communities, and society as a whole, but
they also cultivate and express a variety of important virtues. In following
the Way, one continuously engages in moral self-cultivation (*xiu shen*,
修身): the cultivation of the self or the human person. Even though the
cultivation of the self certainly involves intensive efforts to improve oneself, in order to bring about change in ourselves, and even in order to get
started on the path of self-cultivation, we require the support and assistance of many other individuals over the course of our lives—something
that deeply interested Confucians throughout history. A number of Confucian philosophers argued that this process begins even before we are
born, and continues in a vital way through the work of parents, families,
and other caregivers during infancy and childhood.[7] Entire texts in the
Confucian tradition focus on the way in which specific practices—especially rituals—serve to cultivate our character over the course of our lives,
helping us to develop many different virtues.[8]

The path of moral self-cultivation that defines the Way is difficult; in
the *Analects* 8.7, we are told that, for those who devote their lives to this

---

7. For an exploration of these dimensions of Confucianism, see my *Families of Virtue: Confucian and Western Views on Childhood Development* (New York: Columbia University Press, 2015).
8. Despite their shared concern with this set of issues, Confucians took a wide range of positions on the fundamental character of human nature.

path, "the burden is heavy and the Way is long. They take up humaneness as their burden—is it not heavy? Their way ends only with death—is it not long?" There are, though, clear goals that one works toward as one follows the Way, and in the *Analects* the goal of self-cultivation is made especially clear in Kongzi's conception of humaneness (*Ren*, 仁) and his description of the cultivated person (*junzi*, 君子), which typically designate the highest ideals to which those following the Way aspire.[9] The cultivated person embodies the full range of Confucian virtues, including filial piety, trustworthiness, courage, and wisdom. According to Kongzi, though, despite having attained the depths of moral achievement, the cultivated person continues to exhibit an unwavering devotion to the path of self-cultivation, always striving to become better.

To be sure, the history of Confucianism is long, and it is beyond the scope of the present work to provide an overview, though a few things are especially worth noting, the first of which is the deification of Kongzi. While some have insisted that there was no such thing as "Confucianism" during and shortly after the time that he lived, in fact the followers of Kongzi had a very clear sense that he had preserved and codified a particular set of ideas, practices, and related texts that pointed toward the way of earlier sage-kings. As a result, they referred to "the Way of Kongzi" and defended it against competing ways.[10] As the tradition grew, Confucians continued to respond to, build upon, and frame their work in relation to Kongzi and his teachings. In the Han dynasty (206 BCE–220 CE), people began to venerate Kongzi's spirit. Han emperors began to offer sacrifices at Kongzi's grave and at his family ancestral temple at Qufu. Subsequent emperors in different dynasties continued this practice, and temples devoted to venerating Kongzi and his disciples flourished as well. Alongside the public veneration of Kongzi, an emphasis on personal ancestor veneration—something that Kongzi himself practiced and taught about—was appropriated as an essential ritual as Confucianism flourished throughout history. An emphasis on cultivating the virtue of filial piety—a deep-

---

9. For later thinkers like Mengzi, and in some places in the *Analects*, Ren refers to the virtue of benevolence. I have capitalized "Ren" (humaneness, benevolence) here in order to distinguish it from the term for human being (*ren*, 人).

10. See, for example, references to *xian sheng zhi dao*, 先圣之道 ("the Way of the former sages"), and *Kongzi zhi dao*, 孔子之道 ("the way of Kongzi") in *Mengzi: With Selections from Traditional Commentaries*, trans. Bryan W. Van Norden (Indianapolis: Hackett, 2008), 85 (Mengzi 3B9).

seated respect, love, and appreciation for one's parents and, by extension, one' grandparents, ancestors, and other elders—prevailed as well. But it is important to understand that Confucianism has not gone unchallenged in Chinese or East Asian history. Confucianism competed openly with Daoism and Buddhism throughout its history, and at various points in history each of these three traditions enjoyed the benefits of being the official state religion of China, while the others were marginalized.[11] However, in the twentieth century, Confucianism endured unparalleled persecution first during the anti-imperialist and modernizing May Fourth Movement (1919) and then, much more extensively, during the Cultural Revolution (1966–76). Both of these periods involved aggressive, state-sponsored attempts to root out Confucianism and traditional Chinese values, which were viewed as the cause of many social and political ills. But while Confucian temples were burnt to the ground, in the long run these periods demonstrated just how deeply rooted Confucianism is in Chinese culture. It is a remarkable testament to Confucianism that it withstood such explicit and vehement attempts at eradication. That is not to say that it was unaffected, but it is the case that Confucian values live on in a variety of ways in Chinese and other East Asian cultures; Confucian temples were rebuilt and, as we shall see, today are vibrant places of worship and devotion.

Confucian Religious Practices

In 2010, a controversy erupted in Qufu, the birthplace of Confucius, as news spread that a new Protestant church would be built for the nearly ten thousand Christians who live there. The fact that the pastor of the church was a seventy-fifth-generation descendent of Confucius did little to prevent the building project from being seen as a threat to Confucianism. Ten well-known Confucian scholars, supported by ten Confucian associations and ten Confucian websites, published an open letter protesting building the church in "the sacred city" of Qufu. The debate that followed is captured nicely in the actual media headlines: "Qufu Is Not Jerusalem"; "They Are Nailing Confucius on the Cross"; "Render unto

---

11. In Japan it has also competed with Shinto and the cult associated with the imperial family.

God the Things Which Are *God's*, and unto Confucians the Things That Are Confucians'."[12]

This incident is fascinating partly because it undermines a number of common misconceptions of Confucianism, including the view that Confucianism is not a religion but simply a philosophy or way of life. Another prevalent view—often held in conjunction with the first—is that Confucianism by nature exists harmoniously with other traditions.[13] There is a kernel of truth in each of these claims. As we shall see, Confucianism *is* different from other major religions in certain ways, and partly because Confucianism lives on in East Asian cultural values and practices, many Confucian values are compatible with and even embedded in the values and practices of other religious traditions in East Asia. These kernels aside, however, these views fail to characterize Confucianism accurately. The matter of whether Confucianism—or any tradition, for that matter—is a religion ultimately depends on what one regards as the defining features of a religion. Confucianism has many of the features we normally associate with religions: it has a clearly defined set of rituals, authoritative texts, ethical teachings, a founder who has been venerated through most of its history, and beliefs in spirits or deities. (A belief in ancestral spirits has been shared widely by Confucians throughout the history of the tradition.) Yet it also lacks some of the features religions normally have: Confucianism has no clergy or hierarchy of any kind, there is no centralized or even decentralized authority in Confucianism, and no process for conversion or membership. Does the presence or absence of any or some of these features mean that Confucianism is or is not a religion? It is precisely because the discipline of Religious Studies involves the study of diverse traditions from around the world that virtually all scholars of religion today recognize the difficulty of providing a fully adequate definition of religion.[14] While we can provide a list of widely shared features

12. Sun, *Confucianism as a World Religion*, 175.

13. The view that Asian traditions don't have the same kinds of problems that the Abrahamic faith traditions have, and that they are peaceful, harmonious, and nonexclusivistic, is not uncommon, especially among Westerners. Such views represent a form of orientalism, and fail to characterize these traditions—which have long, complex, and sometimes violent histories—accurately.

14. A broadening of attempts to define religion occurred when scholars of religion came to appreciate forms of religion that did not have a concept of deity. The concept of religion was transformed in the process, and one of the results has been to leave some doubt as to what a fully adequate definition of religion might be. Accordingly, I will not offer a definition of religion, though

of religions, not all religions have all of those features; there are similarities and differences not just in the specific nature of those features, but in which features a religion has. My own view is that Confucianism certainly has enough of the features we normally associate with religious traditions to be regarded as a religion. It is also the case that it *is* regarded as a religion, in practice. In addition to its inclusion in every major world religions textbook, the controversy over the building of a Christian church in the birthplace of Confucius shows that Confucianism sometimes functions very much like other religions in China today: not only does Confucianism at times compete with religions such as Christianity, but there are Confucians who identify Confucianism as a tradition that has a sacred city—a sacred city that would be defiled by building a Christian church there.

The religious beliefs and practices associated with Confucianism have, without question, left an indelible mark on East Asian spirituality. Chief among these are beliefs in the existence of ancestral spirits and the rituals associated with their veneration, which date back much further than Confucianism but took on a definite shape and character as a result of Confucianism's influence. Chinese religious life has long involved belief in a wide variety of powerful spirits, from personifications of natural phenomena to the spirits of dead humans. Of the latter, the more recently deceased have always been particularly important, for they were thought to retain aspects of their personality and character and thus harbored a lively and active concern for their descendants, who could appeal to them for assistance—especially as intercessors with more powerful spirits. In the Confucian tradition—and more broadly in Chinese culture—spirits are not omniscient, omnipotent, or omnibenevolent, nor are they members of a separate realm like heaven; rather, they are more powerful, ethereal members of this realm who can respond to requests from the living. This

---

I treat religion as a "family resemblance" concept here, in the Wittgensteinian sense, by noting a variety of commonly shared features. (For an example of this type of view, see Ninian Smart's discussion of six dimensions of religion. He maintains that not all of these are found in all religions, but that every religion shares in some or all of them to greater or lesser degrees. Wittgenstein called this type of concept a "family resemblance" concept because various traits and features are shared by family members, though every family member does not possess all of those traits. See Smart, *Worldviews* [New York: Charles Scribner's Sons, 1983]. For further discussion of the attempt to define religion, see Keith Yandell, *Philosophy of Religion: A Contemporary Introduction* [London: Routledge, 1999], 16–17.)

view results in what Michael Puett has called "a haunted world," in which ghosts are pervasive and dangerous. As a result, in ancient China "the living regularly performed sacrifices in an attempt to control or mollify the dead."[15] Today in China, having a proper burial and funeral rites that help to make the spirits of the dead content and happy continues to be a widespread practice. In addition, on holidays such as Qingming, large numbers of Chinese people of all ages and backgrounds visit the graves of their ancestors and make sacrifices. These practices were a part of the culture Kongzi sought to revive. Partly because people depended on spirits for help, and partly because they genuinely cared about deceased family members, there was an ongoing concern to keep ancestral spirits happy, beginning at death. Because making sacrifices to one's ancestral spirits was viewed as critically important—not just for individual families but for entire communities who were affected by spirits—having and raising children who would continue to make sacrifices to their ancestral spirits came to be viewed as a religious and moral obligation. Indeed, some Confucians viewed the failure to have children as the most unfilial of actions.[16]

Although cultures throughout the world value filial behavior, East Asian cultures are distinctive for the amount of attention paid to and the unique importance claimed for filial piety. Beginning very early, entire Confucian texts were dedicated to the topic of filial piety—an interest that originally stemmed from the beliefs and practices relating to ancestral spirits. In addition to making the appropriate sacrificial offerings of food and drink accompanied by prayers, music, and often dance, the descendants also had to present such offerings with the proper attitudes of piety, devotion, and gratitude. So, a favorable response from the spirits required people to cultivate certain moral virtues—most notably filial

15. Michael Puett, "Sages, the Past, and the Dead," in *Mortality in Traditional Chinese Thought*, ed. Amy Olberding and Philip J. Ivanhoe (Albany: SUNY Press, 2011), 225. For a comprehensive study of early Chinese religious life, see Puett, *To Become a God* (Cambridge, Mass.: Harvard University Asian Center, 2002).

16. See *Mengzi*, 4A26. For a discussion of the religious view that is presented in the *Analects*, drawn from passages concerning spirits, see my "Religious Thought and Practice in the Analects," in *The Dao Companion to the Analects*, ed. Amy Olberding (New York: Springer Publishing, 2013), 259–91. According to the *Analects*, Kongzi performed ancestral sacrifices with a reverential air (e.g., 10.8), and maintained that one should not simply "go through the motions" but must be sincere and have the right attitudes and feelings when performing rituals.

piety. Kongzi strongly emphasized the ethical function of ancestor veneration and other rituals: when performed properly, these rituals do not just serve to control the spirits; they turn us into better people by helping us to cultivate the virtues that are central to a good life. This emphasis on moral self-cultivation became a defining feature of the Confucian tradition. One's relationships with ancestral spirits, then, were not viewed as radically disconnected from one's relationships with other humans. Kongzi is explicit about this in *Analects* 11.12, when his student Zilu asks how one should serve the ghosts and spirits: "The Master said, When you don't yet know how to serve human beings, how can you serve the spirits?"[17] Kongzi suggests that we cannot serve the spirits properly or in a way that is meaningful until we have learned to properly serve humans, and serving one's parents is one's most pressing ethical obligation. The virtue that is associated with this obligation, filial piety, is a cultivated disposition to attend to the needs and desires of one's parents, and it includes a deep sense of gratitude, reverence, and love.

While ancestral spirits always held a special place in the Confucian tradition, there is another spiritual entity that played an important role in shaping the early tradition in particular, and which has been of great interest to those seeking to compare and connect Confucianism with Christianity. As Ivanhoe points out, early Confucians "did not believe in a creator deity who exists independently of the Natural order, who created the universe *ex nihilo*, and, through revelation, makes its will known in the world. Nevertheless, some important early Confucians ground their ethical claims by appealing to the authority of *tian* 'Heaven,' insisting that Heaven endows human beings with a distinctively ethical nature and at times acts in the world."[18] Confucian conceptions of Tian, 天, have been exceptionally diverse throughout history; while some thinkers saw Tian as an entity that in certain ways resembles a deity, others viewed it as nothing more than the impersonal processes of nature. The origins of Tian appear to derive from a very powerful deity from the Shang dynasty, Shangdi, 上帝, "The Lord on High," who in some contexts was thought

---

17. Zilu goes on to ask about death, and Kongzi answers, "When you don't yet understand life, how can you understand death?"

18. Philip J. Ivanhoe, "Heaven as a Source for Ethical Warrant in Early Confucianism," *Dao: A Journal of Comparative Philosophy* 6, no. 3 (2007), 211.

to be a kind of primordial ancestor who did not have any clear personality or concern for living things, but who possessed a great deal of power over the human and spiritual worlds. Shang religious practices often focused on appealing to nature spirits and ancestral spirits in order to get them to influence Shangdi in ways that would support human efforts. With the rise of the Zhou Dynasty, though, the concept of Shangdi began to disappear, and the distinct though related concept of Tian emerged and eventually replaced Shangdi. Like Shangdi, Tian lacked any clear personality, but unlike Shangdi, it harbored a concern for human beings and occasionally acted in ways that helped them. Kongzi seems to have conceived of Tian as a quasi-personal entity or agent, neither completely personal nor completely impersonal. In the *Analects* it appears to have some person-like attributes, such as having intentions and plans, and the ability to act in the world. For instance, Kongzi maintains that Tian is using him to help return his society to the Way (*Analects* 3.24)—which he sees as Tian's plan for human beings—and that it will protect him from harm so that he can accomplish this mission (7.23, 9.5). Yet we see no clear evidence that it has emotions or feelings, nor does Kongzi interact with Tian. Indeed, Tian lacks many of the personal attributes that are usually ascribed to the God of the Abrahamic faith traditions.

Nevertheless, Christian missionaries to China, including the Jesuits, were enthusiastic about this conception of Tian, and the belief that Tian actually *was* God is seen in the writings of Jesuit missionaries like Matteo Ricci and Protestant missionaries like James Legge, who both read their own Christian beliefs into early Chinese writings, and whose interpretations Christianized early Confucian views as a result.[19] One of the obvious difficulties with their views is that they fail to take account of early Confucian beliefs in spirits. Legge explicitly denied that the early Chinese were polytheists or henotheists because he thought that they regarded other spirits as intercessors, mediators, and ministers to Shangdi or Tian, and thus denied that they were gods.[20] Indeed, he writes that

---

19. For a detailed study of Jesuit encounters with Chinese texts, including Ricci, see David E. Mungello, *Curious Land: Jesuit Accommodation and the Origins of Sinology* (Honolulu: University of Hawaii Press, 1989). For a detailed study of Legge, see Norman Girardot, *The Victorian Translation of China: James Legge's Oriental Pilgrimage* (Berkeley: University of California Press, 2002).

20. James Legge, *The Religions of China: Confucianism and Taoism Described and Compared with Christianity* (London: Hodder and Stoughton, 1880), 16, 29, 70, 254.

"the most ancient and strong conviction of one God" *prevented* the rise of polytheism in China: "We may deplore, as we do deplore, the superstitious worship of a multitude of spirits, terrestrial and celestial . . . but this abuse does not obscure the monotheism. Those spirits are not Gods, and are not called by the divine name." He adds that ancient Chinese beliefs in spirits should not lead us to doubt Chinese monotheism any more than Catholic beliefs in angels and saints leads us to doubt Catholic monotheism.[21] The problem with this view is that there is no suggestion in early Confucian texts that ancestral spirits serve as intercessors, nor is there any suggestion that these spirits have any relationship to or with Tian. This is an important shift from earlier, pre-Confucian understandings of ancestral spirits, which were believed to be capable of influencing Shangdi; but such views pre-date Confucian views of Tian. As impressive as Ricci's and Legge's accomplishments were, on this topic they, like many others, were blinded by their own beliefs, and by their desire to find an implicit form of Christianity in—or at least a natural religion that prefigured or set the stage for—Confucianism.

Perhaps most importantly, the conception of Tian that is seen in early Confucian texts such as the *Analects* and the *Mengzi* did not survive beyond the early period, whereas beliefs about ancestral spirits not only survived but remained remarkably consistent throughout Chinese history up to the present day. If Kongzi's conception of Tian had survived, this concept undoubtedly would help make Ignatian spirituality more accessible to members of Confucian cultures, for in Tian we certainly find a concept much closer to God than ancestral spirits. But beginning with the third century BCE Confucian Xunzi, Tian ceased to be regarded as a being or entity in Confucianism. Ancestral spirits were the primary religious entities that remained a part of Confucian theistic belief—and remained they have, for more than 2,500 years.

Ignatian Spirituality for Confucian Contexts

One of the most significant challenges involved in making Ignatian spirituality accessible to members of East Asian cultures concerns the strong

21. Ibid., 20, 51–53.

emphasis on filial piety and family relationships in the Confucian tradition. While Christianity emphasizes the value of family, there are nevertheless a range of Christian teachings about the family that that stand in tension with Confucian sensibilities. Many of these have been noted by scholars of Confucianism. For instance, Bryan W. Van Norden points out that in the Christian tradition "[a]t times, familial ties seem to be treated as an impediment to perfect virtue and salvation."[22] Several passages from the gospels lend support to this view, including Matthew 10:35–37, in which Jesus says, "For I have come to set a man against his father, and a daughter against her mother, and a daughter-in-law against her mother-in-law; and one's foes will be members of one's own household. Whoever loves father or mother more than me is not worthy of me; and whoever loves son or daughter more than me is not worthy of me." In Luke 9:59–62, when a man whom Jesus asks to become one of his followers replies, "Lord, first let me go and bury my father," Jesus answers, "Let the dead bury their own dead; but as for you, go and proclaim the kingdom of God." And when another man says, "I will follow you, Lord; but let me first say farewell to those at my home," Jesus says, "No one who puts a hand to the plow and looks back is fit for the kingdom of God." Along similar lines, in Mark 3:31–35 when Jesus is told that his mother and brothers are outside asking for him, he asks, "Who are my mother and my brothers?" Then he looks at those who are listening to him and says, "Here are my mother and my brothers! Whoever does the will of God is my brother and sister and mother."

There are many ways of interpreting these passages, some of which make them less anti-family and which, for instance, interpret Jesus as just enlarging our notion of family. Nevertheless, no Confucian text contains statements of the sort that Jesus makes in these passages from the gospels, nor do we get any indication that such views would have been regarded as acceptable in the Confucian tradition. Now, it is worth noting that while there are obvious tensions between the views Jesus expresses in these passages and the views of the family found in Confucian texts, there are also obvious tensions between these views and the views of most Christians today. One might also note that certain aspects of Ca-

22. Bryan W. Van Norden, *Virtue Ethics and Consequentialism in Early Chinese Philosophy* (New York: Cambridge University Press, 2007), 250.

tholicism more strongly emphasize the value of family than many other forms of Christianity, including the Church's teachings on the laity and the vocation of the family, the family as the "domestic church," as well as teachings on abortion and birth control, and the central role and veneration of Mary.[23] However, we should not expect that simply because Ignatian spirituality is situated in the Catholic tradition, this will alleviate the tension with Confucianism on this point, for other aspects of Catholicism create new tensions. For instance, Jesuits (like members of other Catholic religious orders) embrace a life that is inspired in part by the gospel passages discussed above. Additionally, the ordination of celibate men as priests means that only those without spouses and children can hold certain leadership positions. Such a practice is a contrast to other traditions in which the family is central, such as Judaism and Confucianism, and even though these traditions, too, traditionally placed men in positions of authority, having a wife and children was always important and in some cases was required by the tradition. This is seen even in later Confucian criticisms of Buddhists for their vow of celibacy; Confucians found the notion of celibacy abhorrent because they regarded it as a violation of the ethical and religious obligation to have a family.

Here we can see clearly a couple of important key differences between Confucianism and Christianity concerning the family: (1) In Confucianism, one's familial obligations are not a part of one's service to someone or something else, such as God. There is nothing else that ranks above the family in importance or that commands or calls one to have a family—other than one's ancestors, who are, of course, part of the family. (2) The obligation to have a family, for Confucians, applied to everyone. In Catholicism, there is also a vocation to the single life. And as we have seen, Ignatius believed in a priesthood that was set apart from the laity by vows of celibacy and poverty, and that represented a calling higher than others—a view that is supported by passages from Paul's letters. Unlike Catholic priests, select individuals who were called to a higher vocation and thus gave up having a family, the most widely admired and venerated Confucian sages were those who fulfilled their familial obligations. Sage-king Shun, for instance, was celebrated especially because

---

23. See Vatican II, *Lumen Gentium*, sec. 11, on the laity and the vocation of the family, and the family as the "domestic church."

he found a way to get married and have children even in the face of great obstacles, and thus found a way to embody the highest ethical and religious goods of his tradition.

I want to begin by openly acknowledging these important differences between Confucianism and Christianity not only because they highlight some of the reasons why some members of East Asian cultures might be a bit resistant to Christian contemplative practices, but also because I do not want readers to mistake my view here: I am not claiming that the tensions that exist between Confucianism and Christianity do not also exist between Confucianism and the Ignatian tradition. However, I do think the Spiritual Exercises have some helpful resources for addressing these tensions. To begin, in the Exercises, Ignatius emphasizes the fact that Jesus had a human family, and he invites us to enter into a relationship with Jesus first by contemplating the experiences of his parents as they awaited and then experienced his birth, as well as his infancy and childhood. These are not run together for consideration as part of one brief experience in the Exercises, but are each critical parts of the second week. The Contemplation on the Incarnation takes us through the Annunciation and Mary's *Magnificat* (SE 103–7), followed by the Contemplation on the Nativity (SE 110–17). These are each followed by repetitions that allow us to go deeper into the details and lives of Jesus' parents and others who were a part of his early story, and by the application of the five senses (SE 121–26), which opens us up to being fully present in every possible way to this experience. We go on to consider the childhood of Jesus (SE 132–34), and the hidden life of Jesus—the years of upbringing in Nazareth that are only briefly mentioned in the gospels—contemplating the details of how he grew to become a man. These parts of Jesus' story are not often emphasized in Christianity; the teachings of the adult Jesus and Jesus' death on the cross are typically the central focus of Christian education, and indeed many if not most who make the Exercises have never before considered carefully Jesus' early life and his relationship with his parents. And while the story of Jesus' birth is widely known and celebrated, the experience of so intimately entering into the details of the story of Mary and Joseph is one of the truly unique features of the Exercises.

Ignatian methods, and especially the way they incorporate but also

go beyond scripture, lead us to contemplate Jesus' family and his relationships with others (and especially his parents), in these parts of the
Exercises. All Christians, regardless of their background, are typically
struck by this when making the Exercises. Ignatian prayer does not stop
with scripture, and this is precisely what makes the Exercises such a powerful experience when it comes to consideration of Jesus' family and
relationships. If one focuses solely on the content of scripture, there is
much about Jesus' life that one will miss, and this is why even those with
a strong background in biblical study are often led for the first time to
become acquainted with Jesus' parents when making the Exercises. Certain Ignatian methods are pivotal here, especially having conversations
(colloquies) with Jesus' parents and imagining oneself present in the real,
day-to-day details and experiences of Jesus' life and the lives of his parents. His life, on this view, begins with the lives of his parents; we cannot
know him fully without getting to know Mary and Joseph, and they, too,
are worthy of respect, admiration, and emulation. These insights will resonate deeply for those with Confucian sensibilities, and can help to make
Christianity *more* accessible to those coming from cultures that are influenced by Confucianism.

An added dimension of Ignatian contemplation that lends itself to
adaptations of all kinds, including adaptations across cultural and religious boundaries, is the fact that it encourages and allows space for
different individuals to imagine differently. Members of cultures that
strongly emphasize filial piety may imagine Jesus' experience of his father's death and the way this loss affected Jesus and Mary, as well as the
seriousness with which Jesus takes his relationship with his heavenly
Father, through a culturally-specific lens. This is precisely what Ignatius
intended the Exercises to enable, for these different ways of imagining
allow different individuals to form a personal relationship with Jesus—a
relationship that is, for each person, different, as a result of our different
personalities and backgrounds. This is one way in which the Exercises
are especially well-suited for translation to different cultural settings,
just as they are adaptable to people from all walks of life.

Moving beyond the second week of the Exercises, Ignatius shows a
remarkable degree of sensitivity to the unique bond between parent and
child at the beginning of the fourth week, which focuses on the joy and

peace of the risen Christ, and which asks exercitants to contemplate the risen Christ as one who offers consolation—as opposed to contemplating the resurrection as an event. Given the centrality of Mary in Jesus' life, Ignatius believed that the first person to whom Christ appeared simply must have been his mother. In a contemplation that is not found in the scriptures but comes from Ignatius's own imagination, Ignatius asks us to imagine the risen Christ appearing to Mary (SE 218–25): "Here it is how, after Christ died on the cross, his body remained separated from his soul but always united with his divinity, descended to hell. Then, releasing the souls of the just from there, returning to the sepulcher, and rising again, he appeared in body and soul to his Blessed Mother" (SE 219). He asks us "to see the arrangement of the holy sepulcher; also, the place or house where Our Lady was, including its various parts, such as a room, an oratory, and the like" (SE 220). Here Ignatius presents us with what Ivens calls "a moment of natural filial intimacy."[24] Indeed, this contemplation will resonate with those whose lives are informed by Confucian understandings of filial piety.

In addition to specific parts of the Exercises that will resonate with Confucian values, there are also ongoing dimensions of the Exercises that relate to familial sensibilities and are thus particularly accessible. An important dimension of Christianity is the use of familial terms for God and, in Catholicism, for Mary: God is our Father, and Mary is not only Jesus' mother, but our Mother, as well. Especially through the triple colloquy, Ignatius stresses the importance of approaching God the Father with a keen sense of reverence, much as, in the Confucian tradition, one would approach a parent with a sense of filial piety. Additionally, we are all a part of the family of God—something that familial terms for God and Mary emphasize. One thing that Ignatian spirituality explicitly invites us to consider, which is not found in the Confucian tradition, is *vocation*.[25] In so doing, it offers us a different way of thinking about

---

24. Michael Ivens, SJ, *Understanding the Spiritual Exercises* (Leominster, U.K.: Gracewing, 1998), 165. Although he departs from the gospels in taking the first of Jesus' appearances as being the appearance to his Mother, Ignatius is nevertheless following an ancient tradition. On authorities before and after Ignatius who have defended this appearance see Gilles Cusson, *Biblical Theology and the Spiritual Exercises*, trans. Mary Angela Roduit and George Ganss (St. Louis, Mo.: Institute of Jesuit Sources, 1988), 304.

25. For recent work on this topic, including perspectives on vocation from the Ignatian tradi-

family relationships: the decisions we make about marriage, children, and family are, from an Ignatian perspective, all things that we ought to consider in relation to the question of where and whom we are meant to serve. As we saw earlier in this work, the Exercises were never given only to Jesuits or those considering the priesthood; they were always given to lay women and men, as well, even in Ignatius's time. Many who have made the Exercises have found them helpful for making good decisions about marriage and having a family, but all who make the Exercises can use them as a tool for considering how God is calling them as members of a human family. Although Jesuits do not have spouses and children of their own, they have parents, siblings, nieces, nephews, and other family members and close friends; they are also members of a family in the Society of Jesus. Especially in cultures where traditional familial obligations are central—and East Asian cultures are emblematic here—it can be important for people to be intentional in their consideration of family obligations and relationships. It is easy for anyone to take their family for granted, but especially when there are familial cultural practices and expectations that are widely embraced and followed, often uncritically, individuals can easily fail to consider where their vocation lies and how they are being called to use their gifts. The Exercises are a rich tool that individuals can use to consider all of these things, and to seek assistance in bringing greater order to their lives and relationships.

Having considered those resources in the Exercises that relate to the family and that would be especially fruitful in Confucian cultural contexts, I would like to briefly consider a few other dimensions of the Exercises that may be challenging for those who are culturally influenced by Confucianism. In addition to the centrality of filial piety and the family, another important area of contrast between Confucianism and Ignatian spirituality concerns the role of human sin and, ultimately, the fundamental character of human nature. Confucians defended diverse accounts of human nature throughout their history, but even the more pessimistic accounts of human nature—seen, for instance, in the work of the classical Confucian Xunzi—do not express anything like the view that the goodness of creation is gravely wounded by sin. Humans, for

tion as well as Islamic and Jewish traditions, see John C. Haughey, ed., *Revisiting the Idea of Vocation: Theological Explorations* (Washington, D.C.: The Catholic University of America Press, 2004).

Xunzi, are born morally blind, and resemble warped wood that needs to be reshaped but is not fundamentally tainted or seriously wounded by sin; the problem is simply that humans lack moral education and cultivation. Most Confucians throughout history, including Mengzi, Zhu Xi and Wang Yangming, defended more optimistic views, contending for instance that humans have natural tendencies toward virtue or that our nature is fundamentally perfect and that we only need to become aware of our moral nature or to remove the things that are obscuring it, in order to become good. There is an obvious contrast between these accounts and Christian views, which—regardless of whether they are more or less optimistic—take seriously the sinful tendencies that are a fundamental part of human nature. An even deeper contrast between Confucianism and Christianity is seen in the Confucian view that humans are capable of thoroughgoing transformation without divine assistance. Even according to more optimistic Confucian accounts of human nature, this is a difficult task, but we are nevertheless fully capable of transforming ourselves with the assistance of a caring, supportive human community, which includes traditions, rituals, and teachers. Such views are a marked contrast to Christian views, which insist upon the necessity of God's transforming power or grace in our lives. And Confucian views are important to attend to, within the context of contemporary East Asian cultures, which strongly emphasize individual effort and what we can achieve through hard work and persistence.

Both the claim that sinful tendencies are a fundamental part of human nature and the claim that we cannot bring about transformation without divine assistance are essential features of the Ignatian tradition. How might spiritual directors address this tension in ways that will be helpful to those from Confucian contexts, particularly since these themes are central to the Exercises? It is important to make clear that the Exercises are not a program of moral self-cultivation—even though one of the ultimate outcomes of the Exercises may be (and should be) the development of a variety of virtues. Indeed, there is a remarkable contrast between the aims of Confucian moral self-cultivation and the aims of contemplative practices in the Hindu, Buddhist, and Ignatian traditions—all of which concern much more than ethical progress or the cultivation of virtues. The Confucian tradition, in contrast, is centrally concerned with moral cultivation. The Exercises, most fundamentally, are about creating a relationship with God. This relationship and its development ought to have a dramatic impact on one's life, including one's moral development, but it is not identifiable with ethical progress. Personal transformation comes from gazing upon, walking with, and laboring with Jesus; we become more like the One we choose to be with. These are aspects of the Exercises that those who wish to experience Ignatian spirituality need to recognize, and the fact that the Ignatian tradition differs in these ways from the Confucian tradition deepens the potential of the Exercises to offer new and distinctive approaches for those from Confucian contexts. The love and assistance of God is clearly the most significant difference between Ignatian and Confucian approaches, and again, we can see why those who wish to make the Exercises—even in adapted forms that are designed for members of other faiths—need to be open to encountering God.

To this end, one way for those from Confucian contexts to approach the love and assistance of God is to use the love of one's own family members as a bridge to understanding God's love. For instance, the final contemplation of the Exercises (the Contemplation of the Love of God) begins by asking exercitants to imagine themselves "standing before God our Lord, and also before the angels and saints," who are praying for us (SE 232). Exercitants from Confucian contexts may find it especially helpful to begin this contemplation by imagining standing before their ancestors and loved ones who have died. O'Brien suggests that Christians, too, may find it helpful to add such individuals to the heavenly host, contemplating "people who have shown you what loving is all about."[26] By imagining the prayers of those who have the most intimate concern for us, and not just canonized saints, some exercitants will be better able to move toward seeing themselves before God, and to begin to apprehend the depth of God's love. The idea here is not to replace God with family members, but to allow deep familial ties to *enable* exercitants to get into seeing themselves before God, by seeing themselves before family members first.

Another way of approaching the need for divine assistance with those

---

26. Kevin O'Brien, SJ, *The Ignatian Adventure: Experiencing the Spiritual Exercises of Saint Ignatius in Daily Life* (Chicago: Loyola Press, 2011), 250. I have benefited greatly from the insights of Anthony Moore, a veteran spiritual director, on the ways in which this adaptation has benefited Christians who make the Exercises, as well as its potential for those from non-Christian contexts.

from Confucian contexts is to see it as a liberating aspect of the Ignatian tradition. The central aims and purposes of the Exercises directly concern liberation: helping individuals to become free from disordered loves and affections, to become free to make decisions that are grounded in their faith. There is something remarkably liberating in recognizing that one does not have to—and indeed, *cannot*—transform oneself alone. One recognizes one's limitations and the limitations of other humans, as well as of human traditions and rituals. Equally liberating is the full recognition that one is sinful and that this state is a fundamental part of the human condition. It is not that one does not take responsibility for one's sins; to the contrary, the Exercises deal in great depth with this very process. But in recognizing one's sinful nature, one recognizes the necessity of the divine plan that provided that assistance in the person of Jesus Christ. While there is original sin, grace is even more "original." For those who are considering this for the first time or from within the context of a tradition like Confucianism that emphasizes self-cultivation, the opening of the second week and the Contemplation on the Incarnation will be especially important. For as the three divine Persons gaze upon the earth, they do not gaze upon humans who are capable of cultivating themselves in order to bring about their own redemption. Rather, as we hear them say, "Let us work the redemption of the human race" (SE 107), we hear them tell us that this will be a cooperative endeavor that requires our devotion, but an endeavor that we cannot accomplish for ourselves.

Reimagining Confucianism

Throughout this book, I have explored the ways in which the Ignatian Spiritual Exercises might be adapted for members of other faith traditions. But at this point I turn to a different question. What happens if we explore the *other* possibilities suggested by Father Nicolás's words, and try to spell out how "important elements of the Spiritual Exercises . . . can be fruitfully appropriated" by Confucians or those whose lives are informed by Confucianism—without their making the Exercises?[27] As Father

27. Adolfo Nicolás, SJ, "Companions in Mission: Pluralism in Action," Mission Day Keynote Address, Loyola Marymount University, Los Angeles, California, February 2, 2009, http://www.gonzaga.edu/About/Mission/docs/LoyolaMarymountUniversityAddressAdolfoNicolasSJ.pdf, 87–88.

Nicolás asks, "What are the dynamics in the Exercises that non-believers might make their own to find wider horizons in life, a greater sense of spiritual freedom?"[28] In discussing the kinds of exchanges between Jesuits and other faith traditions that can be constructive, he uses the example of how a Buddhist wanted to learn from the Jesuits at one of their schools in Japan "because, as he said, Buddhism doesn't have an explicit and developed philosophy of education, as do the Jesuits, who have been at it for 450 years."[29] I think Confucianism represents an analogous case when it comes to spirituality: Confucianism does not have an explicit and developed set of contemplative practices, as do the Jesuits, and there is much the Confucian tradition can learn from the Ignatian tradition as a result.

Now, it is important to remember that Confucianism has a rich history when it comes to ethical and religious practices. There has been excellent work done on the topic of ritual in early Confucianism, and its role in shaping and expressing a variety of important virtues.[30] Recent work has also sought to extend and adapt these practices for a contemporary setting. Philip J. Ivanhoe argues for the contemporary relevance of a rich variety of Confucian views and practices—from the role of music to traditional forms of greeting—many of which are dedicated to enriching the quality of our everyday lives. As he points out, there are many more views and practices worthy of our attention. He writes,

Focusing on the everyday leads Confucians to develop a range of fascinating views about what we might generally describe as meditation, in the sense of a dynamic, critical, and reflective practice rather than a formal posture-based regimen of training. Much of the work of Confucian self-cultivation requires us to become highly aware, watchful, disciplined, and attuned; we must learn to pay attention to and carefully guide and craft our thoughts, feelings, postures, expressions, and actions to be in accord with the Way. The opening chapter of the *Doctrine of the Mean* (*Zhongyong* 中庸) teaches, "Cultivated persons careful-

---

28. Ibid., 88.

29. Ibid., 86.

30. See, for example, Stephen A. Wilson, "Conformity, Individuality, and the Nature of Virtue: A Classical Confucian Contribution to Contemporary Ethical Reflection," in Van Norden, ed., *Confucius and the Analects: New Essays*, 94–118; Philip J. Ivanhoe, *Confucian Moral Self Cultivation*, 2nd ed. (Indianapolis: Hackett Publishing Company, 2000), 1–14; Van Norden, *Virtue Ethics and Consequentialism*, 101–12; and the essays in *Ritual and Religion in the Xunzi*, ed. T. C. Kline III and Justin Tiwald (Albany: SUNY Press, 2015).

ly watch over themselves" (君子慎其獨). This effort, though, is not purely intro-
spective; the core of the project of cultivating the self lies in the challenge of
developing much greater levels of awareness, attentiveness, and care in regard
to the quotidian aspects of life as well as to one's inner thoughts and feelings.[31]

These themes have been taken up by many Confucians throughout
history. For instance, this line from the *Zhongyong* reminds one of the
Neo-Confucian Wang Yangming's appropriation of the classical Confucian
Mengzi's phrase *bi you shi yan*, 必有事焉 ("Pay constant attention to the
task [of self-cultivation]"), and Wang's exhortation to constantly scrutinize
our thoughts, maintaining an uninterrupted state of inner vigilance: "One
must, at all times, be like a cat catching mice—with eyes intently watching
and ears intently listening. As soon as a single [selfish] thought begins to
stir, one must conquer it and cast it out. Act as if you were cutting a nail
in two or slicing through iron. Do not indulge or accommodate it in any
way. Do not harbor it, and do not allow it to escape."[32] Different Confucians
understood the task of self-cultivation differently—owing partly if not primarily to their different and often competing accounts of human nature—
but they all expressed a profound commitment to the task of attending
closely to, and cultivating, our feelings, desires, intentions, volitions, and
attitudes, in addition to our behavior. And they believed that traditional
Confucian religious practices such as ancestor veneration had a role to
play in this process—although these practices consisted of more than what
we would call worship; as Ivanhoe correctly notes, they also involved contemplative practices such as meditation.

So, what would Confucian contemplative practices look like if we re-
constructed them in a contemporary setting and reinvented them not just
for members of East Asian cultures but for others as well? I believe several dimensions of the Confucian tradition can help us to lead more fulfilling, ethically better lives, but a number of these dimensions of Confucianism are embedded in practices that have not survived. I do not think
it would be feasible or desirable to revive all of them. Instead, my aim
is to outline a reimagining of Confucian contemplative practices based

31. Philip J. Ivanhoe, *Confucian Reflections: Ancient Wisdom for Modern Times* (New York: Routledge, 2013), xxv.
32. Wang Yangming, *Instructions for Practical Living*, sec. 39, quoted in Ivanhoe, *Confucian
Moral Self Cultivation*, 67.

on the values and virtues those practices aimed to cultivate and express: what might reimagined contemporary Confucian contemplative practices that cultivate traditional Confucian virtues look like?

There are many ways in which one might go about a project like this, and many traditions and resources one might draw upon, and I want to be clear from the beginning that I am not arguing that mine is the only viable or successful approach. Given that Confucianism is not a living tradition in the way that it once was, one approach to reimagining Confucian practices is to mine the resources of a vibrant tradition that has preserved and developed a particular set of practices that successfully facilitate the cultivation of the self—even though that is not their only goal. One could turn to the Buddhist or Daoist traditions for geographical and cultural reasons. These traditions, like Confucianism, permeate East Asia and have a history of practices aimed at moral cultivation. But when it comes to contemplative practices, I think Ignatian spirituality is an especially promising resource, because its contemplative practices, like those of Confucianism, are aimed not at eliminating all thoughts and desires, nor at becoming awakened to the ultimate unity of all things, but at helping one *attend to and cultivate* one's desires, thoughts, and feelings *in order to* create and nurture a relationship. In the Ignatian tradition this is most primarily one's relationship with God, but one's membership in a human community and one's personal relationships with Jesus and Mary all have central roles to play in the Exercises. As we have already seen, Ignatian and Confucian ethical and religious views differ in a variety of important ways. But despite these deep and important differences, I think Ignatian spirituality can serve as a unique resource for reimagining the practices that are a part of Confucian moral self-cultivation.

It is worth revisiting Father Nicolás's words here. While acknowledging that the Ignatian Spiritual Exercises are "radically Christo-centric," he went on to "underline this idea that the Spiritual Exercises can be shared by non-Christians. Even though Christ is at the heart of the full experience of the Exercises, it is also true that their structure involves a process of liberation—of opening to new horizons—that can benefit people who do not share our life of faith. This is something I would like to see explored more and more.... What are the dynamics in the Exercises that non-believers might make their own to find wider horizons in life, a greater sense of spiritual freedom?"[33] Confucianism presents an excellent case for putting one of Father Nicolás's claims to the test—namely his suggestion that various aspects of Ignatian spirituality can be "fruitfully appropriated" by other traditions. As we have seen, there are few people who regard themselves as "Confucians," and, while the influence of Confucianism in the cultures of East Asia is unparalleled, Confucianism has not survived as a tradition in the way that other traditions have, and so there are not very many Confucians in need of an adaptation of the Exercises. Among the things that have not survived in Confucianism are the practices that would ordinarily help to define what it means to be a Confucian. Catholics frequently describe themselves as practicing or lapsed, and Jews as observant or nonobservant. But the case of Confucianism differs, because it is not clear what a practicing, observant, religious, or spiritual Confucian would actually do. In the case of Catholics and Jews, religious practices clearly distinguish those who are practicing or observant from those who are not. What religious practices would a practicing Confucian engage in today? In addition to the activities at Confucian temples (which I will discuss in a moment), there are also a wide range of cultural practices, such as participation in the annual tomb-sweeping festival, that can be regarded as Confucian practices. But what about one's daily life—life beyond temple visits and special holidays or festivals? What Confucian contemplative practices might enrich life on a daily basis? And what practices might be adopted by those abroad, without easy access to Confucian temples, or those of different faiths who nevertheless wish to benefit from Confucianism in the same way that members of other faith traditions might benefit from Ignatian spirituality? For if members of other faiths can benefit from the Exercises, surely there are also Confucian practices from which Christians and others might benefit.

The revival of activities at Confucian temples in China today makes clear the degree of interest in the religious and ethical resources of Confucianism. Indeed, in an attempt to revive and reinvent Confucian practices that are no longer alive, these temples are drawing from other religious traditions for inspiration.[34] A new practice that is being em-

---

33. Nicolás, "Companions in Mission: Pluralism in Action," 87–88.
34. Sun, *Confucianism as a World Religion*, 162–63.

braced in Mainland Chinese Confucian temples is writing prayers on prayer cards (*xuyuan qian*, 許願簽) that hang in trees or are displayed on shelves in the temple. The prayer cards are the same size and serve the same function as the *ema*, 絵馬, found in most Shinto temples in Japan—wooden tablets bearing the name of the Shinto temple or god on one side and written prayers on the other. Confucian prayer cards were invented in 2002, after the director of the Shanghai Confucian Temple Administration Office traveled to Japan and was inspired by the prayer cards she saw in Shinto temples there. She returned home and instituted the practice at the Shanghai Confucius Temple, and the practice has now spread to other Confucian temples in China.[35] The emergence of prayer cards is particularly interesting for the present purposes because it suggests that simply reviving or recovering traditional Confucian practices has not been wholly feasible or sufficient for meeting the needs of those who turn to Confucianism today. Other traditions, as this example shows, can play an important role in inspiring and shaping the development of Confucian religious practices.

In light of Confucianism's enduring influence on East Asian cultures and on the religious and spiritual views and practices throughout East Asia, Confucian values and practices can serve as a unique resource for addressing a variety of social maladies. So there are two reasons why I think it is worthwhile to reimagine Confucian practices with the assistance of Ignatian spirituality. First, I agree with Father Nicolás that it is incumbent upon the Jesuit order to share its spiritual riches with members of other religious traditions, because it is a way of "helping souls" by helping people to lead ethically better, spiritually richer lives. Second, I think the Confucian tradition, too, has much to offer us in helping us to lead better lives. In East Asia, for cultural reasons, Confucianism may prove to be a unique resource for helping to address such moral problems as materialism, corruption, and pollution, as well as a failure to attend properly to the richness of a life lived *for others*. The latter is an ideal that is central to the Jesuit tradition, but it resonates deeply with Confucian values, especially the Confucian emphasis on caring for one's family and friends, as well as the wider society of which one is a part.

---

35. Ibid. Unlike paper offerings in Chinese ritual practice, these cards are not burnt but meticulously displayed and then stored after they are taken down.

Confucianism can be an equally valuable resource for those outside of East Asia, including those without any particular cultural ties to it. Both the Ignatian and Confucian traditions would have us attend very carefully to the religious and moral lives of people in order to address the kinds of contemporary moral problems that I mention above; indeed I think both traditions would argue that these kinds of problems cannot be adequately addressed through laws or policies without attending to the religious and moral lives of people.

Offering resources for spiritual renewal and fulfillment is particularly important in the Confucian tradition. This tradition, most especially Confucian self-cultivation, demands much of us. We are to cultivate a wide range of virtues, and this involves not only acting in the right ways, but having the right feelings, attitudes, and intentions, as well. Indeed, the ambitious and rigorous nature of Confucian moral self-cultivation— and the view that our nature is imperfect and needs to be developed or re-formed in various ways—drew criticism from early Daoist thinkers, who accused the Confucians of destroying the original goodness that is a part of humanity, making us excessively self-conscious and heaping destructive layers of socialization on us.[36] One potential remedy for this dimension of Confucian moral self-cultivation might be found in an adapted form of the Jesuit ideal of the *magis,* meaning "more," "better," or "greater."[37] We strive for excellence in our laboring for the kingdom of God; since Christ summons the best from us, we always aim for *magis* responses, not meager responses. Rooted in the virtue of magnanimity, the *magis* is a response to God's generosity: we strive to respond with gratitude and generosity in all that we do. However, the *magis* can easily be misrepresented. It is not about achievement or success as society

36. The early Confucian thinker Mengzi took the view that we need to develop aspects of our nature through moral self-cultivation, while Xunzi maintained that our nature needs to be thoroughly re-formed or re-shaped. For a helpful discussion of the differences between their views (as well as a wide range of other Confucian views on human nature and self-cultivation), see Ivanhoe, *Confucian Moral Self Cultivation,* 29–36. For a translation of the Mengzi, see Van Norden, trans., *Mengzi.* For a translation of the Xunzi, see Eric L. Hutton, *Xunzi: The Complete Text* (Princeton, N.J.: Princeton University Press, 2016). For early texts that criticize Confucianism for the reasons mentioned here, see *The Daodejing of Laozi,* trans. Philip J. Ivanhoe (Indianapolis: Hackett, 2003), and "Zhuangzi," trans. Paul Kjellberg, in *Readings in Classical Chinese Philosophy,* ed. Philip J. Ivanhoe and Bryan W. Van Norden (Indianapolis: Hackett, 2005), 207–54.

37. In what follows I am indebted to Kevin O'Brien's remarks on the *magis* in "The Meaning of Magis" (unpublished paper).

measures it, nor is it necessarily about doing more, for in fact it does not mean doing more things but going deeper in the things one does. There is an important resonance here with the Confucian tradition's rejection of the pursuit of material gain, as well as its insistence that virtues like filial piety and ritual propriety are not simply about performing certain actions, but also and more importantly about one's feelings, attitudes, and the way in which one does those things.[38] If one strives to cultivate oneself in these ways, one works to go deeper, not to do more; so for instance one thinks of ways in which the time spent with one's parents, spouse, siblings, and children might be enriched in *quality*, instead of simply thinking about how to lengthen the list of things one does for them. One of the important amendments we would have to make to the ideal of the *magis* if we applied it to the Confucian tradition would be that the *magis*, for Ignatius, is fundamentally a response to God's abundant generosity toward us. For traditional Confucians, this type of response is inspired not by God's generosity, but by the generosity of one's parents, grandparents, and ancestors—all of whom made one's present life possible through their various choices and sacrifices. It is also a response to the full recognition of what it means to stand in an ancestral line: by striving for what is greater, we express gratitude for the love and sacrifices of those who came before us, but we also prepare the way for our children and grandchildren. This summons the best from us in part because a Confucian understanding of the *magis* involves always remembering that our choices always affect others—thus we must honor those who came before us and prepare the best possible way for those who will follow.

Now, the Jesuits were accused at various points in their history of giving too much weight to the individual's role in bringing about change in herself through the Exercises, and being too Pelagian, not giving adequate weight to the transformative role of God. But as I noted earlier in this chapter, the Exercises center on the idea that although the individual is reaching toward God, it is God who ultimately works in the individual to bring about change. This marks a deep and important difference from Confucianism, although it is worth noting that in Confu-

---

38. See, for example, *Analects* 2.7.

cianism, the idea that one can bring about change in oneself, *by oneself,* is also foreign. Throughout their history, Confucians have insisted that we are ethically transformed only through our relationships with other humans—the dead and the living. There are interesting conceptions of becoming one with something greater than oneself that emerge in the Christian and Confucian traditions from these ideas: The purpose of the Exercises is to grow in union with God, who frees us to make good decisions about our lives and help others. As O'Brien puts it, "Ignatius invites us into an intimate encounter with God, revealed in Jesus Christ, so that we can learn to think and act more like Christ."[39] This conception of oneness is expressed in Jesus' own words: "I am the vine, you are the branches," and in the meaning of his death on the cross. This conception of oneness differs in important ways from living in a manner that reflects a Confucian sense of oneness, in which one's identity is inextricably linked to one's relationships with other humans (especially one's family), and with those who stand in an ancestral line stretching back into the past and into the future.[40] It also differs from Buddhist and Hindu conceptions of oneness, which express monistic metaphysical views. It is important to note, however, that there are also robust metaphysical conceptions of oneness in the Christian tradition, in which union with God through Christ is understood to entail a form of union with distinction, as opposed to the union without distinction seen in monism. The clearest example is the theology and practice of the Eucharist, in which the faithful participate symbolically in Christ's crucifixion and resurrection, and thereby affirm their membership in the body of Christ. The Exercises offer an opportunity to affirm and embrace one's membership in that body. When one makes the Exercises, one strives for a certain type of *oneness*: to be united with Christ on mission by accepting the call to labor not just *for* him but *with* him in the world, in all that one does.

One part of the Exercises that can serve as a fruitful resource for reimagining Confucianism is the daily practice of the Examen, an adaptation of one of the practices outlined in the Exercises that is designed

---

39. O'Brien, *The Ignatian Adventure,* 14.

40. For an insightful study of different conceptions of oneness as well its relevance for us today, see Philip J. Ivanhoe, *Oneness: East Asian Conceptions of Virtue, Happiness, and How We Are All Connected* (New York: Oxford University Press, 2017).

to help us to systematically reflect back on each day and attend to our feelings, desires, and experiences as a way to discern how God is calling us in large and small ways.[41] In contrast with the examination of conscience, which Ignatius outlines in the Exercises and which helps us to name sins, the modern, adapted form of the Examen is rooted in discernment. We can appreciate the difference if we review the five points Ignatius outlines:

The First Point is to give thanks to God our Lord for the benefits I have received. *The Second* is to ask to know my sins and rid myself of them. *The Third* is to ask an account of my soul from the hour of rising to the present examen, hour by hour or period by period; first as to thoughts, then words, then deeds, and in the same order as was given for the particular examination. *The Fourth* is to ask pardon of God our Lord for my faults. *The Fifth* is to resolve, with his grace, to amend them. Close with an Our Father (SE 43).

Contemporary versions emphasize discernment more strongly than knowledge of one's sins, but without neglecting the importance of noticing our sins and asking for forgiveness. For instance, O'Brien divides the five points into praying for God's help, giving thanks for the gifts of this day, praying over the significant feelings that surface as you replay the day, rejoicing and seeking forgiveness, and looking to tomorrow, but the heart of the Examen remains: review the day with God and see what God shows you by attending closely to strong feelings that arise, since God communicates with us through such interior movements. O'Brien suggests,

Pick one or two strong feelings or movements and pray from them. Ask God to help you understand what aroused those feelings and where they led you: Did they draw you closer to God? Did they help you grow in faith, hope, and love? Did they make you more generous with your time and talent? Did they make you feel more alive, whole, and human? Did they lead you to feel more connected to others or challenge you to life-giving growth? Or did the feelings lead you away from God, make you less faithful, hopeful, and loving? Did they cause you to become more self-centered or anxious? Did they lure you into doubt and confusion? Did they lead to the breakdown of relationships?[42]

41. The seminal work that has informed our modern practice of the Examen is George A. Aschenbrenner, *The Examination of Consciousness* (Chicago: Loyola Press, 2007 [reprint of the 1972 article]). See also the recent work on this topic by Mark Thibodeaux, SJ, *Reimagining the Ignatian Examen: Fresh Ways to Pray from Your Day* (Chicago: Loyola Press, 2015).

42. O'Brien, *The Ignatian Adventure*, 76–77.

Ivens notes that Ignatius designed the Examen to "uproot any weeds or thorns that might impede the good seed of the Exercises"—which is to be expected of a practice focused on sin. Modern adaptations of the Examen have broadened its uses in daily life, showing how it can serve as a resource for one's life more generally.[43] Ivens writes that the Examen "facilitates the process of liberation, which must continue through life, from the things that obstruct this action." The modern practice of the Examen underscores the fact that in addition to the process of uprooting "weeds or thorns," a more positive task is central to the Examen, as well; it is "characterized by the development of positive qualities, not just the eradication of negative ones," and this includes the ability to discern God's call.[44]

Even though he practiced it differently than the modern version that is now widely used in Ignatian spirituality, Ignatius regarded the Examen as indispensable, and this view was based on his personal experience with it; he prayed the Examen every hour, and if he had to postpone it because of some more important matter or task, he made it up as soon as possible.[45] This type of practice reminds one of Wang Yangming's account of Confucian moral self-cultivation and how we should make ourselves resemble "a cat catching mice—with eyes intently watching and ears intently listening."[46] Since much of the work of Confucian moral self-cultivation hinges on the extent to which we become aware of thoughts, feelings, desires, attitudes, volitions, intentions, and behaviors and then intentionally work to bring them into line with the *Dao* (the Way), one can see how a practice such as the Examen, which involves reviewing these things systematically each day, would facilitate Confucian moral self-cultivation.[47] Indeed, this type of practice would serve as a helpful complement to Confucian ritual practice in facilitating Confucian self-cultivation. Rituals, as Confucians argued, help to shape (and express) our character in critical ways, helping us to behave in the ways that we should and gradually

43. Ivens, *Understanding the Spiritual Exercises*, 33. For the quote about weeds and thorns, see Martin E. Palmer, ed. *On Giving the Spiritual Exercises: The Early Jesuit Manuscript Directories and Official Directory of 1599* (Saint Louis, Mo.: Institute of Jesuit Sources, 1996), 22.

44. Ibid., 34.

45. Ibid., 33n33.

46. Wang, *Instructions for Practical Living*, sec. 39, in Ivanhoe, *Confucian Moral Self Cultivation*, 67.

47. See *Analects* 1.4.

evoking and then shaping and refining the appropriate feelings in us. But without systematically and carefully reflecting back on our own behavior, thoughts, and feelings, we cannot significantly improve our character. So, for those wishing to practice Confucianism in a contemporary setting, a practice such as the Examen would be extraordinarily helpful. Unlike the practice of prayer cards in Confucian temples, and also unlike more formal versions of Confucian rituals such as ancestor veneration, one could practice a Confucian version of the Examen daily without going to a temple, thus it would be accessible to all. In what follows, I offer instructions for a Confucian practice inspired by the Ignatian Examen:

A Confucian Self-Examination   A general practice of examining ourselves (perhaps for twenty to thirty minutes) helps us to cultivate ourselves, discerning where, in both large and small ways, we are embodying or failing to embody virtues such as filial piety, ritual propriety, humaneness, benevolence, and sympathetic understanding, and achieving or failing to achieve harmony with others, and where and how we might do better.

(1) Resolve to be grateful and honest as you look back on your day. Be attentive to what is happening around, in, and through you, others, and the world.

(2) Review your day and name the things you are grateful for, from the most significant to the more ordinary. Be as specific as possible, making sure to recognize the things that others bring to your life as well as the things you bring to others. Attend closely to your relationships with family members.

(3) After naming the things you are grateful for, reflect back on the feelings that arise as you think about your day. Pay attention to them: did you feel joy, peace, sadness, anxiety, confusion, hope, compassion, regret, anger, confidence, jealousy, self-doubt, boredom, or excitement? Pick one or two strong feelings and contemplate what aroused those feelings and where they led you: Did they make you a better person? Did they make you more generous and caring toward your family? Did they lead you to feel more connected to others or challenge you to grow? Or did the feelings make you more self-centered, anxious, or doubtful? Did they lead to the breakdown of relationships?

(4) Rejoice in the times you were brought closer to others and led to embody virtues such as filial piety, sympathetic understanding, and humaneness, and consider how you could have done things differently in those times when you failed.

(5) Look at your plans for tomorrow. What virtues would you like to embody tomorrow, and what obligations and relationships would you like to focus on? Resolve to think, act, and feel in ways that would make your family proud of you. Make sure to consider your current, past, and future family: from your parents, siblings, spouse, and children, to your grandparents and great-grandparents, to your future children, grandchildren, and great-grandchildren. Consider carefully how your actions and who you are will have an impact on these individuals, even though you may not always be able to see it. Close by reading a favorite passage from the *Analects* or another Confucian text that has meaning for you.[48]

Certain distinctively Confucian features of this exercise are worth noting. The family is an explicit focus, and this includes not only one's current but future family as well as one's ancestors. The Confucian tradition seeks to emphasize the way in which we stand in a lineage stretching back in time and also continuing after we are gone, and this ought to lead us to act in ways that are less self-centered and more mindful of the enduring impact our actions can have. In reflecting on our ties to those who came before us and those who will come after, we are led to recognize more fully our impact on others and their impact on us. An even more striking difference between a Confucian practice inspired by the Examen and the Examen in the Ignatian tradition is that the Confucian exercise I have described here is concerned solely with moral cultivation, and not with a relationship with God or some other entity. The primary aims of the Examen are not ethical in nature, and from an Ignatian perspective the transformative effect it can have on our character is not due to our own efforts but is ultimately owing to God and the transformative power of a relationship with God. As Ivens puts it, "While an element of 'practicality' is a defining characteristic of the examen, it must never be made solely with a view to controlling or changing behaviour but always out of the desire to cooperate in the work God wishes

48. See Thibodeaux, *Reimagining the Ignatian Examen*, on adapting the Examen for different contexts.

to do in oneself, and through oneself for the service of others."[49] Ivens's analysis of the Examen emphasizes this at several points; he notes, for instance, "the need to ask where one has responded or failed to respond to God, rather than to look simply for right or wrong actions."[50] This underscores the critical difference between the Examen and the Confucian exercise that I outline above; indeed, I am not calling this a "Confucian Examen" for precisely this reason: a defining feature of the Examen is that it involves God.

Another Confucian practice that might be reimagined by constructively drawing upon Ignatian prayer comes from the contemplative practices that were traditionally a part of ancestor veneration. For many people in a contemporary setting, traditional ancestor veneration is not something that reflects their actual beliefs, but it is worth considering how contemplative practices might be developed to draw upon some of the ethical goods that are tied to ancestor veneration. In one sense, this is to reimagine or invent new practices, but in another sense, this involves a recovery of the view that Kongzi expresses in the *Analects* concerning ancestor veneration, which clearly emphasizes the role of ancestor veneration in helping us to cultivate our character, morally.

The exercise I describe below is inspired by two different forms of prayer from the Exercises: contemplation and colloquy. Contemplation, as we have seen, involves using one's imagination to place oneself in a setting from the gospels or a scene proposed by Ignatius in the Exercises. The other form of Ignatian prayer I will draw upon is the colloquy: an intimate conversation between the individual and God the Father, Jesus, or Mary, in which we speak very openly and freely, from the heart. In addition to speaking, however, we also leave times of silence for listening.

Confucian Colloquy with an Ancestor   (1) Consider the following line from the *Classic of Filial Piety*: "Remember the ancestors; cultivate their virtue." The *Analects* describes Kongzi observing the rituals that were followed prior to sacrificing to one's ancestral spirits. These included thinking about the deceased, what they looked like, the sound of their voice, and the things they enjoyed, out of a belief that contemplating

---

49. Ivens, *Understanding the Spiritual Exercises*, 34.
50. Ibid., 40.

the emotional life of the deceased deepened one's devotion and filial piety toward one's ancestors. Some also believed that those who properly observed pre-sacrificial vigils would be able to see and hear the ancestral spirit to whom they were sacrificing. Kongzi and other Confucians thought that the act of reflecting on one's ancestors, their challenges and joys, their virtues and vices—and considering how they serve as examples for us to learn from—can help us to become better people.

(2) Choose one of your grandparents or great-grandparents and talk with family members to learn more about that person. If you already know quite a lot about your ancestor, you may simply proceed to the next part of this exercise.

(3) Find a quiet place and think about the individual you have chosen to focus on. Imagine the sound of your ancestor's voice, your ancestor's appearance, favorite places, and favorite activities. Name your ancestor's virtues, and recall in your mind the stories that illustrate those virtues. Imagine that your ancestor is sitting next to you. What would you like to ask? What advice or counsel might your ancestor offer to you?

It is important note that both this exercise and the previous one could be used by those of diverse religious outlooks as well as those who do not identify with a religious tradition. While they are contemplative practices that draw upon the Ignatian tradition in order to cultivate Confucian virtues and values, they are not rooted in or exclusive to a particular theological or religious tradition; one need not have a particular metaphysical or religious view in order for these exercises to be helpful. This makes them very unlike the majority of contemplative practices from the Buddhist, Hindu, or Christian traditions. This makes them also unlike the Ignatian Spiritual Exercises, even though they appropriate Ignatian methods. In addition, these exercises depart from traditional forms of religious practice, such as ancestor veneration, in Chinese culture. One is not attempting to contact the spirits of one's ancestors when one makes the latter exercise, nor is one worshipping them; indeed, one does not even need to believe that they exist as spirits. Rather, the aim of this contemplative practice is to facilitate moral self-cultivation through the use of one's imagination and through reflection on the example of the lives of one's ancestors. What we have here, then, are moral practices which draw creatively upon, and are partly inspired by, religious practices—both the methods of Ignatian spirituality and certain dimensions of Confucian ancestor veneration and moral self-cultivation. This offers us one way of reimagining Confucianism which makes its rich ethical resources accessible to those of diverse beliefs and walks of life, while also taking seriously the Confucian commitment to the role our ancestors ought to play in helping us to lead happier, more fulfilling, ethically better lives. We can also see from these exercises one more way in which the fruits of the Exercises can be shared with members of other traditions.

Suggested Further Readings

Philip J. Ivanhoe. *Confucian Moral Self Cultivation*. 2nd ed. Indianapolis, Ind.: Hackett, 2000.

———. *Confucian Reflections: Ancient Wisdom for Modern Times*. New York: Routledge, 2013.

Philip J. Ivanhoe and Bryan W. Van Norden. *Readings in Classical Chinese Philosophy*. Indianapolis, Ind.: Hackett, 2005.

Conclusion

THIS WORK HAS OFFERED an argument for adapting the Spiritual Exercises in ways that will make them accessible to, and fruitful for, members of other faith traditions. In addition to offering a theological justification for adapting the Exercises for members of other faiths, we have examined the challenges that are involved in this practice, regardless of the specific religious tradition one is adapting for, and various ways of addressing those challenges. While we have looked in detail at Hinduism, Buddhism, and the East Asian cultural contexts that are influenced by Confucianism, the arguments offered here and the model for adaptation that is used throughout apply readily to other faith traditions.

One of the most important lines of argument I have offered concerns the profile of those who would be good candidates for making the full and complete Exercises—for if we attend carefully to the aims and purposes of the Exercises, we will see that not everyone is a good candidate for making the full Exercises (and this, of course, is true of Christians and non-Christians alike). Ignatius stresses the importance, for those who make the Exercises, of "entering upon them with great spirit and generosity toward their Creator and Lord, and by offering all their desires and freedom to him" (SE 5). When applied to the endeavor of offering the Exercises to members of other religious traditions, these remarks suggest that those of other faiths must both exhibit the virtue of magnanimity and also have a desire to encounter not only God, but Jesus Christ; the latter cannot be stressed enough, since traditions such as Hinduism and Judaism involve a relationship with God (variously conceived) but not with Jesus. It is important to note the distinction here between experiencing the Exercises in a shortened form (e.g., an eighteenth-annotation retreat) and their complete form (e.g., a nineteenth- or twentieth-annotation retreat). My argument in this book concerns the more challenging case of the latter, but Christians and members of other traditions alike should be encouraged to experience Ignatian spirituality in other, more accessible ways, including eighteenth-annotation experiences like a weekend or abridged retreat, Lenten and Advent retreats, praying with the Examen daily, or using the imagination to pray with scripture.

It is important to remember that my work here is normative in nature; I am not engaged in the historical or social-scientific tasks of describing and documenting what Jesuits have done—although I have attended closely to and have benefitted immeasurably from the feedback of Jesuits who have given the Exercises to a wide variety of people. Rather, I have presented an argument for *why* this practice is theologically defensible and central to the mission of the Jesuits, and *how* it might best be approached. Throughout this work I have sought to balance the theological task of explaining why the Exercises ought to be shared with members of other faiths with the practical task of specifying in detail what, exactly, one ought to do with the content of the Exercises in order to make it accessible to, and fruitful for, members of other faith traditions. The adaptations that are outlined for Hindus and Buddhists serve as models for how the full and complete Spiritual Exercises can be adapted for members of other traditions: other sacred texts and practices can be added and drawn upon, while the integrity of the Exercises is maintained by leaving the content of the four weeks intact. The chapter on Confucianism presents a model of how the Exercises can serve as a different kind of resource for those of other traditions by making Christianity more accessible, despite challenging differences, and also by inspiring new contemplative practices that draw creatively upon Ignatian spirituality and yet are grounded in another tradition.

In light of the fact that the specific adaptations I outline in this work are for Asian religions, there remains much further work to be done in outlining similar adaptations for Judaism and Islam—particularly since a number of Jesuits have worked to adapt at least part of the Exercises for members of these traditions. It is my hope that this work will serve as a helpful resource for those who pursue this task, for despite the remarkable differences between traditions such as Islam and

Judaism and the traditions of Hinduism, Buddhism, and Confucianism, there nevertheless remain a common set of challenges. While I address my reasons for focusing on Asian traditions in the first chapter of this book, I would like to briefly revisit these issues here in light of the adaptations that I have outlined in the chapters on Hinduism, Buddhism, and Confucianism. As I stated in the introduction, despite the wide-ranging work of Jesuits around the globe throughout their history, there remains a strong tendency to privilege Judaism and Islam in Catholic interreligious endeavors. This is due partly to the fact that these traditions are simply more familiar to most Christians, and partly to the fact that it is easier to engage these traditions since they are all monotheistic, have a shared history, and profess belief in the same God (although they have different beliefs about God)—something that readers of this book ought to appreciate more deeply, having examined the adaptations I outline for other traditions. The tendency to privilege Judaism and Islam is also partly due to an awareness of the violent history of conflict with these traditions, since much if not most interreligious dialogue is motivated by a desire to promote peace. But here we can see clearly how the practice of giving the Exercises to members of other faith traditions differs from other forms of interreligious dialogue: the primary goal here is not to promote peace between religious believers, nor is it to promote religious literacy (although these could certainly be potential benefits). The aim of giving the Exercises is primarily spiritual in nature: we do it to "help souls," to deepen individuals' faith by giving them an opportunity to encounter God and Jesus in new and meaningful ways, and to discern God's summons in their lives. While this can and does have a wide range of practical implications, giving the Exercises is not primarily about putting an end to violence among religious believers, or helping them to understand one another's perspectives more clearly and accurately. There are a variety of worthy interreligious endeavors that work to achieve precisely these ends, but the Exercises differ in their primary aims. One of the implications of this difference is that, unlike some forms of interreligious dialogue, which are best targeted at members of traditions involved in political conflicts (and also at those who have authority and influence), the adaptation of the Exercises for members of other faiths gives us no cause to privilege certain traditions over others, any more that giving the Exercises to Christians encourages us to privilege people from certain backgrounds over others. It was Ignatius's belief that the Exercises can and should be made accessible to people from all walks of life, and Jesuits who have given and adapted the Exercises in exceptionally wide-ranging settings have demonstrated the value of this practice.[1] Just as we see Jesus addressing and reaching out to those of all backgrounds in the gospels, we, too, are called to do the same.

The chapters of this book that focus on Hinduism and Buddhism demonstrate the extent to which it is easier to adapt the Exercises for theists compared with non-theists, and monotheists compared with polytheists. While adaptations of the full and complete Exercises for Jews and Muslims face unique challenges because of the differing views about Jesus, I nevertheless suspect that it will, in most cases, be easier to adapt the Exercises for Jews and Muslims who are interested in encountering Jesus (and thus who fit the profile of those who would be good candidates to make the Exercises) than it is for non-theists. Jews and Muslims already view God as their Creator and Lord, and they see many aspects of their lives and creation as gifts from God. They also believe that God calls to each of us, and that we ought to listen and respond generously to this call. At the same time, in addition to highlighting just how central theism or belief in God is to the Exercises, this work also demonstrates why Father Nicolás calls the Exercises "radically Christo-centric." This is why I argue that those of other faiths who wish to make the Exercises need to have a desire to encounter Jesus as he is understood in the Christian tradition if they are to proceed through all four weeks of the Exercises. While one could use parts of the Exercises simply to deepen a person's relationship with God, Jesus is central to most of the movements of the second, third, and fourth weeks. And while one could create a new set of exercises that would last four weeks, replacing most of the content of the Exercises with non-Christian scripture while making use of Ignatian methods, this would be to engage in a different creative task than *adapting* the Exercises. As I argued in chapter 2, the view that one can *adapt the Exercises* in a way that removes or decentralizes Jesus in the second, third, and fourth weeks is problematic for several reasons. I want to stress, though, that although

---

1. See, for example, the work of Joseph Tetlow, SJ, a Jesuit of the New Orleans Province who has worked tirelessly to make the *Spiritual Exercises* available to diverse populations.

I suspect that it might be easier to adapt the Exercises for Jews and Muslims (compared with non-theists and polytheists) using the model I have outlined in this book, that is *not* to say that such a task would be easy. Additionally, because Judaism and Islam explicitly reject Christian views of Jesus, I suspect that there would be fewer Jews and Muslims who would be interested in encountering Jesus personally through the Exercises and thus fewer Jews and Muslims who would be good candidates for making the full and complete Exercises, compared with adherents of other faith traditions. Indeed, it is unlikely that a devout or committed Jew or Muslim would be interested in encountering Jesus personally through the Exercises, because she would not believe that Jesus *could* be encountered in this way; and that is because members of both religions take many central Christian beliefs about Jesus to be false. Similarly, there are good reasons to think there would be fewer philosophical Buddhists who would be interested in making the Exercises (since most of them are not theists), compared with Hindus and theistic Buddhists.

The larger point I am making is that the nature of a person's religious beliefs matter greatly in determining whether certain contemplative practices will be attractive, feasible, or beneficial to him or her. My aim in this work is not to privilege the Exercises over other contemplative practices and uncritically encourage members of all traditions to make the Exercises; to the contrary, given the nature and content of the full and complete Exercises and the investment of time and energy on the part of spiritual directors and exercitants, I think we ought to think carefully about who is a good candidate. My general argument in this work is that the Exercises ought to be made accessible to more people around the world, including those of other traditions. But retreat houses should not function as businesses, selling retreats to anyone who is interested and willing to pay, as is the practice with many other kinds of retreats that are based on the contemplative practices of other traditions. Yoga and Zen teachers are more plentiful than those trained to give the Exercises, which makes this type of practice more feasible for them, but as this work makes clear, there are good reasons to think that the Ignatian Spiritual Exercises warrant a different approach. Yoga and Zen both lend themselves to very broad accessibility. This is due largely to the beneficial physical practices associated with yoga, which were stripped away

from their religious content and now stand alone for most Western practitioners of yoga; as a result, no particular religious beliefs or commitments are required on the part of practitioners in such circles.[2] In the
case of Zen practice, the emphasis on emptying the mind decentralizes
religious belief, which is why it is not uncommon for a cross-section of
Western Zen practitioners to include those of widely varying religious
beliefs, including members of other religions. The Ignatian tradition differs in these respects. While Ignatian spirituality can serve as a helpful
and meaningful resource for many different kinds of people—seen for
instance in how the Examen can be used to create an exercise that would
benefit those who are informed by the Confucian tradition—the full and
complete Exercises, because of their irreducibly Christocentric content,
will be feasible for a narrower set of people.

One of the most obvious challenges facing an implementation of
the proposal that the Spiritual Exercises should be offered to members
of other faith traditions is that there currently are not enough individuals trained to offer the Exercises even to Christians who are interested in
them. This of course is not a new challenge to those in Jesuit circles.[3] It
underscores the need for good training programs for those who discern
a call to share the Exercises by giving them to others. It would also be
helpful if these training programs included resources on how to adapt
the Exercises for members of other faith traditions, but this is an admit-
tedly ambitious proposal, since programs of this sort work very hard just
to train people to give the Exercises to Christians. Nevertheless, in order
to respond to the challenge that Father Nicolás offered when he proposed that we find ways to share the Exercises more widely, those who
give the Exercises will need a background that enables them to adapt the
Exercises in more diverse ways. So it may be that we need to begin this
process by looking more closely at how Jesuits and lay spiritual directors

2. There has been a backlash against secular Western appropriations of yoga in India, and
criticism from within conservative Christian circles in the West, as well. While the former is rooted
in a concern about the secularization of yoga (which fails to preserve its integrity), the latter is
rooted in the view that yoga can never be detached from its original religious aims (and thus that
it should not be practiced by Christians).

3. As Father Nicolás points out in his 2009 speech, Ignatius and his first companions saw
themselves as following in the footsteps of Jesus' own disciples. As Jesus said to those first disciples, "The harvest is plentiful, but the laborers are few; therefore ask the Lord of the harvest to
send out laborers into his harvest" (Lk 10:2).

are trained, and how they might be better prepared to share the Exercises with members of other faiths.

Jesuits normally do not, as part of their education, complete substantial training in any religious tradition except Christianity.[4] This might seem puzzling, given that Jesuits have often been on the cutting edge of educational progress, and also given the history of Jesuit encounters with other cultures and religious traditions. It is unsurprising though, given that the latter has been in the mission field, which for most of its history aimed at conversion (which, at least to a more traditional way of thinking, made learning about other religions less important). While Jesuits typically complete a master's degree in theology, their theological training continues to consist almost entirely (and sometimes exclusively) of Christian theology. While Jesuits can take classes in other religions, such courses typically represent a very small part of their training. This is a missed opportunity, for it means that many Jesuits are left to learn on their own—or with very little formal study—about the other religious traditions they will encounter in the places they will live and serve. If the Jesuits wish to adapt the Exercises for members of other faith traditions, one essential step will be to offer serious training in other faith traditions to Jesuits. I am intentional here in saying "serious training;" it will not be enough simply to require a token "World Religions" course, or encourage Jesuits to spend time at a Zen center. Jesuit seminaries already do quite well incorporating the work of Catholic theologians with an interest in interreligious dialogue, but Jesuits ought to study other faiths in detail with real specialists in those traditions. This could be done formally at the graduate level—something that would require re-thinking the composition of the faculty and course requirements at Jesuit schools of theology—or, at least initially, through summer seminars hosted by Jesuit theology centers and led by specialists in other traditions. Ideally, this training would include some comparative work, which would give Jesuits the opportunity to relate what they learn about other traditions to their home tradition. Such changes make sense not only in relation to the task of adapting the Exercises for members of other faiths; Jesuits with a stronger background in other traditions would be better prepared

---

4. The obvious exceptions are those who become specialists in other religions.

to serve around the world in settings that are more diverse today than they ever have been. Indeed, this is a practical reform that seems long overdue and that has been advocated by some Jesuits considering their decade-long program of formation. It is certainly in keeping with the spirit of the *magis*, for in learning deeply about other traditions, we embrace a ministry that will lead to greater universal good—which is what Ignatius instructed Jesuits to do when he urged them to "Go and set the world on fire!"

There are also important reasons why Jesuit institutions ought to take an interest in translating the Exercises for members of other faith traditions. For universities and schools with a diverse faculty, staff, and students—and here we should recall Father Nicolás's story about the Buddhist faculty member who noted how Jesuit work on education could serve as an important resource—it can often be a challenge to generate and sustain support for the Jesuit identity and mission of a place. The Exercises may be the richest resource available to us for doing this at Jesuit institutions, for they allow individuals to experience firsthand the ways in which the Ignatian tradition can enrich lives. This in turn helps people of diverse backgrounds to see how they might contribute to and participate in—and also be served by—the Jesuit institutions of which they are a part. The Exercises kindle in us a desire to become multipliers. They also have a way of demonstrating for us how religious institutions can be liberating (rather than constricting). Offering members of Jesuit institutions of higher learning the opportunity to experience the Exercises—regardless of their backgrounds—is perhaps the most effective way to ensure the preservation and growth of the Jesuit character of an institution. Diverse institutions, then, must consider adapting the Exercises in order to share them with members of different faiths. This is an example of what it means to live on the frontier that Pope Francis described, proclaiming the gospel so that it is understandable and meaningful for the people, and helping them to find what Father Nicolás described as the "wider horizons in life" that the Exercises can help to unlock.

At the heart of Pope Francis's call to members of different faith traditions to "build unity *on the basis of* our diversity of languages, cultures, and religions" is the idea that we should not seek only to emphasize what we share in common, but we should utilize the unique resources of each of our traditions as a starting place for healing and unity. The Spiritual Exercises, as we have seen, offer us one such resource that is firmly grounded in the Christian tradition and yet holds great potential for those of different faiths. In offering others the opportunity to deepen their spiritual lives through the Exercises, we are responding to what Pope Francis calls the urgent need "to see once again that faith is a light, for once the flame dies out, all other lights begin to dim. The light of faith is unique, since it is capable of illuminating every aspect of human existence."[5] The possibility of sharing the Exercises with members of other faiths gives new meaning to the Ignatian goal of "setting the world on fire," and reminds us that we are each called to share the light with all, for "Faith is passed on, we might say, by contact, from one person to another, just as one candle is lighted from another."[6]

5. Francis, *Lumen Fidei*, Encyclical Letter, June 29, 2013, http://w2.vatican.va/content/francesco/en/encyclicals/documents/papa-francesco_20130629_enciclica-lumen-fidei.html, sec. 4.
6. Ibid., sec. 37.

Bibliography

Alphonso, Herbert, SJ. *Discovering Your Personal Vocation: The Search for Meaning through the Spiritual Exercises*. New York: Paulist Press, 2001.

Ames, Roger T., and Henry Rosemont, Jr., trans. *The Analects of Confucius: A Philosophical Translation*. New York: Ballantine Books, 1998.

Aschenbrenner, George A., SJ. *The Examination of Consciousness*. Chicago: Loyola Press, 2007.

Benedict XVI. *Address of His Holiness Benedict XVI to the Fathers of the General Congregation of the Society of Jesus*. February 21, 2008. https://w2.vatican.va/content/benedict-xvi/en/speeches/2008/february/documents/hf_ben-xvi_spe_20080221_gesuiti.html.

Brackley, Dean, SJ. *The Call to Discernment in Troubled Times: New Perspectives on the Transformative Wisdom of Ignatius of Loyola*. New York: Crossroad, 2004.

Braun, Erik. *The Birth of Insight: Meditation, Modern Buddhism, and the Burmese Monk Ledi Sayadaw*. Chicago: University of Chicago Press, 2013.

Bresnan, Patrick. *Awakening: An Introduction to the History of Eastern Thought*, 3rd ed. Upper Saddle River, N.J.: Pearson Prentice Hall, 2007.

Burrows, Ruth. *Essence of Prayer*. Mahwah, N.J.: HiddenSpring, 2006.

Cline, Erin M. "Religious Thought and Practice in the Analects." In *The Dao Companion to the Analects*, edited by Amy Olberding, 259–91. New York: Springer Publishing, 2013.

———. *Families of Virtue: Confucian and Western Views on Childhood Development*. New York: Columbia University Press, 2015.

Clooney, Francis X., SJ. "Inside-Out with Fr. Nicolas." *America Magazine*, February 3, 2008. http://americamagazine.org/content/all-things/inside-out-fr-nicolas.

———. "Learning to Learn Interreligiously: In Light of the *Spiritual Exercises* of St. Ignatius of Loyola." *Asian Christian Review* 2, no. 1 (2008): 67–83.

———. "Learning Our Way: Some Reflections on the Catholic–Hindu Encounter."

In *Catholicism and Interreligious Dialogue,* edited by James L. Heft, SM, 89–108. New York: Oxford University Press, 2012.

Costelloe, M. Joseph, SJ, trans. *The Letters and Instructions of Francis Xavier.* St. Louis, Mo.: Institute of Jesuit Sources, 1992.

Cusson, Gilles. *Biblical Theology and the Spiritual Exercises.* Translated by Mary Angela Roduit and George Ganss. Saint Louis, Mo.: Institute of Jesuit Sources, 1988.

D'Costa, Anthony, SJ. *The Call of the Orient: A Response by Jesuits in the Sixteenth Century.* Mumbai: Heras Institute of Indian History and Culture, 1999.

D'Costa, Gavin. "Christian Theology of Religions." In *The Routledge Companion to Modern Christian Thought,* edited by Chad Meister and James Beilby, 661–72. London: Routledge, 2013.

Documents of the 31st and 32nd General Congregations of the Society of Jesus: An English Translation of the Official Latin Texts of the General Congregations and of the Accompanying Papal Documents. Translated by John Padberg. Saint Louis, Mo.: Institute of Jesuit Sources, 1977.

Documents of the 34th General Congregation of the Society of Jesus: The Decrees of General Congregation Thirty-Four, the Fifteenth of the Restored Society and the Accompanying Papal and Jesuit Document. Edited by John L. McCarthy, SJ. Saint Louis, Mo.: Institute of Jesuit Sources, 1995.

English, John J. *Spiritual Freedom: From an Experience of the Ignatian Exercises to the Art of Spiritual Guidance,* 2nd ed. Chicago: Loyola Press, 1995.

Fagin, Gerald M., SJ. *Putting On the Heart of Christ: How the Spiritual Exercises Invite Us to a Virtuous Life.* Chicago: Loyola Press, 2010.

Fleming, David L., SJ. *Draw Me into Your Friendship: A Literal Translation and a Contemporary Reading of The Spiritual Exercises.* Saint Louis, Mo.: Institute of Jesuit Sources, 1996.

Francis. *Lumen Fidei.* Encyclical Letter. June 29, 2013. http://w2.vatican.va/content/francesco/en/encyclicals/documents/papa-francesco_20130629_enciclica-lumen-fidei.html.

———. *Letter of His Holiness Pope Francis to the Grand Chancellor of the 'Pontifica Universidad Catolica Argentina' For the 100th Anniversary of the Founding of the Faculty of Theology.* March 3, 2015. http://w2.vatican.va/content/francesco/en/letters/2015/documents/papa-francesco_20150303_lettera-universita-cattolica -argentina.html.

———. *Interreligious Meeting, Address of the Holy Father, Ground Zero Memorial, New York.* Sept 25, 2016. https://w2.vatican.va/content/francesco/en/speeches/2015/september/documents/papa-francesco_20150925_usa-ground-zero.html.

Ganss, George E., SJ, trans. *The Spiritual Exercises of Saint Ignatius*. Saint Louis, Mo.: Institute of Jesuit Sources, 1992.

Girardot, Norman. *The Victorian Translation of China: James Legge's Oriental Pilgrimage*. Berkeley: University of California Press, 2002.

Gula, Richard. *Reason Informed by Faith: Foundations of Catholic Morality*. New York: Paulist Press, 1989.

Habito, Ruben. *Living Zen, Loving God*. Somerville, Mass.: Wisdom Publications, 1995.

———. *Healing Breath: Zen for Christians and Buddhists in a Wounded World*. Somerville, Mass.: Wisdom Publications, 2006.

———. *Zen and the Spiritual Exercises*. Maryknoll, N.Y.: Orbis Books, 2013.

Haight, Roger, SJ. *Christian Spirituality for Seekers: Reflections on the Spiritual Exercises of Ignatius Loyola*. Maryknoll, N.Y.: Orbis Books, 2012.

Harmless, William. *Mystics*. New York: Oxford University Press, 2008.

Haughey, John C., ed. *Revisiting the Idea of Vocation: Theological Explorations*. Washington, D.C.: The Catholic University of America Press, 2004.

Hick, John. *An Interpretation of Religion*. New Haven, Conn.: Yale University Press, 1989.

Hutton, Eric L., trans. *Xunzi: The Complete Text*. Princeton, N.J.: Princeton University Press, 2016.

Ivanhoe, Philip J. *Confucian Moral Self Cultivation*, 2nd ed. Indianapolis: Hackett, 2000.

———, trans. *The Daodejing of Laozi*. Indianapolis: Hackett, 2003.

———. "Heaven as a Source for Ethical Warrant in Early Confucianism." *Dao: A Journal of Comparative Philosophy* 6, no. 3 (2007): 211–20.

———, ed. *Readings from the Lu-Wang School of Neo-Confucianism*. Indianapolis: Hackett, 2009.

———. *Confucian Reflections: Ancient Wisdom for Modern Times*. New York: Routledge, 2013.

———. *Oneness: East Asian Conceptions of Virtue, Happiness, and How We Are All Connected*. New York: Oxford University Press, 2017.

Ivens, Michael, SJ. *Understanding the Spiritual Exercises*. Leominster, U.K.: Gracewing, 1998.

Johnson, Elizabeth. *Abounding in Kindness*. Maryknoll, N.Y.: Orbis, 2015.

Johnston, William, SJ. *Christian Zen: A Way of Meditation*. New York: Fordham University Press, 1987.

———. *The Still Point: Reflections on Zen and Christian Mysticism*. New York: Fordham University Press, 1989.

————. *The Mirror-Mind: Zen-Christian Dialogue*. New York: Fordham University Press, 1990.

Keenan, James, SJ. *Moral Wisdom: Lessons and Texts from the Catholic Tradition*. Lanham, Md.: Rowman and Littlefield, 2010.

Kennedy, Robert, SJ. *Zen Spirit, Christian Spirit: The Place of Zen in Christian Life*. New York: Bloomsbury Academic, 1995.

————. *Zen Gifts to Christians*. New York: Bloomsbury Academic, 2004.

Kjellberg, Paul, trans. "Zhuangzi." In *Readings in Classical Chinese Philosophy*, 2nd ed., edited by Philip J. Ivanhoe and Bryan W. Van Norden, 207–54. Indianapolis: Hackett, 2005.

Kolvenbach, Peter-Hans, SJ. "Cooperating with Each Other in Mission." Address at Creighton University, Omaha, Nebraska, October 7, 2004. http://online ministries.creighton.edu/CollaborativeMinistry/Kolvenbach/Cooperating .html.

————. "The Service of Faith in a Religiously Pluralistic World: The Challenge for Jesuit Higher Education." In *A Jesuit Education Reader*, edited by George W. Traub, SJ, 163–76. Chicago: Loyola Press, 2008.

Kline, T. C., III, and Justin Tiwald, eds. *Ritual and Religion in the Xunzi*. Albany: SUNY Press, 2015.

Legge, James. *The Religions of China: Confucianism and Taoism Described and Compared with Christianity*. London: Hodder and Stoughton, 1880.

Mascaro, Juan, trans. *The Upanishads*. New York: Penguin, 1965.

McVeigh, Michael. "Profile: Father Adolfo Nicolas." *Province Express*, February 21, 2007. https://web.archive.org/web/20080122063407/http://www.express.org .au/article.aspx?aeid=2305.

Melloni, Javier, SJ. *The Exercises of St. Ignatius and the Traditions of the East*. Leominster, U.K.: Gracewing, 2013.

Michel, Thomas. "Crossing the Frontiers of Faith: GC34 and Interreligious Dialogue." *Review of Ignatian Spirituality* 28-3, no. 83 (1996): 19–24.

Miller, Barbara Stoler, trans. *The Bhagavad-Gita*. New York: Bantam, 1986.

Mitchell, Donald W. *Buddhism: Introducing the Buddhist Experience*. New York: Oxford University Press, 2002.

Mungello, David E. *Curious Land: Jesuit Accommodation and the Origins of Sinology*. Honolulu: University of Hawaii Press, 1989.

Newman, John Henry. *An Essay on the Development of Christian Doctrine*. Notre Dame, Ind.: University of Notre Dame Press, 1994.

Nicolás, Adolfo, SJ. "Companions in Mission: Pluralism in Action." Mission Day Keynote Address, Loyola Marymount University, Los Angeles, California,

February 2, 2009. http://www.gonzaga.edu/About/Mission/docs/Loyola
MarymountUniversityAddressAdolfoNicolasSJ.pdf.

O'Brien, Kevin, SJ. *The Ignatian Adventure: Experiencing the Spiritual Exercises of Saint Ignatius in Daily Life.* Chicago: Loyola Press, 2011.

O'Hanlon, Daniel J. "Zen and the Spiritual Exercises: A Dialogue between Faiths." *Theological Studies* 39 (1978): 737–68.

O'Malley, John, SJ. *The First Jesuits.* Cambridge, Mass.: Harvard University Press, 1993.

———. "How the First Jesuits Became Involved in Education." In *A Jesuit Education Reader*, edited by George W. Traub, SJ, 43–62. Chicago: Loyola Press, 2008.

Palmer, Martin E., ed. *On Giving the Spiritual Exercises: The Early Jesuit Manuscript Directories and Official Directory of 1599.* Saint Louis, Mo.: Institute of Jesuit Sources, 1996.

Pascal, Blaise. *Pensées and Other Writings.* Translated by Honor Levi. New York: Oxford University Press, 1995.

Paul VI. *Nostra Aetate.* Declaration on the Relation of the Church to Non-Christian Religions. October 28, 1965. http://www.vatican.va/archive/hist_councils/ii_vatican_council/documents/vat-ii_decl_19651028_nostra-aetate_en.html.

Proudfoot, Wayne. *Religious Experience.* Berkeley: University of California Press, 1985.

Puett, Michael. *To Become a God.* Cambridge, Mass.: Harvard University Asian Center, 2002.

———. "Sages, the Past, and the Dead." In *Mortality in Traditional Chinese Thought*, edited by Amy Olberding and Philip J. Ivanhoe, 225–48. Albany: SUNY Press, 2011.

Rahula, Walpola, trans. *What the Buddha Taught.* New York: Grove Press, 1974.

Reiser, William, SJ. "The *Spiritual Exercises* in a Religiously Pluralistic World." *Spiritus* 10 (2010): 135–57.

Rotsaert, Mark, SJ. "When Are Spiritual Exercises Ignatian Spiritual Exercises?" *Review of Ignatian Spirituality* 98 (2001): 29–40.

Shahar, Meir, and Robert Weller, eds. *Unruly Gods: Divinity and Society in China.* Honolulu: University of Hawaii Press, 1996.

Skeehan, James, SJ. *Place Me with Your Son: Ignatian Spirituality in Everyday Life.* Washington, D.C.: Georgetown University Press, 1991.

Smart, Ninian. *Worldviews.* New York: Charles Scribner's Sons, 1983.

Smith, Carol Ann, SHCJ, and Eugene F. Merz, SJ. *Moment by Moment: A Retreat in Everyday Life.* Notre Dame, Ind.: Ave Maria Press, 2000.

Spence, Jonathan. *The Memory Palace of Matteo Ricci.* New York: Viking, 1984.

Standaert, Nicolas. "The Spiritual Exercises of Ignatius of Loyola in the China Mission of the 17th and 18th Centuries." *Archivum Historicum Societatis Iesu* 81 (2012): 73–124.

Sun, Anna. *Confucianism as a World Religion*. Princeton, N.J.: Princeton University Press, 2013.

Tetlow, Joseph, SJ. *Choosing Christ in the World*. Saint Louis, Mo.: The Institute of Jesuit Sources, 1998.

———. *Making Choices in Christ: The Foundations of Ignatian Spirituality*. Chicago: Loyola Press, 2008.

Thibodeaux, Mark, SJ. *Reimagining the Ignatian Examen: Fresh Ways to Pray from Your Day* Chicago: Loyola Press, 2015.

Van Norden, Bryan W., ed. *Confucius and the Analects: New Essays*. New York: Oxford University Press, 2002.

———. *Virtue Ethics and Consequentialism in Early Chinese Philosophy*. New York: Cambridge University Press, 2007.

———, trans. *Mengzi: With Selections from Traditional Commentaries*. Indianapolis: Hackett, 2008.

Veltri, John, SJ. *Orientations*. Vol. 2, *A Manual to Aid Beginning Directors of the Spiritual Exercises according to Annotation 19*. Guelph, Ontario, Canada: Loyola House, 1981.

Wilson, Stephen A. "Conformity, Individuality, and the Nature of Virtue: A Classical Confucian Contribution to Contemporary Ethical Reflection." In Van Norden, ed., *Confucius and the Analects: New Essays*, 94–118.

Yandell, Keith. *Philosophy of Religion: A Contemporary Introduction*. London: Routledge, 1999.

Index

A World on Fire: Sharing the Ignatian Spiritual Exercises with Other Religions was designed in Frutiger Serif, with Aisha Latin display type, and composed by Kachergis Book Design of Pittsboro, North Carolina. It was printed on 60-pound House Natural Smooth and bound by Sheridan Books of Chelsea, Michigan.